MIND SPACE

MIND SPACE

Discovering Meditation Without the Meditator

Ronald E. Purser

DHARMA PUBLISHING

Mind Space
Ronald E. Purser

ISBN 9780898003499

Library of Congress Control Number: 2025949607

Page 12 photo: Pickpik Royalty Free (https://www.pickpik.com/theravada-buddhism-monks-at-tibet-tibet-monks-wondering-buddhist-monk-1092269.

For information, write Dharma Publishing
2425 Hillside Avenue, Berkeley CA 94704

Printed in the USA by Dharma Mangalam Press
Ratna Ling, 35755 Hauser Bridge Road, Cazadero CA 95421

10 9 8 7 6 5 4 3 2 1

CONTENTS

Dedication

For all who have struggled with striving,
with the restless search for fulfillment,
with the feeling that freedom is always deferred,
may these pages remind you that the ease you seek
has never been elsewhere.

PREFACE

For years, the word mindfulness has floated across our culture like a magic cure, promising more than it could deliver. Corporations claimed it would soothe stress and sharpen performance. Public schools rolled out programs to keep students focused. Some politicians even mused that if enough people meditated, society itself might grow calmer. But in practice, mindfulness was sold as a way of coping, not questioning. It helped us adapt to the very conditions that were exhausting us. My book *McMindfulness* exposed this flaw, showing how an ancient practice was hollowed out and repurposed for productivity and compliance.

That critique struck a chord, but it left a harder question hanging: if mindfulness isn't enough, what lies beyond it? As a palliative, it treated symptoms without touching the roots of our malaise. The problem is not just stress or burnout. It runs deeper: we moderns have grown alienated from the very dimensions that make life possible. What we need is not another coping mechanism, but a way of reimagining what it means to be conscious, embodied, and alive in time and space.

That question brought me back—though I had never fully left—to a body of work that has shaped my life since I was young. In the mid-1980s, as a twenty-something student wandering into the Nyingma Institute in Berkeley, I first encountered a strange and luminous book by Tarthang Tulku: *Time, Space, and Knowledge*. It was unlike anything I had read. Not quite Buddhist philosophy, not psychology, not metaphysics, but something else entirely: a new *vision*, a fresh medium of inquiry into the nature of reality.

When it first appeared in 1977, *Time, Space, and Knowledge* (*TSK*) landed in fertile ground. The human potential movement was flourishing, Asian traditions were streaming into the counterculture, and many were searching for alternatives to consumerism. *TSK* sparked attention. The text was adopted in over a hundred university courses, was translated into several languages, and even intrigued a group of renegade physicists at UC Berkeley restless with the limits of quantum orthodoxy.[1,2,3] To many, *TSK* felt less like another import from the East and more like a homegrown experiment in expanding inquiry itself.

I joined a small, year-long program where we worked through the book line-by-line, practicing its exercises and immersing ourselves in retreats. What struck me was that it asked for no belief, no conversion, no new "ism." Instead, it opened a new way of seeing. Space was no longer an empty backdrop but a living dimension. Time was not a merciless juggernaut but a dynamic unfolding. Knowledge was not just information but an innate intelligence waiting to awaken. These glimpses felt radical and intimate, as if reality had turned inside out.

Tarthang Tulku himself emphasized that *TSK* was "not intended to be a presentation of traditional Buddhist thought."[4,5] Though rooted in his background, he offered it as a visionary medium in a Western idiom, capable of speaking across philosophy, science, and religion.[6]

Even so, I followed the arc of many seekers in that era. I sat in Zen halls, traveled to India, immersed myself in meditation, and eventually became an ordained Korean Zen teacher. For all their richness, these practices carried a limitation that grew clearer over time. Meditation could bring calm, and even fleeting peace, but the gap between "meditation" and "life" remained. Sitting practice simply did not heal the deeper wound: the existential angst of "never enough": never enough time, never enough space, never enough clarity. Too easily, it became another project of the inner manager, the "self-as-meditator," tracking progress and measuring attainment. Retreats even turned into quiet competitions, with practitioners wearing their ability to sit motionless like a badge of honor. The irony was plain: a practice meant to free us from striving often became one more performance of control.

This realization opened the way back to *Time, Space, and Knowledge*. Where meditation taught me to manage mental states, *TSK* invited me to question the very frame of reality itself. Instead of calming the storm, it asked me to look up and ask what the sky might be. That recognition gave rise to this book.

Mind Space is my attempt to render the daring vision of *TSK* in a language that speaks to contemporary readers: seekers, skeptics, and the simply curious. It is not a manual of techniques or a scholastic commentary, but an invitation into a new atmosphere of knowing. What follows is not my own system of thought, but a re-presentation of a vision first articulated by Tarthang Tulku. You'll encounter bolded quotations from the *TSK* book throughout, placed as touchstones to guide each chapter and convey the texture of the original.

This volume explores the first part of that vision, the theme of Space. Later volumes will turn to Time and Knowledge, completing the arc of the work. My hope is that *Mind Space* serves as a companion, an invitation to test the vision, glimpse its possibilities, and see whether its questions speak to your own life.

BEYOND THE PERSONAL

This is not only my story. Half a century ago, Tarthang Tulku wrote in the Preface to *TSK*, "The disharmony in our lives is reflected in our attempts to control the environment.... The effects of our limited perspectives upon the environment are becoming increasingly obvious." What seemed then like a prescient warning has become our daily reality.

The ecological crisis, the social media treadmill, the endless chase for productivity and growth—these are not random pathologies but symptoms of a deeper blindness. Because we have only a narrow understanding of time, space, and knowledge, we live as if something essential were always missing. We feel it as restlessness, stress, a constant hunger for more. Modern life reinforces this blindness, turning us into perpetual consumers: insatiable in our appetites, propelled forward by an economy that promises fulfillment just around the corner but rarely delivers. Entire societies are caught in cycles of distraction. We check our phones hundreds of times a day, feed on curated images, measure our worth by 'likes'. With the rise of artificial intelligence, we now face an even greater danger: the temptation to outsource our own intelligence to algorithms. Beneath this churn lies a haunting sense of estrangement. We accept it as the "human condition," yet it is not inevitable. As Tarthang Tulku observed, "we have a basic insufficiency of space to live in, of time to use it, and knowledge to enjoy it." That insufficiency is not natural; it stems from our narrowed vision.

We treat space as empty, time as scarce, and knowledge as information to hoard. These assumptions confine us to a disenchanted world of control and separation. The result is not only an ecological and technological crisis, but a meaning crisis itself. The vision of *Time, Space, and Knowledge* insists that it doesn't have to be this way. What if space were felt as alive and generous, time as an unfolding possibility, knowledge as the radiance of awareness itself? What if the very dimensions we ignore are the source of the freedom we crave?

Our malaise does not come from a failure of willpower or even morality, but from a failure of vision. By expanding how we experience space, time, and knowledge, we discover a freedom not dependent on acquisition or achievement but arising within experience itself.

HOW TO APPROACH THE EXERCISES

One distinctive feature of this book is the presence of exercises. Some are drawn directly from *TSK*; others are adaptations reframed for contemporary readers. They are not my inventions. They belong to the vision first articulated by Tarthang Tulku in 1977. My role is to re-present them in an accessible voice, with commentary to help those encountering this vision for the first time.

These exercises are not designed to produce predictable results or incremental progress. They are invitations to shift how we notice and know. Like turning a kaleidoscope, a small shift in angle can rearrange the whole pattern. The aim is not to arrive somewhere else, but to see more clearly where we already are.

This book unfolds in two voices: prose and practice. The prose offers context and reflections; the exercises serve as apertures, doorways to test and feel. They are companions, not separable tracks: reading without practice risks abstraction, while practicing without reflection risks fixation. Read together, they create a rhythm.

If you have practiced meditation, you may feel tempted to treat these as another technique to master. Suspend that impulse. Meditation often comes with an agenda: to calm the mind, to gain insight, to reach a state. The exercises here subvert that logic. They are not about mastery, endurance, or achievement but about play, experiment, and curiosity. As Tarthang Tulku once said, "Practice is a tool. The real question is what vision you have."[7]

Some exercises will feel natural; others awkward. Difficulty is not failure; it is often a doorway. Strange phenomena may arise, but the point is not to collect them like trophies. The point is to see how deeply our knowing is structured and how it can shift when we release our grasp. Over time, these exercises seep into daily life, while walking, resting, working, or pausing between breaths. They invite us to notice what is already here, but differently.

WHY MIND SPACE? WHY NOW?

Why insist on space? Because our age is marked by contraction. We live as if space were scarce: calendars overfilled, minds crowded with stimulation, language betraying us with phrases like "no space," "no bandwidth," "no room to breathe." No wonder burnout feels like drowning, anxiety like being trapped, depression like being crushed.

This contraction plays out not only personally but collectively. Our politics fracture into tribes. Our digital lives compress us into thumbnail avatars. Our economy drives us toward infinite consumption on a finite planet. Climate collapse, polarization, and mental health epidemics are all, in some sense, crises of space.

We have forgotten that space is not nothing. Space is what allows relations to unfold, breath to enter the lungs, creativity to emerge, love to stretch between two people, ecosystems to thrive. To ignore space is to cut ourselves off from the ground of being.

To reawaken a felt relationship with space is not escapism but realism. When we soften our attention, when we widen the aperture of mind, space reveals itself as fullness, alive and radiant. This book offers a vision that meets us where we are and practices subtle enough to shift daily life. These invitations don't demand withdrawal but encourage small shifts that can make even ordinary moments gleam with clarity.

Mind Space points to an intimacy with reality already available, but long overlooked. Mind is not sealed inside a skull, space is not a dead void. Mind is spacious; space is mindful. To sense this is to discover that being human is not exile from reality, but participation in its inexhaustible richness.

RETURNING TO WHAT WAS NEVER LOST

If *McMindfulness* named the problem, *Mind Space* is my attempt to propose an answer. That earlier book critiqued how mindfulness was hollowed out into a productivity tool. It struck a nerve, but it left me with a deeper question: if not mindfulness-as-coping, then what?

That question kept circling me, and the orbit grew tighter when I began teaching at Dharma College. In truth, I had never truly left this vision; it ran like a subterranean current, shaping my life beneath the surface. Standing before a roomful of students, reading aloud the words that had first startled me in my twenties—*space is not nothing*—I saw faces shift. I realized I wasn't simply revisiting an old text but returning to a living vision. Teaching TSK revealed what I had missed: this was never meant to remain private. Given the urgency of our time—the collapse of meaning, ecological unraveling, cultural fragmentation—I returned with new eyes.

We are living through a time of contraction. To recover space is not a luxury. It is survival, and it is joy. This book is my invitation into that recovery. *Mind Space* is not a manual of answers but a set of invitations: words, reflections, and exercises offered not to master but to play with, to see what shifts.

This book is not about joining a lineage or mastering a practice. It is about rediscovering what has always been present, hidden in plain sight: the openness of space, the liveliness of time, and the intrinsic clarity of knowledge. Nothing needs to be added or attained. What is required is only the willingness to notice how near it already is.

CHAPTER 1

A New Vision of Reality

Each morning, millions of us wake to a barrage of notifications. Before our feet touch the ground, we are already pulled into the day's demands: inboxes pinging, headlines flashing, calendars overflowing. We tell ourselves this is just modern life. But beneath the surface, something deeper gnaws at us.

I hear it in conversations about distraction. Friends admit they can no longer focus long enough to finish a book, or even a long article, without reaching for their phone. I hear it, too, in conversations about climate change. One friend told me she had stopped reading the news because every headline—floods, wildfires, extinctions—left her sleepless. "I recycle, I try to bike instead of drive," she said, "but it feels like bailing water from a sinking ship with a teaspoon." What lingers is not only worry but helplessness: the sense that even in face of planetary emergency, ordinary human presence and action don't count.

These are not isolated anecdotes. They reveal a deeper fault line in our cultural imagination. We've learned to see ourselves as skin-encapsulated individuals moving across a stage of linear time. In this disenchanted frame, we are isolated selves navigating an external, largely insentient world. Separation, distance, power, and control set the terms; space and time shrink to little more than background coordinates for human affairs. No wonder meaning frays. No wonder we end up alienated, from one another, from the living world, and from our own depth.

Living within this milieu of alienation, we find ourselves in the midst of a profound meaning crisis. The word "crisis" is not used lightly. It marks both danger and opportunity, a turning point when something fundamental is at stake. To speak of a meaning crisis is to name not only rising anxiety, polarization, and ecological collapse, but also the deeper wound beneath them: a civilization that has lost touch with the ground of reality itself.

> **Space and Time are not simply backgrounds or supporting mediums for our ordinary pursuits and experience; they can provide a very special and direct form of nourishment for our 'humanity' or human nature.**
>
> *Time, Space, and Knowledge* by Tarthang Tulku (1977)

THE MECHANISTIC INHERITANCE

Since the European Enlightenment, the dominant cultural story has pictured the world as a vast machine, made up of parts to be measured, predicted, and controlled. This mechanistic vision gave us science and technology of extraordinary power, lifting millions out of poverty and expanding horizons of knowledge. Yet what once seemed liberating has also narrowed our sense of reality.

Time was recast as a resource to be managed. Space became a container to be owned and filled. Knowledge was framed as an instrumental tool for extraction and control. Human beings themselves were redefined as producers, consumers, and now data points in a restless cycle of optimization. The cost of this worldview is everywhere. Loneliness and anxiety climb to epidemic levels. Attention fractures under digital saturation, leaving many unable to rest or focus. Inequality deepens, while polarization corrodes civic life and trust in institutions. And beyond the human sphere, the planet itself groans: biodiversity loss, accelerating climate disruption, cascading ecological tipping points.

At its heart, this inheritance has produced not only external crises but an interior hollowing. A kind of cultural nihilism takes root. We grow clever and powerful yet estranged from the very ground of being. Beneath daily routines, an undertow of existential anxiety tugs at us. It shows up in a thousand small ways: the constant rush of "never enough": never enough time to meet obligations, never enough space to breathe, never enough clarity to feel at ease in our own lives. Thus, so much of modern life feels claustrophobic. Stress is the symptom, but the root wound is lack of room. We have accepted this anxious orientation as the "human condition," but it is not inevitable, being the downstream effect of a cramped worldview, one that trains attention to lock onto objects, tasks, and results while rendering the spaciousness they depend on almost invisible.

When a single feather and a thousand worlds
Are equally this Space,
Who can say which contains which?
Who can find limits
To life's richness?

Chapter One

MIND SPACE

This book proposes a different starting point: *Space.* Not space as a blank container or empty void, but as a living presence—open, dynamic, surprisingly intimate. When we soften our fixation on "things," space shows up as the quiet support of everything we perceive. It isn't passive. It shapes experience and is shaped by it, a stillness with its own vibrancy. Even a small shift in how we relate to "solidity" can ripple through our lives, easing the sense that we must forever manage, control, and defend.

Think of a painting. The colors and figures hold the eye, but without the canvas they would collapse. Or consider music: we hear the notes, but it is silence that carries them. The same with words on a page: the letters catch our attention, but it is the white of the paper that makes them legible.

So too in our lives. Space is not an empty backdrop. It is the quiet partner of every moment. To overlook it is to live pressed against surfaces; to notice it is to feel a loosening, a widening, a quiet sufficiency.

The escape from our tight, managing stance is not to abandon the world but to *open it*—to notice the spaciousness we've been moving through all along. As attention relaxes, objects become a little less heavy, a little more translucent, like light on water. Even the body, even the "me," can be felt as appearing *in* this wider field rather than standing apart from it. The result is not spacing-out but an increase in presence, ease, and responsiveness.

If we taste this—even briefly—we sense a different kind of freedom. Not the freedom of choosing faster or controlling more, but the freedom of not being bound in the first place: the freedom of openness itself. That freedom doesn't come from mastering a technique or perfecting a self-improvement plan. It comes from recognizing and participating in the dimensions that already support our being.

Mind Space is an invitation to loosen that frame. It asks us to question what seems most obvious: *where* and *how* experience shows up. What if space isn't simply "where things are," but an active partner in how things appear? What if the self is less a solitary agent and more a pattern arising within a web of relations? When we start from these questions, the world grows more intimate and more alive; the feeling of exile eases. Being human becomes less a burden of isolation and lack, and more a direct expression of an inexhaustible richness.

In the pages ahead, we'll slow down and look at space from the inside out. We'll explore how our attention frames reality; how the "solid" world is co-created by habits of seeing; and how simple shifts in posture, sensing, and inquiry can widen our span of awareness. Along the way, we'll keep our feet on the ground: no esoteric vocabulary required, no allegiance to a religious tradition demanded. The point isn't to escape into abstraction, but to change our felt relationship with the world we're already living.

> **Central to the very heart of reality, a beautiful vision is available—when we can 'see' without adopting limiting positions. This vision concerns Space, which is primordially peaceful, open. In its openness, it is an open-ended accommodating of various views, all welling up, floating and gathering within Space.**

THE RECOVERY OF VISION

This is a book about recovering vision, not as heroic transcendence, but as everyday participation. It is not escape, nor some lofty attainment. It is the simple act of noticing, discovering that the fabric of experience itself is already more open, more vibrant, more responsive than we realized.

The promise is modest and radical at once: *more room* in the very places our lives feel tight; *more ease* in the very moments our attention contracts; *more meaning* in the activities that have gone flat. To recover vision is to rediscover we are not exiles in an alien universe, but participants in a reality that is, at its root, spacious and alive.

We rarely think of ourselves as visionary beings. Instead, we treat perception as if it were a simple matter of "looking out" through the senses, receiving what is already there. The world appears as ready-made: objects with shapes, colors, and textures; people and places with fixed properties. Behind the eyes, we assume, sits a perceiver, the "me" who sees. This seems so obvious that we mistake it for reality itself.

But this stance is less natural than it feels, being the inheritance of a worldview that casts us as bystanders gazing at a mind-independent world. Our senses become transparent windows, our knowing reduced to grasping and managing objects. This "instrumental gaze" has given us extraordinary powers of prediction and control. Yet it has also narrowed our range of vision, severing scope, meaning, and empathy. The very orientation that fueled mastery has left us blind to deeper dimensions, a blindness that now shows up as the meta-crisis of alienation and nihilism.

And yet, many of us have glimpsed something beyond this narrowed frame. A night sky so immense it silences thought. A moment of stillness where peace feels boundless. A sudden joy in harmony with music, nature, or another being. However fleeting, such moments open a lucent horizon—a sense that reality is more spacious, more alive, than our concepts allow.

These are not fantasies or escapes. They are reminders that vision can be recovered. To open the mind "360 degrees" is to release knowing from its exclusive fixation on objects and positions. What emerges is not abstraction but a wholeness-knowing that sees space and time as already unified, dynamic, and nourishing.

This is what *Mind Space* points toward: a reawakening of vision that restores us to a wider ecology of being. It is not about withdrawing from the world but about inhabiting it differently—with a clarity that renews meaning and a presence that feels like coming home. This book is for anyone who has felt the claustrophobia of modern life and wondered whether another way of being is possible. It is for those who sense that beneath distraction, anxiety, and contraction lies a possibility of openness and creative freedom that is our natural birthright.

The chapters ahead won't offer a new self-improvement program or a set of quick fixes. Instead, they will invite a reorientation—a loosening of the inherited lens that binds us to narrow ways of knowing. We will begin with space, not as abstract geometry but as lived presence. We will see how our bodies, perceptions, and even our sense of time are shaped by the openness we ignore. We will test this not as theory but as experience, through shifts of attention and subtle experiments in perception. To enter this inquiry is to risk seeing differently. It is also to rediscover a dimension of belonging that has been with us all along.

CHAPTER TWO

The Presence of Space

Step into a crowded café at midday and the air itself seems to thicken. Tables are pressed shoulder to shoulder. The hiss of espresso machines and the rise and fall of voices fold into a blur. You feel the press of bodies, the weight of too many impressions converging in too small a frame. Then step outside. The sudden rush of sky, the sweep of air between trees, the simple fact of open space—your body exhales before you know it. Something palpable shifts. Nothing new has been added. You simply encountered openness.

We move through such contrasts every day, though we rarely pause to notice the silent partner beneath them. A subway car at rush hour versus a quiet park bench. A cluttered inbox versus a blank page. A fluorescent-lit office versus a trail opening to the horizon. What shifts in each case is not only the scenery but the presence of space. And yet, despite its constancy, space slips past awareness. It seems like nothing—a backdrop, a void, an absence behind the "real" business of things.

We all know the relief of stepping into openness, yet in daily life we almost never notice what makes this relief possible. Our attention rushes toward things—the screen, the task, the person in front of us—and seldom lingers in the medium that holds them. Space recedes into the background, as if it were only an empty stage on which the real action of life takes place.

This habit runs so deep that we rarely stop to ask how it is that we locate or identify an object in the first place. Space is treated as a void, while things are assumed to be solid and unquestionably real. Because this assumption goes unchallenged, experience hardens. The world appears as a set of fixed objects, and their solidity feels beyond dispute.

But this is not just an abstract point. Much of our stress and defensiveness comes from feeling trapped in a world of fixed things—things we must manage, control, or avoid. The possibility that these "things" are not as final as they appear is surprisingly liberating: not because we escape the world, but because the world itself begins to thaw. Even a slight shift in how we sense solidity can ripple through the way we meet life.

We also tend to treat space and time as neutral backdrops: space as the "where," time as the "when." We are born into what seems like a pre-established world, already fixed in place, independent of how we know it. These assumptions run so deep they feel natural, even inevitable.

To question them can feel abstract or disorienting, but that discomfort is not a mistake. It's the sign that our most basic certainties are being gently unsettled. And it leads directly to the most insistent certainty of all: the "I." This "I" asserts itself constantly: *I know. I am here. This is my body.* Identity feels like a fixed point from which experience is narrated and controlled. The "I" is always pushing to the foreground, declaring, *this is how it is.* But is it really?

> **Whatever we do, wherever we go, whatever happens on this crowded surface of interactions constituting our world, there is also the sky. The sky is perhaps the simplest example of space, but it is a very important symbol as well. No matter how tangled, crowded,**

and intense our activities might be, the sky is present too—directly above everything.

THE SKY

The sky is our everyday symbol of boundlessness, a constant reminder, simple and disarming. It accepts everything: clouds, planes, storms, even smoke. It cannot be hoarded or exhausted, and is never absent. One upward glance reminds us of what habit obscures: space is not nothing, but the very condition that allows everything else to be.

On a clear day, the sky can lift our mood. When we look up, or out toward the horizon, it appears as a canopy stretching across our sight, enveloping our vision in openness. Even while life unfolds on the seemingly solid ground beneath us, the sky is a presence that evokes release. For many, hiking to high ground and gazing beyond into the distance brings a visceral sense of freedom, a freedom of awareness without limits or boundaries.

The sky, then, is more than a backdrop; it is a living simile for space itself. Its openness can nourish us and offer a first taste of spaciousness, especially against the press and crowding of daily affairs. Yet the vision of space reaches further, pointing to dimensions that are deeper, subtler, and more transformative than the mere expanse of the visible sky.[8]

And yet, even though we intuit that space, like the sky, can be a gateway to freedom, we rarely register it. From childhood, we are trained to look at things: to identify, classify, acquire, and manage. Perception becomes a searchlight, always fixed on objects. The open expanse that allows those objects to appear fades into invisibility. But beneath every surface, space has not disappeared.

Inside or beneath the opacities and hard surfaces which define us and our encounters, there is also space. Intangible, immeasurable psychological spaces constitute the person whose body we see as definite and localized.

We imagine ourselves bounded, contained by skin. Yet breath flows through wide, hollow paths; blood courses through open vessels; atoms are mostly emptiness. Even thoughts are not stacked like bricks. They arise in an inner atmosphere; as quickly as they arrive, they dissolve. What we call "self" is not sealed but porous, suspended in a wider atmosphere. To notice this directly is simple: pause. Instead of chasing your next thought, feel the openness in which it appears. Watch it pass back into silence. Without that subtle spaciousness, continuity would never hold.

Why, then, does life so often feel cramped and pressured? Because the way perception is structured narrows the aperture. What shows up as "objects" depends on the particular stance or focus we bring. Hold to a given perspective, and reality crystallizes into things arranged before us. Shift the perspective, and what appears changes with it.

HOW WE FRAME EXPERIENCE: FOCAL SETTINGS

Think of how a camera works. Twist the lens and the scene shifts: a flower in the foreground springs into sharp focus while the landscape behind it blurs into haze. Adjust again and the horizon comes into clarity, while the flower dissolves into softness. Nothing in the world has changed, only the focal setting of the lens.

Our minds work in just this way. Perception is not neutral, as if the world simply streams into us "as it is." Experience depends on where we set the aperture of attention. A narrow setting makes particular objects pop into salience, while the surrounding field fades to invisibility. A wide setting includes more context, letting things appear against the background that holds them. But because we are rarely taught to notice this, we live as if the current focal setting were the only one possible.

You can feel this in moments of strong emotion. Think of being caught in anger. The "I" burns at the center, and the object of anger—someone's slight, someone's tone—fills the whole screen. Other dimensions of the situation drop out. It doesn't matter that the person is tired, that the day has been difficult, that they are also complex and vulnerable. In the heat of the moment, anger narrows the aperture until only the offense remains in sharp focus. The whole world shrinks to "me" versus "them."

That is what a contracted focal setting feels like: tight, absolute, claustrophobic. It generates a sense of certainty—*this is how it is*—but it's a certainty purchased at the price of blindness. Other possibilities, other meanings, even other feelings are excluded from view. Life reduces to a pinhole through which only the self and its objects of fixation can be seen.

This narrowing is not just an individual quirk. Our entire culture encourages it. We learn to pay attention to things we can manage, count, buy, or control. Work deadlines, performance metrics, and digital feeds all demand that attention tighten, that the aperture closes down to a narrow strip of "what matters." No wonder we so often feel pressed and reactive: we are moving through the world with a constricted view, and the world contracts to match it.

And yet, just as a camera can adjust, so too can attention. A focal setting is not destiny. Shift it, and reality shifts with it. When the aperture widens, context comes alive. Anger softens when we take in more of the person we are angry at: their body language, their vulnerability, their humanity. Stress diminishes when we see the task not as an isolated threat but as part of a larger rhythm of activity, a wider pattern that includes pauses, relationships, and supports. Even the sense of self grows lighter when the lens opens enough to reveal the space in which the self arises.

At any level of analysis, objects appear only because a very precise focal setting is maintained. This is not simply a philosophical curiosity, it is a practical key. It means that what we take as fixed and solid can be reconfigured by changing how we look. The solidity of the world is, in part, a function of our focus.

> **Our perceptions of various spaces and 'things' reflect different levels and types of analysis. For any given level of analysis, there is the appearance of 'objects' only because a very precise 'focal setting' or perspective is maintained.**

Consider how science discovered the atom. What once seemed solid and indivisible, matter itself, was revealed to contain vast space, hidden energies, surprising depths. Something similar happens in perception when we widen the aperture. The dense and impenetrable softens into something more spacious. The fixed becomes fluid. What seemed to press on us as absolute turns out to be provisional, a surface that conceals depths.

This is why focal settings matter so much. They do not just determine what we see; they shape how we feel, how we think, how we act. A contracted focal setting breeds defensiveness, stress, and reactivity. A more open setting allows flexibility, empathy, and freedom.

You can experiment with this right now. Bring to mind a small irritation: perhaps an email unanswered, a slight from a friend, a worry about tomorrow. Let it fill the screen of your mind for a moment, as it so often does. Notice how the body tightens, how the "I" at the center contracts around it. Now, without pushing the irritation away, widen the aperture. Include the space of the room, the sounds around you, the rhythm of your breath. Feel how the irritation still exists, but no longer defines the whole scene. It is one part of a larger picture. Even a small widening creates more room to breathe, more freedom to choose how to respond.

Other possibilities of space emerge in intimate connection with each thought, each sensation, each surface. Our lives are not locked passageways. They are layered strata, within which new spaces become available whenever the focal setting shifts.

The challenge is that our ordinary habit is to overlook space entirely, fastening instead on things. We dismiss openness as nothing, treating the interval between objects as meaningless. But this is precisely what keeps us locked into lower space: a world of opaque surfaces and solid objects, crowded with problems to manage. By recognizing that even the way we focus constructs this density, we loosen its hold.

This perspective may feel abstract at first, but the implications are personal. Much of what suffocates us—stress, defensiveness, the pressure of being "me"—is intensified by a narrowed focal setting. By learning to widen and vary the aperture of attention, we discover a capacity for freedom already hidden within perception. The world becomes less a fixed array of solid things and more a living tapestry, fluid and alive.

Just as opening the camera lens lets in more light, widening attention lets in more life. The shift does not need to be dramatic. Even a small widening creates more room to breathe, more freedom to choose how to respond. A shift in how we look can shift the very texture of what we call reality.

EVERYDAY GLIMPSES OF SPACE

But focal settings are only the surface of something deeper. Beneath our ordinary ways of looking lie more hidden habits, assumptions so intimate we rarely notice them at all. We don't just focus too narrowly; we take for granted that the world we see is the world as it is. This unquestioned stance, so natural it feels like common sense, forms the blind spot of our perception.

A small shift in the way we look can widen the lens. The ordinary world, seen differently, reveals hidden layers of openness. Around objects, between events, within perception itself, space begins to shimmer.

It may be possible to discover a kind of space in some intimate connection with each thought, each sensation, each surface, and each conceptual category which constitutes our lived world.

This vision is radical, but not remote. Space is not merely above, in the sky, or "out there" among the stars. It threads through everything, including the most ordinary of moments. Each sensation arises within it. Each thought floats in it. Even the very feeling of being "me" occurs in an atmosphere generous enough to hold it. We glimpse this most easily in moments of awe. Standing before a mountain ridge, boundaries soften. Listening to music that seems to dissolve time, the body breathes differently. Gazing at the night sky, we sense immensity. Such moments may feel exceptional, yet they are already woven into our lives. Space does not arrive only in grandeur. It is present in the pause between words, in the silence after a breath, in the stillness of an unoccupied room.

This spaciousness can be tasted directly. Let attention drift for a moment from these black marks to the white page that holds them, to the air touching the skin, to the room around you. Nothing has changed, yet something eases. There is more room.

When this openness goes unnoticed, life contracts. The absence of space shows up in confusion, conflict, imbalance, and a general sense of strain. We know this wound, and we long for its healing. Even the smallest recognition—a full breath, a glimpse of horizon—restores us because it restores contact with openness.

Understanding itself can become a kind of space. When perception shifts into new focal settings, the very act of seeing differently becomes expansive. This understanding is not a neat conclusion but an atmosphere. Imagine a conversation where someone truly listens. Their attention doesn't press in; it widens. In that opening, words find their shape. Insight arrives not as a trophy won but as air shared. Knowledge is not simply information possessed. It is the felt presence of openness.

THE BLIND SPOT OF NAÏVE REALISM

Most of us move through the world with an unquestioned sense that we are simply looking "out" at reality. We assume that the eyes function like windows, receiving images of a ready-made world, and that perception is nothing more than registering what's already there. This stance is so natural it rarely even occurs to us that it might be an assumption. It feels like common sense: I open my eyes, and the world appears.

Philosophers call this *naïve realism*, the conviction that things exist "out there" just as we see them, independent of how we know them.[8] It is a mental posture as deep-seated as the feeling of gravity. Yet modern science, from neuroscience to cosmology, tells a very different story.

Take neuroscience. A leading researcher of consciousness puts it bluntly: perception is a "controlled hallucination."[9] The brain is not a passive receiver but an active constructor. It takes sensory signals and interprets them against expectations, predictions, and prior models of the world. The red of an apple, the solidity of a chair, even the constancy of your own body are not raw facts delivered to the mind but carefully generated interpretations. The world seems stable because our focal settings lock us into a particular mode of construction, one that hides its own activity.[10]

This is not to say that the world is unreal, but that what we take to be self-evident—"this is just how things are"—is in fact deeply mediated. We take it for granted that what we perceive as a solid and familiar world of objective things has no relationship to meanings, to our *figuration* of phenomena.[11] The use of this term figuration is intentional, as it conjures associations related to figments of our imagination. Our limited vision of reality deludes us into a naïve belief that the meanings we rely upon for making sense of a familiar world are not the output of a focal setting, figments of our imagination, but simply the way things really are. In everyday life, though, we rarely feel this. We act as if what appears before us is solid, fixed, independent, and unquestionable. The very framing of experience vanishes into transparency.

Cosmology adds another irony. We live in a universe where, according to our best physics, more than 80 percent of what exists is not matter at all but "dark energy" and "dark matter": mysterious forms of space-filling presence we barely understand.[12] At the subatomic level, what appears solid is mostly emptiness, structured fields of probability. And yet, when we wake in the morning and look at our bedroom, we see solidity everywhere: walls, furniture, objects to be used. In practice, we inhabit a world of density, where space seems absent, incidental, irrelevant.

This is the blind spot of naïve realism. On the one hand, our science tells us the universe is saturated with space, mystery, and openness. On the other hand, our habits of perception treat space as nothing, a mere absence between things. We live within openness but experience only density.

Language itself betrays this paradox. Listen to the metaphors we use every day: "I need more head space." "I feel blocked." "She invaded my space." "I'm hemmed in." "Give me room to breathe." Without realizing it, we describe our inner lives in terms of space, as though our very well-being depended on it. And it does. These idioms reveal an intuition we usually overlook: space is not nothing. It shapes how we feel, how we relate, how we know.

Consider the sense of being "boxed in" by obligations. The phrase points to something physical, yet the pressure is psychological. Or think of what we mean when we say someone has "presence." We don't mean their body is larger. We mean they carry an openness, an ease, that affects the space of a room. Even in casual speech, we acknowledge that space is active and relational. But when it comes to how we consciously frame reality, space vanishes again into the background.

This backgrounding of space is not just an intellectual oversight. It has consequences. If we treat the world as a collection of fixed things, isolated and solid, we meet it with corresponding attitudes: control, defense, acquisition. We clutch at objects as if they were ultimate; we cling to the self as if it were permanent. The result is tension, stress, a chronic contraction of being. But if we ease that hold, if we question the assumption that space is merely emptiness, we may find the very structure of experience shifts.

Try a small experiment. Look around the room you're in. Pick out an object: a book, a glass, a chair. Notice how the mind immediately fixates on the thing: its function, its use, its solidity. Now let your attention widen to include the space around it: the air, the intervals, the openness in which the object rests. Without space, the object could not appear at all. Let your gaze soften and notice how the object and the space are inseparable, each defining the other. You may feel a subtle release, as if the object itself has grown lighter.

This kind of shift does not demand abstract speculation. It is simply a matter of noticing the unnoticed. Our usual mode of perception hides its own assumptions: that space is irrelevant, that things are ultimate, that the "I" at the center is fixed and in control. These assumptions are so close, so intimate, that we do not see them as assumptions at all. But once they are called into question, the spell of naïve realism lifts, and other possibilities emerge.

In what may sound like a radical claim, space is not a void but an active dimension of knowing. It is the field that allows appearances to arise and dissolve, the openness that sustains the very possibility of experience. To recognize this is not to deny the world but to deepen our engagement with it. For in the end, what we overlook most is also what holds us most completely.

Space is not something to be earned or achieved. It is already here, sustaining you now. To notice it is to feel a loosening, a widening, a sufficiency that is not contingent on circumstance. Even the "self," so often carried as a heavy freight, is revealed as an appearance within openness: fluid, provisional, free to shift.

This recovery of vision is not heroic transcendence but everyday participation. To look up at the sky, to sense the pause between breaths, to notice the room around the word, to allow surfaces to grow transparent are small gestures. Each points toward vastness. To live from that vastness is to feel less like an exile and more like someone who has come home.

SPACE IS NEVER ABSENT

For now, it is enough to notice that space is not absent. However much we overlook it, space quietly sustains every breath, every perception, every thought. What seemed like nothing reveals itself as the very condition for everything. To sense this, even briefly, is to feel a loosening. The world grows less rigid, the self less confined. A little more room appears: room to breathe, room to respond, room simply to be. In this openness, the pressures of "me" and "mine" lose some of their weight, and what feels like a burden begins to feel more like participation in a greater openness. This is not a technique or a skill to master, but a shift of seeing. Space has been here all along, waiting in the background of our experience. To recognize it is to recover a freedom that no circumstance can take away.

In the next chapter, we will follow this recognition more deeply. For space is not only "out there," in the sky above or in the intervals between objects; it is also the ground of our embodiment, the matrix within which we say, "I am here." What does it mean to be located, to inhabit a body, to feel ourselves somewhere? And how might the very sense of being "here" already open into a greater spaciousness?

CHAPTER THREE

Seeing Through Walls

On certain afternoons, a city feels like a long corridor. The sidewalks narrow where scaffolding pushes people into single-file. Storefront glass stacks reflections in layers: your face overlaid on traffic, a bus sliding through the ghost of your shoulder. You sense the press of buildings as weight, as if the air itself were thickened into panels. Then, turning a corner, the street opens to a small square and a sudden wash of sky. Something in you drops. Nothing "happened," and yet everything changed. You didn't add an object to the scene; you lost a wall.

Boundaries shape our experience in ways we rarely notice. Some are physical, such as the walls of a room, but many are psychological or cultural: the roles we occupy, the deadlines we follow, the routines we rarely question. These boundaries give us orientation, but when they harden, they begin to feel like prisons. We keep reinforcing them, seeking more control, more structure, more certainty, and then wonder why our lives feel constricted.

The problem is not lack of effort. Modern life is already full of effort: efficiency programs, self-improvement plans, endless cycles of optimization. But effort applied within the same frame only tightens the frame. Real change begins when we notice how the frame itself is constructed and maintained. By questioning those assumptions, what once felt like a solid wall begins to function as an entry point into something wider.

> **If we employ new 'focal settings' and see the way they work, we can come to an overall understanding which itself is a kind of space. Moreover, this 'understanding', which is also a 'space', explains, expresses, and *is* everything.**

A paradox sits at the heart of ordinary experience. We treat the solid surfaces of our world, bodies, things, situations, as final and regard space as mere blankness between them. Yet when an opening gives way to sky, the relief arrives not from adding one more thing but from a shift in how the field is felt. No new object appears; rather, a presence that was hidden in plain sight is recognized. The relief is spatial: a widening inside and out. This presence is not mystical; it is the most practical thing. A meeting feels less adversarial when you notice the room that holds the people. A hard conversation softens when you include the silence around the words. A knotted emotion unwinds the moment you stop clamping down on it and give it a little room to move. In each case, space stops being a nothing and becomes a partner.

We resist this shift because our cultural training is object-oriented. From childhood, we learn to find, name, categorize, and own. This object-centered orientation was adaptive for survival, but it also set the stage for a dualistic stance: a knower over here grasping at things over there. The world comes to feel like an inventory of possessions to be secured, managed, or defended. What once kept us safe becomes a wall that keeps us confined. By treating appearances as solid objects, we reinforce the presupposition of a separate subject who must control them. The very lens we trust to reveal reality ends up narrowing our access to it.

This same pattern shows up in meditation. Many meditators approach practice like endurance athletes, bracing ourselves against discomfort, as if the point were to outlast distraction. We white-knuckle our attention, trying to freeze the mind into stillness. Perhaps on retreat, such effort can produce moments of calm, but it leaves intact the deeper presupposition of a self-agent responsible for generating peace. When ordinary life resumes and agitation returns, we blame ourselves, convinced that the failure lies in us. But the real problem is structural: practice framed as achievement only tightens the grip of the self-as-doer. True opening begins when this subject–object polarization softens and the mind is no longer imagined as a separate knower. Then mind is revealed as translucent within and as Great Space: spacious, dynamic, and not owned by any agent at all. This calls for a gentler option: letting the world be less hard. Letting, however, is not passivity. Rather, think of letting as the gentle discipline of loosening what simply does not need to be tight and tense, begun by noticing the very atmosphere in which things appear.

Consider the moment a crowded café empties. Before, your attention was caught by objects: cups, voices, faces. After the café empties, the first and most palpable change is the quality of openness. The air has more room. Even your body is included differently, as if your shape were drawn in light against something generous enough to hold it. That generosity is not an idea; it is a felt dimension. And the most striking thing is how ordinary it is.

If we stayed only with the vocabulary of the everyday, we might say we are "getting some space." But this phrase masks the radical shift at stake. The world as we ordinarily know it is structured by a lens that highlights objects while relegating the background to a blank. We mistake that blank as empty or irrelevant, but in fact it is decisive. What seems like "nothing" is the very condition that allows appearances to arise. To begin to sense that the background is articulate, that it contributes to how things appear, is to loosen the grip of object-fixation and glimpse a more participatory field of experience.

This is why even small shifts of orientation can have transformative effects. We do not need to add new content to enlarge our world, just as a room does not need more furniture to feel spacious. What it needs are windows. In lived experience, windows open when attention relaxes its contraction around objects and lets the wider surroundings enter. This might mean attending to the margins of vision, letting the air around your shoulders come alive, or noticing the silence that makes words intelligible. It might mean softening the posture of the self: easing the jaw, releasing the back of the heart, sensing the body less as a sealed container than as a ripple within a larger sea. These are not techniques to "produce space," but invitations to recognize the spacious dimension already implicit in every experience.

Language easily betrays us here. Because we are trained to think of space as a container or worse, as empty nothingness, when we hear that "space matters" it can sound like a metaphysical claim to be argued for or against. But the point is experiential, not doctrinal. If we attend to the field of awareness itself, we begin to notice a shift in how things appear. The more openness is felt, the less solidity has to be defended. What arises is not vagueness but a quiet relief: objects do not disappear but find their natural place within a wider expanse.

SPACE IS PROJECTING SPACE INTO SPACE!

"Space is projecting space into space" seems utterly absurd in relation to conventional views. But the vision is not concerned with adhering to the presuppositions, or abiding by the rules of conventional views. This contemplation on space can act like a perceptual massage, or even a deep unsettling, of our ordinary focal setting. As a new vision unfolds, our common-sense consensual reality is shaken from its reliance on inherited assumptions about existence. What we are embarking on here runs counter to the most basic assumption of the "world at large."

A story may help us appreciate just how radical this shift can be.[13] Imagine living in the Dark Ages, walking along a beach with a very wise friend. Troubled, you ask: "Does the earth go on forever in all directions? If I were to sail out on the sea, would I fall off the edge?" Your friend, who comes from a far-distant future, reassures you: "The earth does not go on forever, and you will not fall off the edge." But this sounds preposterous. It is simply common sense that the earth is flat; what other option could there be?

Patiently your friend tries to explain that you are seeing the question the wrong way, that the Earth is a sphere, and if you walked all the way around it you would return to where you started. You find this ridiculous. You point to the horizon: "Look. It's flat! The water stretches on forever!" Immersed in the conventional view of your time, you cannot even imagine the possibility of a globe.

Something similar holds true for us. We are steeped in conventional views of space and have no reason to believe otherwise. The provocation "Space is projecting Space into Space," may sound as absurd to us as a spherical Earth once sounded to a medieval mind. Yet this is precisely the invitation: to discover that our most basic assumptions about reality may be only local habits of perception, not unshakable truths.

We should also be careful with the word "ground." If we imagine a platform on which reality sits, we have simply moved the wall. A better image is a *groundless ground*: not a slab beneath appearances, but the open condition in which appearances arise and dissolve. It will resist grasping. It can be known, but not handled. You cannot move it because you are moving in it.

> **But rather than attending to this infinite and transcendent character of space, intellectual energy busies itself with trying to keep up with the infinite wealth of information to be had about objects. Meanwhile space, unlike objects, remains infinite in a way that is untrackable and ungraspable.**

There are many ways to miss this. One is the hyperactive mind, which has often been caricatured as a monkey jumping from branch to branch. The overused "monkey mind" image is clever, but incomplete. Imagine instead the monkey's actual world: a canopy of dense branches, fruit flashing at the edges, the constant need to leap. The monkey's attention is busy with objects—this twig, that fruit—so busy it forgets the tree. It forgets the trunk and the ground in which the tree roots. The monkey is agile and quick, but its world is small. It is not "wrong"; it is enclosed.[14]

This is how many of us live: bright and efficient inside the canopy of tasks, rarely noticing the larger ground that allows everything to grow at all. We are not punished for this so much as cramped by it. The body gives us hints in the language of pressure. The psyche gives us hints in the language of "never enough." The culture amplifies both and sells us solutions that keep us leaping. What breaks the spell is the rediscovery of ground, not as an object to be found, but as the open condition that never left.

> **While space around objects may seem appropriate, necessary, and restful, space within objects may appear a little bewildering. And space considered by itself may appear meaningless, or perhaps even forbidding.**

At first, given our relatively fixed reaction patterns, to progress in understanding by contemplating objects is difficult. Directing attention to space itself is thus more helpful. Even on this ordinary level, space is not a 'nothing', and attending to it can be a potentially powerful and salutary engagement of human awareness. The first time you try, it may feel like looking for something that isn't there. Then you realize: of course you cannot "see" openness the way you see a cup; you can only feel how space lightens the seeing. Space is intuitively felt and sensed, not grasped. It is recognized more by its effects: the release of muscular tension, the easing of a thought's gravity, the way a difficult moment becomes breathable when the margins return. In this recognition, space ceases to be background and begins to show itself as the hidden partner in every appearance.

One workable approach is to treat space not as another "thing" to notice, but as a direction of attention. Ordinarily, our focal setting privileges objects and pushes their background into invisibility. By shifting the setting, by deliberately opening to the margins, the intervals and boundaries, or the silence between sounds, we discover that the so-called background is not passive but formative. Attention widens, and with it the sense of enclosure lessens. The body, too, registers this change: edges grow porous, the breath circulates more freely, gravity feels like support rather than pressure. None of these maneuvers are exotic. They are a return to something the body knows.

Awareness is no longer a spotlight pressing outward from a fixed point; it unfolds, transforming from a narrow spotlight into the soft, omnidirectional glow of a lantern. What seemed peripheral proves essential, for it is in these margins that space shows itself as the hidden partner of appearance.

The corridor metaphor helps us chart three phases of return. In the first, we move through the world as if confined to narrow hallways. Distinctions feel absolute: object or no object, me or not-me, now or not-now: *either/or knowing*, dualistic logic that divides reality into hard categories. Like a blade, it cuts cleanly, but at the cost of isolating knower from known.

In the second phase, corridors sprout windows. Boundaries still function, doors still swing, walls still stand, but thresholds become as interesting as rooms. Surfaces show their ambiguity: they divide, yet they also connect. Edges articulate relations, letting forms breathe. This is *either/and knowing*: a mode that admits ambiguity without panic. Perception begins to shimmer, and the world discloses that presence and absence are not opposites but complementary expressions of a deeper field.

In the third phase, the very image of the corridor gives way to a new architecture: rooms within rooms, vistas opening through archways, the kind of building where standing in one place you sense nine others. Here boundaries arise and dissolve within a single continuum. This is *both/and knowing*, what some traditions call non-dual awareness. Space and appearance are no longer two. Just as waves are the sea's expression, appearances are the continuum's articulation. Nothing is denied: solidity still holds a cup, a wall still stops a hand. But the burden of carrying the world as a pile of separate bricks falls away. Space needs no support.

Seen in this way, each phase is more than a stage of error to be discarded. Even the most rigid dualisms are already symbolic gestures of a deeper truth. To say "this, not that" is also to trace a boundary line, and every boundary presupposes the larger field in which it is drawn. Either/or knowing, though confining, preserves within its sharpness the hint of a space it cannot fully exclude. Ambiguity, likewise, is not just confusion. It is the first stirring of space within the hard shell of dualism, the recognition that edges can also open. In both/and knowing, this latent presence is allowed to flower: distinctions no longer obstruct but participate in the play of non-duality.

> **One very useful and positive consequence of such ambiguity is that even conventional dichotomies themselves preserve, in a symbolic or 'inspired' sense, expressions of a higher order unity.**

The corridor, then, is not simply left behind. Its walls, thresholds, and its very architecture can be read as symbolic expressions of space itself, expressions that, when attended to, point beyond themselves. Dualisms and ambiguities become invitations: ways the continuum of Great Space discloses itself even within the most ordinary structures of perception.

None of this needs to be believed. It asks to be tested. The tests are small and specific: Pause at a window and let your attention rest on the part that isn't glass. Feel how the opening changes your body, even before a thought about "view" arrives. Read a paragraph and, before you turn the page, sense the white that made the letters legible. Then notice the way the mind wants to skip the white to get to the next black. Who, exactly, is rushing?

When a difficult emotion swells, try loosening the surround. Let the feeling have a larger space. Refuse the mind's demand that you pick a side—am I calm or upset?—and instead let both coexist. Training in spacious seeing is training in this capacity: to let multiple truths sit together without forcing them to cancel each other out.

There is a temptation, however, to turn all this into metaphysics. The mind wants a single conclusion: the world is solid or not; space is something or nothing; the self is real or an illusion. But the invitation here is operational rather than doctrinal. Widen the horizon and watch solidity relax its hardness. Relaxed solidity is kinder, more creative, less frightened. That is enough.

Still, language has work to do. One phrase continues to tug: *Space projecting Space into Space!* The words can sound like poetry or nonsense, depending on perspective. But taken as instruction, they are neither. Rather, this statement suggests that what appears as "space" at the ordinary level can be taken as a symbol for a more primary openness, one that expresses itself in every appearing, whether or not we notice. If you let the phrase repeat under your breath—walking, waiting, washing dishes—it becomes less of a statement and more of a tuning fork. You might notice your breathing becomes deeper, while your shoulders lose a millimeter of height. The eyes may stop pointing and fixating. The jaw may relax. You didn't make the walls disappear; you discovered they were never barriers at all, but expressions of the openness that lets them appear.

To keep this grounded, consider how often our fiercest problems are problems of enclosure. A creative block is not the absence of ideas; it is the presence of too much self against the task at hand. A conflict is not always a mismatch of values; it is often the inability to create a space where two values can breathe together long enough to recognize their common ground. Burnout is not just too much to do; it is a way of doing that clamps down on everything it touches until the life goes out of it. In each case, the habit is to add more: more effort, more argument, more caffeine. In each case, the repair begins when you remember space is projecting space into space!

The repair can be social as well as personal. Organizations that only optimize tasks soon become psychic prisons of compliance. The best leaders understand design: they create space where creative tension can surface without tearing people apart. Classes that treat knowledge as cramming information create good test takers and poor learners. Teachers know that "less is more," that the real curriculum needs oxygen and room to breathe. Families that run on schedules, rushing from one activity to another, forget how to linger. The most nourishing moments arrive when someone refuses to rush the conversation and lets the silence do what only silence can.

Seeing through walls is not the same as walking through them. The fantasy of invincibility bears glamour: obstacles vanish at command, we pass untouched. But the freedom available here is humbler, in the end, more reliable. We need not violate the conditions of the world to feel free in it. We need to meet those conditions with a wider lens. Sometimes the lens widens on its own. A parent waits in a hospital corridor, roof lights buzzing, the ceiling's panels, the floor's grid, the long line of closed doors. Then the nurse returns with a sentence, "She's okay." Nothing in the corridor has changed, yet the field is transformed. What had been a prison of surfaces opens into relief.

At other times, the widening is learned. A violinist remembers that music is not in the notes themselves but in their relation to silence, and lets the rests lengthen by a breath. A programmer steps away from the screen, and in the rhythm of walking his dog, the problem resolves itself. In each case, the objects remain, but awareness loosens its grip on them, and the background, once invisible shows itself as formative.

Because the field is always present, practice can start anywhere and anytime. Include the periphery of your vision while reading. Let a little of your attention rest behind you as you listen to a friend. When you catch yourself insisting—this problem, this person, this worry—let your insistence be the cue to soften the edges. The cue is not a reprimand; it is a hand on your shoulder that remembers the open sky.

Across all of this runs a deeper correction. We are trained to experience the self as a hardened center of experience: *I* see; *I* think; *I* act. Reality becomes a stage with a spotlight on a singular protagonist, and everything else is either prop or threat. When the wider expanse is allowed in, the spotlight becomes daylight. The "I" does not vanish so much as change its job. It stops being the manager of a crowded corridor and becomes a participant in a wider ecology. Agency softens into responsiveness. Knowing stops cutting everything it touches and begins to include.

A quiet courage is required to live this way. A corridor is reassuring: you know where "you" stand and where the walls are. An open expanse is trickier, because it asks you to trust what cannot be grasped or possessed. But courage here is not rigidity; it is composure within openness. It is the confidence that you can stand in a room open on every side and discover that stability comes not from the walls, but from space itself.

Etymologically, "courage" comes from the Old French *corage*, from Latin *cor* for "heart," meaning the innermost feelings, spirit, or temperament. This root reminds us that courage is rooted not in external structure or certainties, but in the heart's capacity to stay present, open, and unclaimed by what shows up. To shift our focal setting, to move from object-fixation into space's revealing background, is to let the heart trust the unseen architecture of awareness.

All of this may sound abstract until the next crisis, when you need a wall to lean on. Then it helps to remember that solidity is not the enemy. It is only one possible mode of perception. Walls give form to rooms. Doors give meaning to passage. Structure is how openness articulates itself so that a life can be lived. The problem is not form. The problem is forgetting Space.

> **In our usual experience we are directed away from contact with the infinite dimensions that are available to us. Thus, we are not flowing—floating—properly. Our senses, ideas, and physical capacities are blocked in some ways.**

Forgetting Space means settling into "lower space," the narrow corridors and crowded enclosures that have shaped our habits of perception. Within these confines, life becomes a matter of coping with walls, of leaning against them for support, or of pushing against their limits. Yet, these lower spaces are not absolute barriers but symbolic expressions of Space itself. The opaque surfaces we take as solid obstacles, and even the mental blocks we call frustration or fatigue, are themselves configurations of a more primary openness. The very walls that seem to hem us in are already made of Space, and so they can open to Great Space.

Courage in the face of difficulty, then, is not bracing harder against the walls but recognizing their provisional nature. Estrangement from each other, from nature, and even from ourselves is not a final verdict on our humanity; it is the trace of a constricted focal setting. To "flow-float properly" is to rediscover that we are not meat-bodies stranded in a hostile world, but beings already participating in infinite dimensions of Space, Time, and Knowledge. When this recognition dawns, blockages unfreeze, energies circulate, and the walls of identity lose their power to name who we are.

What is promised here is not escape but a new vision of reality: a way of inhabiting life at its most fundamental level, where limits reveal themselves as invitations. By evoking a greater understanding, we begin to see that what appeared as walls were thresholds all along, expressions of the very openness that supports our authentic destiny and creative purpose. Space, Time, and Knowledge have our backs.

One of the most reliable ways to remember is simply to look up. Not because of saving grace in altitude, but because the sky demonstrates what openness is. It accepts everything: clouds, wires, planes, storms. It cannot be hoarded or exhausted. It is never absent. One upward glance, and the body recognizes itself as drawn within, and sustained by, an openness it did not create.

From there, subtler "skies" come into view: the margin of a page, the pause in a sentence, the breath's brief balcony between in and out. The small thaw in the jaw before you answer. The space around a decision where the question shifts from "What do I want?" to "What gives this room more room?" These are not ornaments of experience; they are reminders of how perception can reset its focal setting. If you keep at this, something quieter than triumph enters your days. Not the victory of walking through walls, but the ease of seeing through them. Anger still visits, but it no longer needs to be a hallway without doors. Sorrow still comes, but it can sit with you gazing out a window. Even joy stops shouting and starts flowing.

In the old way, the world must be carried and maintained. In the new way, the world carries itself. Work remains, cups to wash, emails to send, people to love, but the work unfolds within a room not built by us, a room we do not have to hold aloft with a clenched jaw or fist. When narrowing returns, a single sentence can serve as a reminder: from most conventional points of view, the phrase "Space projecting Space into Space" seems useless or absurd. But it is not a doctrine to accept; it is a trial to run. Direct attention to openness, and watch how reality shifts its register. The walls remain, but the outlines shine. They become surfaces through which knowing can move; sometimes, they vanish altogether.

We mistake the gift of such vision when we think the point is to escape. The point is to *inhabit*: to inhabit the room already larger than its furniture, to inhabit the day already floating in the sky, to inhabit a self that is less a fort and more a clearing. This is not withdrawal from the world. It is a return to the kind of participation that makes the world livable.

CHAPTER FOUR

The Space of Embodiment

Imagine standing on a quiet stretch of beach. The sand is warm beneath your feet, the horizon stretching endlessly ahead. Now picture your body, not as the familiar outline contained within skin, but as vast as the scene itself. Arms as wide as the coastline, legs like pillars sunk into the sea, the chest rising with the rhythm of waves. The simple thought experiment may sound fanciful, yet its effect is immediate: the sense of "me" expanding beyond the familiar contours of flesh and bone.

We've been taught to take objects as primary, bodies, tools, tasks, problems, and to treat space as a passive stage on which things appear, collide, and disappear. That assumption has survival value.[15] We eat apples, not space; navigate sidewalks, not atmospheres. Yet it comes with a cost: experience hardens and the world feels dense, compartmentalized, heavy to carry. We try to manage our way through it by adding more, more control, more technique, and more self-improvement, without questioning the lens that makes life feel small in the first place.

We can open to a new vision by catalyzing new ways of knowing that invite a different entry point. Rather than preaching a new belief, we will engage in a set of direct experiments: "try this and see." These exercises tilt our attention away from the usual focus on things, challenging our taken-for-granted certitudes, and gesture toward the openness that holds them. What changes is not the world but the way it shows up: what seemed like walls and opaque partitions begins to behave like windows and transparent outlines. The difference is not escape; it is full engagement with immediacy.

What follows is a sequence that begins with the body, our most convincing "thing," and opens it step by step, not by denial but by direct inspection. Each practice is immediately experiential. Between them, we'll pause to name what is shifting conceptually, so you can follow the arc without losing the thread of felt experience. In this way, practice and perspective work together: the exercises open the focal setting; the framing shows why this loosening matters.

> **Our bodies are a central focus for our experiences as human beings. Therefore, it is important to carefully examine what typically makes up our conception of a 'body'—for the 'typical' is taken for granted all too often. . . . A fresh perspective, grounded in 'felt reality,' thus may emerge from a kind of experiential review and challenge of our usual preconceptions.**

Exercise One: The Giant Body

Let your body expand in imagination until it overlaps with mountains, rivers, sky. Don't push detail; feel the reach. Let your sense of "me" widen with the image: arms spanning valleys, chest lifting with the tide, feet planted as if the earth were your floor.

It may begin as visualization, but its effect isn't limited to imagery. The familiar conviction that "I" lives inside a small contained outline starts to loosen. The body's edges blur into the space around them. You become less of a compact unit and more of a ripple in a wider presence. What changes is not ownership, but orientation. Instead of being a "me" that *has* a body, there is a body-as-space, a self that feels more like an expanse than enclosure.

Reflection

Close your eyes. Imagine your body filling the room. Let the room become too small and your body spill into the building, then beyond, into the horizon. Don't force anything. Just allow the expansion. Notice what happens to breath, posture, and mood. Do the same problems feel as heavy when carried by a body as vast as the sky?

REIFICATION VERSUS RELIEF

Why does this simple expansion matter? Because our ordinary way of knowing reifies, literally "thing-ifies," whatever we notice. We perceive, name, fix. The body becomes an object among objects. Identity clings to it like a badge. With that move, experience tightens: the self as a compact thing must defend its boundaries against other compact things. In that contracting, appearances harden into discrete "things," and the distinction between knower and known hardens with them. In this way, space itself is cast as worthless, irrelevant, nonexistent.

When we think of "what's real," we almost always mean *objects*. A chair. A tree. A cell phone. A body. They are solid, tangible, and, so it seems, self-contained. This orientation is so deep that we rarely pause to ask how these objects appear at all or what makes them *stand out*. We treat space as absence, a blank nothing that simply frames the "real stuff in the real world." But what if that assumption blinds us to half of reality?

The Giant Body exercise begins to loosens this reflex. The exercise does not ask us to deny the body, but rather to dilate it, allowing a taste of spaciousness that doesn't have to be earned or defended. Even a brief taste is instructive: the sensation of "more room" is not a reward, it is a clue. Space isn't a luxury, it is the condition of appearance. Paradoxically, every "something" depends on this supposed "nothing." The outline of your hand is visible only because of the space around it. A melody is heard only because silence supports it. The body you inhabit only makes sense because it is surrounded, penetrated, and sustained by space.

Exercise Two: Internal Details

Turn inward. Instead of a solid mass, feel the body as cavities, chambers, currents: lungs as vaulted spaces, bloodstream as rivers, nerves as filaments. Wherever you expect a wall, explore for pathways. Look for where air flows, where warmth moves, where sensation flickers and fades. The body is less a sealed container than a living weather system, an ecology of exchanges.

Now, let these internal spaces expand the way the outer horizon did. The chambers grow more airy; the rivers of blood more fluid; the membranes more permeable. It is not a feat of imagination so much as a reorientation: you are noticing space where you once saw only surface.

Reflection

Let the breath show you the shape of inner space. Follow the in-breath into the lungs as if you were walking into a cathedral's nave. Follow the out-breath like a tide going out. Then widen the attention to include the whole torso as open volume. What happens to the sense of "inside" and "outside" when the body is felt as an open field rather than a solid, dense form?

Our way of relating to our bodies is often very rigid and tends to restrict our potential as embodied beings. Our attitudes and investigations of the body often perpetuate either a mechanical or a 'ghost in the machine' perspective.

Chapter Four

AMBIGUITY AND ATTENTION

Ordinarily, we take the body to be a compact, solid container. But when we intentionally shift the focal setting and widen the scope of attention, it feels and appears porous. Air flows in and out, blood circulates, signals pulse. The body is less a sealed and consolidated vessel than a living, dynamic flow of relations. Because ordinary knowing is pointed toward perceiving objects, reification creates, in addition, a dualistic opposition between knower and known. We not only think we *have* a body, we imagine the body as a fixed object. With that assumption, the knower positions itself apart from what is known. It is as if "I" observe "my" body from behind the eyes.

An even more vivid image depicting our ordinary stance is like a "ghost in the machine," an isolated subject peering out from a compartment in the head. Another image is the *homunculus*, a little internal observer thought to be the true "self," sentient and conscious, surveying both the body and the world from a hidden control booth.[16] Within this picture, the body itself is demoted to an object, just another "thing" among things to be managed or explained.

This way of knowing restricts awareness to the supposed isolated observer and cuts us off from a more intimate and integrated sense of embodiment. From such a cramped perspective, what counts as "known" must always be objects, surfaces, or insentient systems. Even when we relate to other beings, what we notice is primarily their physical bodies, not the liveliness of their knowing. The result is a frozen mind–body dualism: a way of relating not only to ourselves but to our surroundings, and especially to the natural world, that is marked by estrangement.

But this frozen picture can be thawed. The more we open to liveliness, clarity, and intimacy, the more the rigid categories of "body," "mind," and "world" begin to lose their grip. Awareness no longer needs to be trapped inside the skull, looking out. It can return to the body as flow and to the world as a relational field. In this thaw, ambiguity becomes a doorway: the recognition that the body is both perceiving and perceived, both subject and object. It is in such ambiguity that a more fluid, participatory knowing can take root.

This simple exercise, if you can even call it that, loosens the duality. As internal details open into space, the rigid split between observer and observed weakens. The body is not "out there" to be inspected, nor "in here" as property. The second exercise also introduces a subtle skill: allowing multiple truths to sit together. The body is solid enough to keep you from walking through walls; yet, on closer inspection, it is pervasively open: alveoli, sinuses, capillaries, interstitial fluids, and vast neuronal spaces. Both are real, neither cancels the other. The mind typically flips between these realities as if they were mutually exclusive. What if, instead, this coexistence was the point? The body can be felt as object *and* as space, depending on how attention is set. Learning to let these modes coexist is not indecision; it is embracing ambiguity as a provisional mode of a wider intelligence.

From here we can transition into a larger question: what if ambiguity itself is not a failure of perception, but a gateway? Our inherited worldview has taught us to prize clarity, to cut the world into sharp binaries: either something exists (the object) or it doesn't (space = nothing). Reality is parsed into opposites: life/death, subject/object, presence/absence.

This "either/or" logic has evolutionary survival value, but it is also narrowing; it has kept us alive, but it does not necessarily help us flourish.

Ambiguity, by contrast, opens another register of knowing. Think of the famous optical illusion sometimes called *My Wife and My Mother-in-Law.* Some people see the young woman (wife) instantly; others see the old woman (mother-in-law). Both interpretations are encoded in the same lines, yet neither figure exists *in* the lines themselves. What we perceive arises through interpretation: the brain's best guess at meaning.

Ambiguity is not error. It is the sign that perception is framed by more than one possibility.

If you perceive the young woman, you cannot simultaneously see the old woman. They coexist and are unified, but at a higher level that is difficult to see directly. What the mind can manage instead is a quasi-dualistic switching back and forth. Yet this ambiguity admits their presence together. This is why artistic forms like poetry, music, and metaphor are so nourishing. They thrive in the ambiguous zone, where meaning is not locked down, where object and space comingle. They offer a lived taste of openness that logic alone cannot.

You might wonder, isn't this all too abstract? What difference does it make if objects are "really" space? Again, the difference shows up in the body. When we insist on dualistic knowing, the body contracts. Space is excluded, and experience feels crowded, pressured, confined. Stress, anxiety, and defensiveness thrive in this mode.

But when ambiguity is allowed, when we admit that objects are not as absolute as they appear, the felt sense of our body can radically change. Indeed, it is our conception and familiar sense of the body that is the locus of experiential reality. We are not seeking a mystical experience but rather a heightening of our perception. Even a simple shift of focus, from relating to our body as an object to the space around it, can be felt directly as relief.

Our body can simultaneously appear solid, reliable, protective; and at the same time radically open, fluid, and spacious. The problem is that our attention usually narrows, forcing us into one register or the other. The exercise invites us to let both stand side by side, not as a contradiction but as an expansion. To dwell in such ambiguity is to learn that reality is layered, shimmering, not exhausted by any single reading.

This is where "focal settings" becomes practical. We habitually narrow the lens: select, isolate, and fixate. Space fades to background, and things take center stage. By relaxing the focal setting, we don't lose resolution; rather, we gain context. Internal details become less like components of a machine and more like luminous nodes in a field. The exercise fosters precisely that shift.

Exercise Three: Location and Presence

Ask a simple question: where am I? Point to the chest. To the head. To the eyes from behind with which you "look out." Keep asking the question. Each point dissolves into sensations: pressure here, warmth there, pulse somewhere. None of these sensations is the "I" you expect to find. The map doesn't reveal an address. Let the question become open rather than agitated. If "here" won't hold still, perhaps "I" isn't a pin on a board but an event, something that shows up with certain conditions and dissolves when the conditions shift. If presence doesn't have a single location, what is it?

If we try to determine our position by pointing to the body, we only point to an appearance, an appearance itself is conditioned by space. The 'I' is not found there.

This is more than wordplay. The certainty of "I am here" undergirds our every thought and action. But when pressed, "here" dissolves. The "I" that was supposed to occupy it slips away. Instead of being disorienting, this realization can be freeing. Presence no longer clings to a pin on a map. It begins to feel more like a ripple in openness. The Giant Body exercises have begun to unseat the most insistent assumption of all: that self and body coincide as a fixed point.

The inquiry can deepen. If "I" cannot be located in chest, head, or inner image, then where am I really? The point here is not to seek a tidy solution or answer. Instead, this exercise reveals the insufficiency of the very question. The "I" is not a thing to be pinned, and space is not a container in which it sits.

Location is a concept; it cannot serve as a basis for reality. It is space which makes location possible, but space itself is not locatable. This signals a turning point. The very structure of our identity—"I am here, you are there"—rests on assumptions that collapse under scrutiny. And when they collapse, something shifts: what was rigid becomes permeable, what was final becomes provisional.

Reflection

Repeat the statement "I am here." After each repetition, ask softly, "Where is here?" Point if you like, but keep noticing that you only point to appearances, not an owner. Let the question grow friendly. If "I" can't be located, does that mean I'm missing or that the way I've looked all along has been too tight?

A SCHEMA OF RELATIONS: HIGHER SPACES

We can sketch the shift like this. In our default mode, object and space are sharply divided: things exist, while space is the emptiness between them. We have been speaking of this as the "either/or" lens. With a gentle widening, ambiguity enters: object and space coexist; surfaces are also edges and thresholds. This is an "either/and" lens. With deeper ease, the distinction softens further: appearances are not other than the space in which they arise—not two separate things—yet without collapsing into sameness. This is not a metaphysical claim to be believed but a perceptual fact to be tested: the more openness can be felt, sensed, and embodied, the less solidity needs to defend itself. The result isn't vagueness but a kind of primordial relief.

> **This invokes a picture of concentric or nested spaces, each space more 'accommodating' than those below or inside. When we first attempt to move to another space, due to the relative opacity or intolerance of our present space, it seems that we have to push and force, to 'break the rules' of our level in order to 'break out'. A strict logic of alternation usually seems to be in force—either things are 'this way' or 'that way'.**

We might picture this movement as a series of concentric circles, each ring opening into a wider one. At higher levels, appearances as objects and the space that allows them are no longer separate. Objects are space and space reveals objects. These higher spaces are qualitatively different in character: more open, more inclusive, more accommodating. Importantly, higher does not erase or destroy lower. Just as the sky can completely accommodate storm clouds that temporarily obscure the sun, higher space can hold the distinctions, boundaries, and tensions that shape our ordinary perception, without losing its openness.

This means that "higher" is not about climbing into some far-off realm or otherworldly domain; not a "there" in contrast to "here." Rather, higher spaces are already present, woven through our experience, waiting to be noticed. Their transcendence lies not in escape but in accommodation. They include what came before, the way a room includes the furniture within it, while also offering a larger dimension in which those furnishings can be rearranged or reimagined.

In our yearning for transcendence, we often begin with what can be called a "breakout mentality." Practice feels like a struggle of will: a determined effort to burst through the walls of confinement and catapult ourselves into freedom. We imagine the task in heroic terms: "Here I am, trapped in a stifling space. I must break through." Striving becomes the fuel; expectations rise. We long for a dramatic breakthrough.

But this urgency still belongs to the logic of lower space. The very sense of being hemmed in sharpens the desire to escape, keeping attention bound to the walls. We strain and push, as though openness were a distant destination to be reached by force. What is missed at this stage is that higher space is not elsewhere. It does not have to be stormed or conquered.

This is a key point in the vision: higher spaces are not otherworldly territories, but more inclusive dimensions of the very space we already inhabit. They can fully accommodate the patterns of lower space, its boundaries, oppositions, and distinctions, without being limited by them. Just as the sky can contain both clear light and storm clouds, higher space is never diminished by what it accommodates.

Still, when we first shift focal settings, the movement can feel like pushing against the walls of a too-small room. Habits resist; perception insists that things must be one way or another. Early glimpses of openness can seem jarring or destabilizing. Ambiguity unsettles certainty, and we may long for the old clarity of binary distinctions. But as understanding matures, the unfamiliar begins to feel less threatening. Ambiguity reveals itself as accommodation; the sense of "being between" dissolves into the sense of "being within." What once felt foreign starts to seem natural, even inevitable. Looking back, our earlier perspective appears constricted, like breathing through a straw after tasting mountain air.

The genius of higher space is that it does not denigrate lower space. Instead, it enfolds and reinterprets it. Boundaries, forms, and conventions continue to appear, but they are no longer taken as absolute. They become translucent outlines within a wider expanse—provisional rather than final. This reframing is not just philosophical. It points to the possibility of a radically different experience of reality: more fluid, more accommodating, less bound by sharp edges.

To live in this way is to inhabit a more inclusive dimension of being. Experience is not carved into isolated chunks but allowed to unfold as continuum, a shimmering play of boundaries that are never quite final. This is what it means to "cross over" into higher space: not a departure to somewhere else, but an arrival into a more profoundly expansive mode of consciousness.

But notice a trap here. The moment we begin to sense that something more spacious is stirring, the mind wants to conceptualize and domesticate it into familiar terms. We ask, "What does this mean for me? How can I understand these infinite dimensions from where I stand now?" That is precisely where we risk getting stuck. Any idea born from the narrow frame of lower space will only reproduce its limits.

This is why certain philosophical questions—existence versus nonexistence, life versus death—prove impossible to resolve within the confines of ordinary space. They were never meant to be settled on that terrain. What is required is not a sharper argument but a different mode of seeing, one in which the very oppositions that generate the puzzle begin to lose their relevance. Some questions are not solved; they dissolve when the ground that sustains them is left behind.

Consider our most basic assumption: we exist as solid objects, standing forth in space, vulnerable to the threat of not existing. The Latin root of "exist" means "to step out, to stand forth," which is how we picture ourselves: as discrete figures stepping forward on the stage of life, with space reduced to a backdrop. Because we identify with this solidity, we cling to existence and recoil from its opposite. From this recoil grows a fundamental insecurity, a restless hunger for reassurance, not a mere biological drive for survival, rather an existential craving born from fear of vanishing. Such primal craving shapes our lives more than we realize, creating a sense of being ungrounded, always slightly at risk, as if there were a black hole at the center of our being that no achievement, possession, or relationship can ever fulfill. We keep moving, seeking, grasping, looking for anchors in things that themselves are impermanent. This is the "monkey mind" at work: never still, swinging from one branch of experience to the next, mistaking frenetic activity for fulfillment.

Higher space does not deny this insecurity. It includes it, reinterprets it, and opens a door. What once appeared as an implacable craving for existence begins to look more like a signal pointing toward openness. The hunger itself is revealed as an invitation to drop into a deeper groundless ground, a space in which existence and nonexistence are no longer opposites, but part of a wider play of being.

BREATHING ROOM

Pause for a moment. Notice your body as it is, without trying to change it. Sense the surfaces you normally take for granted: skin, bones, weight. Let yourself feel their density, their opacity. This is the familiar world of enclosure, the sense of being bounded and pressed by circumstance. Then, without discarding that sense of solidity, widen your attention to the air around you. Feel the simple fact that your body is already in space, already supported by openness you did not create. The walls of the room, the edges of your own body, even the limits of thought itself may feel like barriers, but they are also thresholds. Space allows them all.

Stay with this contrast: the heaviness of density alongside the ease of openness. Do not force them to reconcile; simply allow them to coexist in your awareness. Notice how the pressure eases when you grant yourself permission to inhabit both dimensions at once. This is the invitation of higher space: not to erase what is solid, but to sense the vast and deep continuum in which solidity itself takes form. As you linger in this contrast, you may begin to glimpse the possibility that even what seems opaque has more to show.

In the following chapter, we explore what happens when density itself begins to reveal outlines, when the familiar solidity of the body is not only buoyed by space but begins to shine within it.

CHAPTER FIVE

Shining Outlines

At the end of the last chapter, we lingered on the contrast between density and openness. Solidity presses, space releases, yet they coexist in every moment. That contrast is a doorway. Description alone cannot take us through it. If we stop at the threshold, we risk confusing the map for the territory.

Imagine writing the word *water* in the sand. The letters may be neat, carefully inscribed, their strokes clear in the sun. But they will never quench thirst. Words about water are not water. The metaphor is ancient, yet it speaks directly to our predicament: explanation is not the same as experience. A map can guide you to a spring, but unless you drink, you remain thirsty.

Space is like this. We can measure it in physics, define it with mathematics, praise it in poetry, or reduce it to metaphor. We can describe it as emptiness, container, void, or backdrop. Yet none of these accounts means that we actually feel space as an immediate dimension of experience.

This chapter turns from map to territory, from words to presence. The body becomes our starting point, not as a fixed container, but as a surface on which new lines can be drawn. These are not rigid boundaries but shining outlines: translucent, alive, revealing a more spacious way of knowing. The problem is not that we lack concepts of space. We have plenty. The problem is that concepts too easily become substitutes for encounter. It is like standing before a window, tracing its frame with a finger, and mistaking that for stepping outside.

To live within concepts of space is to live indoors, surrounded by diagrams of windows. To live with space as presence is to walk outdoors, where the sky opens above and breath expands on its own. The difference is not subtle—it is visceral. One leaves us confined and restricted, the other restores us.

And yet, the shift is delicate. Our habits are deeply set. For years, even decades, we have trained attention to cling to objects: things to fix, solve, defend, consume. In that mode, space remains background, an absence. The invitation now is to turn attention differently, to let space itself become vivid. That shift cannot be achieved by force. It is more like relaxing into a view you hadn't realized was already surrounding you.

This is why the practices ahead matter. They are not meant to add yet another layer of theory. They are designed to help us loosen the fixation on density long enough for translucence to shine through. The body becomes our laboratory, not because it is a puzzle to solve, but because it is already our most intimate ground of appearance. To reimagine the body as outlines, as thresholds, as radiant edges within openness, is to begin learning what it means to inhabit space directly.

The transition from concept to encounter is always a crossing. We leave behind the safety of "aboutness" and step into immediacy. At first this can feel disorienting, like walking out of a darkened theater into full daylight: eyes straining, senses overwhelmed. The very strangeness is a sign that something real is happening. To steady ourselves in this crossing, it helps to begin close to home. The body is the most intimate of landscapes, yet we mostly know it through surfaces and routines. We identify with its weight, its aches, its appearance in the mirror. We rarely sense it as a living interplay of relations, a play of boundaries and flows.

This chapter invites us to explore the body in just this way, not as a fixed thing, but as an unfolding into spacious knowing. The exercises that follow are not abstractions. They are simple methods for loosening the solidity of form so that we can glimpse the openness that pervades it. Think of them less as instructions to "get right" and more as invitations: doors you can walk through at your own pace, each leading into a wider room. With that spirit, we begin.

> **[to] thaw out our world of appearance and to regain the 'knowing' that has been somehow frozen in the process of building this world, we need to learn what we ourselves are. We must work with—and thaw out—what we apparently have close at hand.**

Exercise 4: Just Interactions and Shining Outlines

Begin again with the body, not as a single, solid object, but as a gathering of countless living structures working together. Notice how every structure depends on another: bones supporting muscles, muscles drawing on blood, blood carried through branching vessels. What we usually call a "thing" is, on closer attention, more like a crossroads of interactions. Each part is itself made of smaller patterns, which in turn are made of smaller ones still.

As you follow this inward unfolding, let the familiar sense of solidity thin out. The surfaces that once seemed like barriers can now be felt as permeable boundaries that both define and connect. With patience, these edges may even begin to appear less opaque, showing themselves instead as *shining outlines*: luminous traces that hold their shape yet invite passage. They are not walls but shimmering interfaces, translucent boundaries alive with possibility.

From here, experiment with a gentle freedom. Imagine you can move through these shining outlines, passing from one region to the next without obstruction. Let the body show itself no longer as a solid thing, but as living layers of interwoven traces and flows.

Assume a position outside the body, and view it in this translucent aspect, a nesting of outlines within outlines. Try to encompass all of the body's organization simultaneously within this vision. Consider the possibility of entertaining this vision without its being limited to a single angle or point of view; try to see the body from all directions and levels simultaneously.

Reflection

To glimpse the body in terms of shining outlines is to undo one of our deepest habits: the conviction that form must equal solidity. Normally, edges signal limits: where something stops, where a wall keeps us out, where a body ends and the world begins. But when those edges glow as outlines rather than hard barriers, perception shifts. We see definition without confinement, clarity without closure.

This shift opens a paradoxical freedom. The body remains precise—heart here, lungs there, bones beneath skin—yet its boundaries no longer *feel* final. Each outline is provisional, a meeting point where inside and outside touch. The body is not so much an isolated structure as a constellation of luminous thresholds, shimmering with their own aliveness.

It is a little like reading music. On the page, black marks trace exact forms—notes, rests, rhythms. Yet those outlines are not the music itself; they are shining guides, invitations into sound. The notes are both precise and open, defining possibility without enclosing it. In the same way, the outlines of the body can be experienced as invitations, not limits, markers that point toward a deeper resonance, a vibration already moving through us.

In this mode of seeing, even ordinary perception begins to feel more spacious. A thought is not just a thought but a glowing trace arising in awareness; a sensation is not a sealed-off thing but a radiant edge between body and world. The practice is not about dissolving into vagueness. It is about discovering a new kind of clarity: sharpness that shines and shows, but does not imprison.

Shining outlines remind us that form and space are not adversaries. They interpenetrate. When we recognize this, our own sense of self changes. Identity ceases to be a fortress defended on all sides. Instead, it becomes a set of outlines too, bright enough to be seen, open enough to be crossed and permeated.

We are used to treating "things" as givens. We take their solidity for granted, as if their density were self-evident. Our eyes confirm what we think we know: objects are stable, fixed, opaque. Even our own visual organs, the eyes themselves, are taken as just more "things," reliable instruments reporting on a solid world. This kind of knowing is passive; it accepts that the way things appear is actually how they are. The purpose of these practices is to begin destabilizing that fixation. What seems most obvious, that things are hard, dense, and unchanging, is precisely what can dramatically unfreeze under the scrutiny of experiential inquiry. By shifting our attention and using the power of inquiry, we will begin to notice that "things" are not so inert. The body, for instance, is not a lump of solid flesh but a complex, living process, a network of exchanges, flows, and interactions. The body is dynamic and alive as motion: breathing, circulating, neuronal firing, dissolving.

When we see in this way, we are already moving toward a more visionary kind of knowing. Instead of being locked into passivity, we enter a more dynamic engagement. "Things" become events, relations, interactions—never simply what they seemed. And from this shift, translucence begins to appear not as an exception or an anomaly, but as a more accurate reading of the nature of appearances. Forms do not vanish; they grow lighter, brighter, more intra-relational, less absolute. Their outlines shimmer, hinting that they are both themselves and something more.

This new capacity to see not just "objects," but the openness (and the dynamic), lets them arise, preparing us for the next step: the release of the body into space itself.

Exercise 5: Released to Space

Bring to mind the giant body once more. Let it appear now as an immense constellation of translucent outlines: nested systems within systems, every contour luminous. These outlines should not remain as faint sketches. Brighten them. Let them grow vivid, alive, and ungraspable, shimmering with an ecstatic quality that lifts the whole image beyond heaviness.

Now, allow your awareness to move directly into the outlines themselves. Instead of boundaries that separate, feel them releasing, becoming permeable. Each line dissolves into space, until the entire image releases into a vast openness—intensely alive, but without fixed form. There are no points of view, no measured regions, no fixed coordinates. The outlines have vanished, not into absence, but into a dimension of pure space: radiant, unqualified, boundless.

Reflection

This exercise asks us to reimagine the body, not as a fixed thing but as a score unfolding in real time. At first, the outlines may appear faint, as if a single instrument is playing in a quiet register. Then, as they brighten, something like a crescendo builds: the outlines grow luminous, ecstatic, and alive. They cease to be barriers and instead resonate like passages of music, each contour carrying you forward.

Think of it as an original composition. Nothing is prescripted. The music emerges in the moment—spontaneous, fresh, as if you were hearing it for the first time. The outlines shimmer like notes that rise, swell, and then dissolve back into silence. In the same way, the body's boundaries intensify, only to release into the openness that has always been present.

Here the usual perspective of "me in here" looking at "the body out there" is left behind. The knower and the known no longer sit apart. The body is not reduced to an object of analysis, heavy and opaque, but revealed as wondrous and energetic—alive as space itself. The release is not annihilation but resonance: outlines shining and dissolving into openness, like a final chord that lingers in the air. What remains is not emptiness as absence, but emptiness as living space: radiant, immediate, and inexhaustible.

Notice what is released here: not just the sense of "the body" as an object, but the dictates of perception that insist things must be enclosed to exist. In this wider space, nothing is lost. Aliveness intensifies, even as boundaries fade. The body is not annihilated; it is revisioned as an expression of space itself. The more we touch this, the less we cling to the fear of dissolution. Release is not erasure. Far from it, release is the discovery of a natural freedom.

> **The 'space' is unlike ordinary space, being free from the qualities and presuppositions that are ordinarily attached to space. It is also unlike ordinary 'things' as they are usually understood. We have, however, reached it by an exploration of 'things.' So perhaps 'things' could actually be said to be, fundamentally, nothing but this 'space' or openness.**

RENDERING WALLS AS TRANSPARENT

Sometimes it feels as though we are penned in by invisible walls. These walls are not made of stone, but of assumptions, preconceptions, and habits of mind, our insistence that things are solid, our conviction that "inside" and "outside" are fixed. We push against them daily, and they push back, leaving us caught in collisions with what seems immovable.

Through the previous exercises, we have initiated a new way of knowing, like seeing through walls by rendering them transparent. Not shattered, not replaced with new ones, but rendered so open that the very idea of "inside" and "outside" no longer applies. In such moments, the sense of being boxed in begins to dissolve. What once appeared as resistance becomes pliable, even luminous. This gesture, "rendering the walls transparent," is not about entering some distant otherworld. It is a way of loosening the grasp of lower space, where every surface seems like a limit and an endpoint. Transparency here doesn't mean the disappearance of boundaries, but their transformation. Surfaces still appear, yet they are less obstructive, more responsive, as if they carry the imprint of our own natural capacity to relax.

This is one glimpse of what the TSK vision calls Great Space. As you probably can surmise by now, Great Space is not a "thing" to be found elsewhere, not some exotic condition distinguished by the absence of concepts. Rather, it is the very openness that allows concepts to arise, without being bound by them. However, from the vantage of lower space, it may feel radically different, even remote. Yet from within its own dimension, Great Space is natural and simply accommodating, capable of allowing boundaries and distinctions without being limited by them. More importantly, this openness doesn't require us to suppress thought or to declare war on our concepts. The issue is not whether we think or not, but the quality of our thinking atmosphere. What is our mind space like? Is it contracted, stale, reactive? Or is it fresh, clear, bright, like air after a storm? Great Space does not negate thought; it reconditions the mental climate so that thought becomes fluid, creative, and life-serving.

We may have already had brief tastes of this. Times in nature, when the ordinary chatter of mind fell away, leave a simple presence of wonder; a sunset whose colors erased our commentary; a mountain vista that seemed to open the heart by dissolving the usual categories of "me here, world there." These moments are not mystical in any remote sense. They are intimate previews of a more profound relaxation into space.

To live this way is to discover that the things we once took as heavy and confining can become workable, even light. The walls are not demolished, but we no longer collide with them. They are transparent enough to let us move with ease, and in their translucence, they reflect our own capacity to blend and bend to the situations at hand—to 'flow-float' with skill and grace. This is the atmosphere in which we now enter the next exploration: learning to sense how even the opaque can reveal itself as open and how what once seemed dense and final can be experienced as alive *with and as* Space.

Exercise 6: Opacity and Translucency

Return again to the giant body you explored in the earlier exercises. Let it appear now in its most solid and dense form. Sense the thickness of bones, the weight of muscles, the resistance of skin. Let opacity register fully, how we ordinarily experience the body: as substantial, firm, even heavy.

Now, without dismissing that density, recall its other face. Allow the body once more to shimmer in translucency, outlines bright and open, structures no longer barriers but thresholds. Notice how these two visions, the dense and the transparent, can both be present as valid experiences (remember the young/old lady figure). Ask yourself: does anything in the opaque version truly prevent it from being open? Can solidity itself be another way that space shows up?

Reflection

We usually think of solidity and openness as polar opposites. One cancels the other. But here, the practice hints at something subtler: opacity and translucency may both be expressions of Great Space. Like two movements in a piece of music—one heavy, grounded, percussive; the other light, airy, melodic—they are distinct yet joined in a single composition.

What shifts is not the body itself but our way of knowing and attending. A rigid gaze isolates, carving the world into things. A more relaxed seeing allows form to breathe and move, until even density carries a quiet spaciousness. When the body is experienced as translucent outlines, it is easy to feel openness. When experienced as solid mass, it seems harder. Yet if you listen closely, even the solid carries echoes of space, like bass notes resonating beneath higher tones.

This reflection suggests that the opposition between solidity and openness may be less final than we imagine. Perhaps every surface has translucence enfolded within it, and every opacity is another rhythm of space. The invitation of this exercise is not to prefer one over the other, but to sense and appreciate the continuum they share.

BEYOND OPACITY

When we compare the dense, opaque body with the translucent body of space, it is tempting to imagine we are moving between two separate realities. One feels undeniable, solid; the other provisional, visionary. But the point is subtler. What we call "solidity" and what we call "openness" are not distinct universes. They are perspectives that shift depending on how wide the aperture of attention opens, how the lens of the focal setting frames what is given. The difference lies less in what is "out there" than in how awareness positions itself, and in that shift, the ordinary can begin to glow with an unexpected spaciousness. Solidity is no longer the final word; it is an expression of a more primary spaciousness.

Seen this way, even opacity is part of space. The dense and the open, the bounded and the boundless, are not enemies. They are modulations of the same unbounded reality. The more we can relax into this, the less pressure there is to hold onto one perspective or view as being absolute. Solidity and openness can be felt together, not as contradictions, but as mutual harmonies within a single continuum.

A THROUGH-LINE FOR PRACTICE

Seen as a whole, the six exercises presented so far form a gentle but decisive arc:

1. Expand the felt body until the idea of a tight enclosure no longer dictates identity.
2. Discover the inner body as a landscape of cavities and currents rather than a sealed crate.
3. Explore the unfindability of a single "point" of presence—the failure of the pin-on-a-map self.
4. Re-read boundaries as shining outlines, interfaces rather than barricades.
5. Let even the luminous outlines dissolve into space that is vivid without being locatable.
6. Learn to hold solidity and translucency together as two textures of one space.

The arc is cumulative but non-linear. You may find that Exercise Six retroactively illuminates Exercise One; or that a day of interiors (Exercise Two) delivers the insight that "here" won't hold still (Exercise Three). Treat the sequence not as a ladder to climb but as a set of windows to open. Each window admits air to the same house.

The work of Exercises 1–6 has carried us into a new terrain. Step by step, we have learned to see the body less as a fixed object and more as a constellation of relationships: open, translucent, spacious. Exercise 6 left us with a crucial question: if both the dense, opaque body and the translucent body are equally "space," what does that imply for how we actually live and know ourselves?

Answering this question requires an even greater shift. Until now, our exploration has treated the "giant body" primarily as a physical organism, a system of interacting parts that can be opened, brightened, and released into space. That perspective has been powerful, but it is not enough. To move further, we must recognize that the body is not just an object of inspection. It is a lived reality: personal, intimate, inseparable from the one who supposedly observes it.

This next stage calls us to bring the observer into view. What does it mean to approach the giant body not only as a structure, but as an embodied person? How does our very act of observing shape what appears? These questions strike at the roots of our sense of "being someone," a self who stands apart, watching and evaluating.

The coming chapters and exercises will challenge that stance. They will press us to ask whether the self as "bystander" is truly separate, or whether it, too, arises within a wider and more inclusive space. This is where the inquiry into space begins to open into the nature of our own subjectivity. What we discover may unsettle our familiar sense of location, but it also holds the promise of revealing a more unbounded dimension of knowing. The translucent boundaries we glimpse here, these shining outlines, are not an end but a beginning. They open into deeper questions of perspective and presence, drawing us toward Great Space.

Chapter Six turns directly toward this territory. It extends the giant body practice into the realm of psychology and lived embodiment. We will explore the play of body, mind, and thought as they interweave, and we will begin to sense how even the "self-as-observer" participates in the same openness we have been tracing. If earlier exercises have shown us how walls can become transparent, the next ones will show us that the one who thought they were trapped inside is also less solid than imagined.

CHAPTER SIX

Spaceland

In the last chapter, we discovered how even the walls of the body could be made translucent. Structures once felt to be opaque opened into outlines, thresholds, and space itself. But this was never the end of the journey. What happens when we turn that same investigative light on the one who has been looking all along?

Until now, we have worked with the image of the giant body as though it were an object of inspection: lungs, nerves, veins, bones, all shimmering into openness. Yet to continue this inquiry, we must face a deeper challenge. For the body is not just a structure; it is also the basis for our sense of being a *person*. The body is lived, inhabited, and felt, entangled with thought, memory, and identity.

A radical question comes into focus: Is the "person" as continuous, enduring, and self-contained as we assume? Or could personhood itself be another appearance, another pattern arising within space?

> **Despite appearances, the person is not a continuous being, born once and for all in a world. Rather, the 'person in a world' could more accurately be seen as a tendency toward consolidation ... a frozen pattern of successive moments.**

This is where the inquiry into space begins to open directly into the nature of subjectivity. First let's define a "person-in-a-world" with the help of a compact field guide.

A Field Guide to Focal Settings

This compact "field guide" summarizes the focal settings we slip into without noticing. Each focal setting acts like a stage: it frames appearances, organizes meanings, and cues us into certain roles. It shapes what counts as real, who we think we are, and how the world appears—yet it usually stays invisible. We don't step into a setting the way we enter a room. We live inside it without noticing, as though it were the only world available.

But settings are not fixed. They can shift, loosen, and sometimes collapse. Each exercise in this book is less about adding a new skill and more about exposing the frame that was already shaping perception. Once seen, the setting itself can soften, and new possibilities appear. The following sketches are not exhaustive, but they will serve as a map we can return to in later chapters.

Lower Space / The Default Chamber

Think of a cave or vault, where meanings echo off the walls. Thoughts, judgments, and memories ricochet in closed loops, creating a sense of heaviness and confinement. Here, self and world appear sealed off from each other, bound in partitions. Life feels bound by walls that aren't really there, yet still seem to hem us in.

Idolatrous Settings

Within this chamber, meanings do not just echo; they crystallize. Abstractions congeal into "things" and are mistaken for concrete realities. Space seems like a neutral container, the self like a fixed inhabitant, the world like a stock of solid objects. In this "vault" of meanings, provisional designations become idols: they feel final, unquestionable, self-standing. We bow to our own mental constructs, mistaking signs for what they signify. This is the habit of taking shadows on the walls of the cave as reality.

The Bystander

The self stands apart as spectator, manager, or controller. This stance feels safe, as if distance offered security. But it also isolates, making us outsiders to our own life. The bystander holds up the world at arm's length, never noticing it was already moving without supervision. Here the self is always "on duty," supervising thoughts, emotions, and actions, trying to manage life as a project. This setting produces the sensation that without constant control, things will fall apart.

Openings

Every chamber has its cracks. Even in lower space, light filters through: a pause between thoughts, a breath of beauty, a gap in the loop. These translucent moments show us that no setting is airtight. They are thresholds, brief but real, that hint at a wider space.

Life still unfolds, but less as a burden to be managed than as a dance already underway. The cave shows its cracks; light filters in.

Nondual Settings

Beyond all these orientations lies a shift where "setting" itself loosens. The divide between self and world, inside and outside, begins to dissolve. Reality presents as a seamless play of appearances, not staged from a vantage point, but arising on its own. Here, intimacy is uncontrived, and participation replaces performance. The cave, the chamber, the vault dissolve into openness.

These sketches are not exhaustive, but they mark the terrain we keep circling: caves of echoing thought, idols made of meanings, the bystander's distance, the cracks of opening, and the intimacy of non-dual presence. What seems absolute, self, world, distance, time, is already colored by the stance we occupy. To catch ourselves inside a chamber is already to notice its walls. To notice the walls is to glimpse the openings. And to glimpse the openings is to sense that another kind of space was here all along. Each chapter offers another way to notice how settings shape us, how, through cracks and openings, they can also release us. With this map in hand, we can now look more closely at how the sense of "self" and "world" crystallizes, the subject of the four views that follow.

BEYOND THE FROZEN PATTERN: FOUR VIEWS OF PERSON-IN-A-WORLD

Before we move deeper into the practices of this chapter, it helps to pause and look carefully at the picture of personhood that most of us carry around, usually without question.

In ordinary life, we take the story of personhood for granted. First, we presume there is already a world, a stable container of space and time. Then, at a certain moment, an individual is born into that preexisting world. Cells divide, an organism develops, a baby appears, and eventually an adult takes shape. After decades of persistence, that person dies, and the world continues without them.

This story feels natural because it mirrors our own experience. We look at old photographs and feel, "That was me. I have changed, but I am still the same person." We imagine time as a line, with "my life" as a continuous thread running across it, stretched from birth to death. Even science appears to confirm this picture: causes precede effects, DNA guides development, neurons fire in sequential chains.

From this angle, space and time seem neutral and fixed, the reliable backdrop on which the drama of our lives unfolds. We, as embodied persons, are the actors, moving across the stage until the curtain falls. But built into this conventional view is a dichotomy we rarely notice: existence versus nonexistence. I exist now; once I did not; one day I will not again. We live with this tension as if it were a fact of reality rather than an assumption baked into our lens.

The vision we are exploring here challenges this familiar picture, not with dogma but by offering a sequence of views that progressively unsettle the "frozen pattern." Each view is like a step melting the ice of a "frozen pattern," the rigid frame that tells us who we are and what kind of world we live in:

1. The Ordinary Worldview

This is the view we all inherit. A person is born into a preexisting world of space and time, shaped by prior conditions. We grow, persist through causal continuity, and eventually die. Space and time serve as neutral backdrops. The world itself seems too stable to be changed by our brief appearance.

2. A Pattern Derived from Openness

From another angle, the world we take as solid is less stable than it seems. Its apparent continuity is an arbitrary consolidation, a pattern that actually draws its energy from a more open dimension. Linear sequences of cause and effect are not absolute—they are just one way of stitching appearances together.

3. The Ongoing Tendency to Freeze

Looking deeper, even this apparent consolidation never fully solidifies. What looks like a continuous person in a continuous world is actually a fluid patterning, crystallizing moment by moment into the appearance of stability. Identity is not fixed but an ongoing condensation.

4. Nothing Separate from Space

The most radical shift dissolves even this. There is no frozen pattern opposed to openness, no thing that needs to be thawed. Worlds, things, and persons are never separate from space in the first place. The boundaries we take as ultimate are not barriers but already part of a more accommodating openness.

Each of these perspectives can feel bewildering, as though we've slipped into another dimension. That's where the metaphor of *Flatland* becomes illuminating.[17]

A Visit to Flatland

Imagine, for a moment, the two-dimensional world of Edwin Abbott's *Flatland*.[18] Its citizens are geometric shapes, sliding across a plane. They know only length and width, no height. A square lives his life among triangles, circles, and polygons, convinced that flatness is all there is. One night, a mysterious visitor arrives: a Sphere from the three-dimensional world.

Sphere: You believe your world is the whole of reality. But I come from another dimension, one that gives rise to yours.

Square: Nonsense! I see only lines and angles. Everything is contained in the plane. There is no 'above' or 'below.' Your words are absurd.

Sphere: Then let me show you. Watch as I pass through your world.

The Square sees a circle appear, grow larger, then shrink and vanish.

Square: A trick of perspective! A circle that grows and shrinks, that's all. Why call it a dimension?

Sphere: Because what you saw was only a slice of me. You cannot yet perceive my full shape, but without my dimension, your plane could not exist.

To Square, the claim of another dimension sounds absurd, even dangerous. This scene offers a parable for how the four views of personhood unfold, and we can track their conversation to illustrate how the four views take form:

First View: The Ordinary World

Square insists: I was born when my sides appeared. I will die when they vanish. The plane is eternal, the world stable. Beyond this, there is nothing. This is our ordinary view: a self born into a preexisting space-time, persisting until death.

Second View: The Pattern Draws from Openness

Sphere tells Square: Your flat world is not self-sufficient. Its stability depends on a wider dimension you cannot yet see. Square protests, but begins to notice how lines and angles, once thought absolute, seem to shift when the vantage changes. The solidity of Flatland wavers. Just so, our world of causal sequences may be less absolute than it appears, deriving energy from a more open dimension.

Third View: The Tendency to Freeze

Sphere continues: Even your own body is not continuous. You crystallize moment by moment, traced anew each instant.

Square protests: But I *feel* continuous. I wake each day the same Square!

Sphere answers: That continuity is a story your world keeps telling itself. Look closer: identity is not fixed but a condensation, freezing and unfreezing within openness.

Square begins to glimpse that the apparent stability is a moment-by-moment crystallization. Identity is not a permanent polygon but a tendency, freezing and unfreezing within the wider field.

Fourth View: Nothing Separate from Space

At last Sphere declares: There has never been a separation. Your lines, your plane, even you are already inseparable from space. There is nothing to overcome.

Square is stunned: If that is true, then my walls, my boundaries, are they illusions?

Sphere: Not illusions, but appearances within openness. They are real enough, but provisional. They do not confine you. The plane itself, the lines, the shapes, everything is already an expression of space. There is no rigid barrier to overcome, no ultimate wall.

Square's entire world, and Square himself, are already inseparable from the openness. For Square, these revelations are destabilizing. They unsettle the inherited certainty that Flatland is the whole of reality. But they are also liberating. What once seemed a prison of rigid lines now shimmers as an expression of a more generous dimension.

The 'person' is then a summary notion describing the overall attempt to set up a frozen pattern or series of instants connected in an exclusive manner, in contrast to a more open and inclusive 'space'.

The parable captures something central about our own sense of self. Like Square, we ordinarily assume that identity is continuous and secure: *I was born, I have persisted, and I will die when my body dissolves.* This is the first view, the ordinary conviction that a person is born into a preexisting space-time, continuous until death. But as the second view suggests, our stability is not self-sufficient. Just as Square's plane depends on a higher dimension he cannot see, our world of linear causality may derive its very energy from a more open dimension. What feels stable may be contingent, patterned from a larger field of openness.

The third view pushes further. Our sense of continuity, like Square's confidence that he wakes each day "the same Square," is revealed as a crystallization: a condensation that freezes moment by moment. Identity is not a permanent polygon but a tendency toward consolidation, a habit of mind that takes transient patterns and binds them into the story of a solid "self." This *consolidating tendency* is the drive to freeze what is fluid, to string together successive instants until they seem continuous and absolute. From this view, the "person in a world" is not a fixed being but a patterning, an ongoing effort to hold open uncommittedness in place as if it were permanent.

Finally, the fourth view declares that there has never been a true separation. Square's lines and walls, the very plane, are already inseparable from space itself. Likewise, what we call body, world, and even "self" are not obstacles to openness but expressions of it. Here, the consolidating tendency completely relaxes and dissolves. What appeared frozen is seen as translucent, already pervaded by space. Nothing needs to be overcome; there is no "elsewhere" to reach.

Read in this way, the story of Flatland is more than a parable of dimensions; it is a mirror held up to the very process of personhood. Out of an original "openness uncommittedness" emerges a tendency toward patterning. Feelings, images, and associations coalesce, forming the sense of a bounded self facing an external world. That self is not a fixed entity but a provisional crystallization, repeating itself from moment to moment. Like Square, we take the consolidation as absolute, forgetting the openness that subtends it.

Now we can return to our own embodiment. To consider the body as lived is to notice how the "self-as-observer" is woven into this very patterning. It is not outside the weave, directing the show from some homunculus in the head. It too is crystallized within the same openness. The next set of exercises invites us to feel how body, mind, and thought co-compose "you in a situation" and then to gently open even that composition.

Exercise 7: Body-Mind-Thought Interplay

Explore a wide variety of typical activities and situations: social interactions, entertainments, learning experiences, various sorts of work or labor, and emotional highs and lows. In each situation, notice that its overall character and nature are reflected in your own psycho-physical embodiment. Observe the complex interrelationship between sensations, 'mind', thoughts, emotions, and body which constitutes 'you in that situation'. For instance, the mind receives input; it thinks thoughts; these thoughts bear an emotional dimension; and emotions are embodied in particular physical areas (the stomach, the throat, and so forth). Such embodiment leads to sensations that again tie in with particular emotions, memories, thoughts, and so on.

Investigate the psychological and physiological mechanisms and interactions in as much detail as you can. Such an investigation may require that you treat your own body as a 'giant body', traveling through it once again as a tiny observer.

Reflection

Keep this exercise flexible and unscheduled. Try it in a staff meeting, on a walk, while cooking, during an argument, in a quiet hour. What matters is the *patterning*: how a situation recruits sensations, images, micro-postures, and storylines that together feel like "me-here-now." Don't force insight; track the choreography. With practice, you may come to notice:

- How the "me" of one scene (capable/tense/studious) is not identical to the "me" of another (tender/guarded/performative).
- How quick the inner manager is to take credit or assign blame.
- How labels—*my thought, my body, my mood*—harden fluid processes into compartments.

Each time you catch the labeling hardening, loosen it by asking, *What's the texture here? Where is it felt? What else is happening in the field?*

> **Thoughts, concepts, and distinctions are the product of a 'space' which could be considered similar to an enclosing chamber that filters and inhibits input from the 'outside'—casting shadows and causing echoes or impingements, bombardments, and fragmentations to occur within its walls. Space should accommodate, be open to, and make room for things. But in our ordinary space, 'making room' has become 'making a room'—lower space is like a walled enclosure.**

INSIDE THE CHAMBER OF LOWER SPACE

This image of a chamber, filled with shadows and echoes, gives us a vivid picture of how lower space operates. It is not an abstract description but an experiential one: the sense of being hemmed in by our own thoughts, caught in feedback loops that reverberate endlessly. Anyone who has lain awake at night replaying conversations or anxieties knows the claustrophobia of this echo chamber.

Lower space does not merely describe an external condition; it is enacted in the interplay of body, mind, and thought. Our sensations, our emotions, our ideas all arise within a mental environment already structured by boundaries and partitions. The "walls" are not physical, yet they are felt: the pressure of expectations, the echoes of past judgments, the bombardment of distractions. Instead of offering relief, this space folds in on itself, layering concept upon concept until we drown in complexity.

> **It is as if we were being manipulated by a sort of local petty official, whose power actually derives from a larger government and whose actions express the will of that government. This petty official does not inform us of the source or purpose of his commands—maybe he himself is governing clandestinely—and so we cannot correctly judge our situation.**

Attempts to simply "quiet the mind" or "be present" rarely touch this deeper dynamic. To sit inside an echo chamber and command the sounds to stop is to misunderstand the architecture. What needs to be seen is how the walls themselves are shaping the experience: how lower space, by filtering and enclosing, generates the very dissonance that unsettles us.

This is why the exercise of exploring body–mind–thought is not just psychological analysis. It is a way of noticing how the enclosure itself is built, how sensations spark emotions, emotions spark thoughts, thoughts return to the body, and the cycle continues, tightening the chamber walls.

Recognizing this dynamic lightens the heaviness. The very act of seeing the pattern from within begins to thin the walls.

The recognition and the possibility that our mental "walls" are not absolute but patterns that can thin and open sets the stage for the next inquiry. They are not barriers we must smash through, but patterns we can render more transparent. When echoes lose their density, when shadows thin, what seemed like a closed room reveals itself as permeable. If the echo chamber of thought is not the whole story, what else might emerge when its outlines begin to soften? Even small moments of relaxation in attention, even a slight widening of our aperture, can show that the walls we take as given are, in fact, translucent. And that translucence is a foretaste of Great Space.

> **If these walls can be somehow rendered transparent without thereby setting up new walls and points of view, the notion of inside and outside is thus deactivated, and the experience of internal collisions and interactions ceases. This is then something like Great Space.**

In the previous exercise, we saw how the structures of body, mind, and thought can feel like chambers, environments that reverberate with feedback and ricochet. We can take this one step further by now seeing how "making room" becomes "making *a* room." Boundaries harden; partitions arise; compartments freeze in place. What could have been an open expanse of participation becomes enclosed, divided into inside and outside.

The suggestion now is radical: if the partitions we take as real were thawed out and seen through, the collisions that dominate our ordinary sense of self would lose their force. Instead of ricocheting off boundaries, experience could settle into openness. This is the flavor of Great Space.

There is a warning here, too. We cannot chase Great Space as though it were an object, a hidden "it" waiting in hiding somewhere else. To do so is only to construct more subtle walls. Words, metaphors, even the term "Great Space" itself are at best provisional. The point is not to nail down another concept, but to feel directly the possibility of a space without inside and outside, already 'here,' closer than we think.

This shift from "making a room" to rendering the walls transparent prepares us for the next step. If body, mind, and thought have appeared as opaque compartments, what happens when we open their boundaries the way we opened the body in earlier exercises? What if the surfaces of mind itself became translucent, their partitions dissolving into space? That is the invitation of the next exercise: to track the body–mind–thought interplay, and then to let each component grow transparent until the whole structure of "the person" opens into space.

Exercise 8: The Translucent Person

Continue to track the body-mind-thought interplay sketched out in Exercise 7. As you do this, gently move into the space or region that is the 'body', 'mind', or 'thought' component of the experienced interplay between 'body and mind' or 'mind and thought', and so on. Open up the opaque surfaces and partitions that define each component. Carry on this response to the presence of 'body,' 'mind,' and 'thought' until all instances of their appearance are completely translucent, as in Exercise 4. Then complete this process by opening up the translucent outlines themselves until the entire interplay disappears in a kind of openness or 'space'.

Reflection

This exercise invites us to see that what we call "a person" is less a fixed identity and more a shimmering interplay of body, mind, and thought. Normally, these appear as separate compartments: sensations in one box, emotions in another, thoughts in still another. Each feels opaque, walled-off, and solid. By letting their surfaces become translucent, we glimpse how artificial those separations are. The "person" ceases to be an object located inside the skin and skull. Instead, personhood becomes more like an open constellation: dynamic, relational, not easily bounded. To rest even briefly in this openness is to sense that the self we defend so fiercely is not a fortress, but a pattern of translucence already pervaded by space.

BEYOND PARTITIONS: A GLIMPSE OF GREAT SPACE

Exercises 7 and 8 ask us to notice the interplay of body, mind, and thought and then to open even those compartments until they too became translucent. At first glance, this exercise might look like a lesson in self-analysis, cataloguing how thoughts trigger emotions, how emotions show up in the body, how bodily tension loops back into thought. In part, it is. But this was not just an exercise in perception, but a gesture toward something much more profound: the possibility that what we call "the person," our embodied sense of being, is itself only a provisional enclosure. The walls of body, mind, and thought, which seemed so necessary to our identity, can become transparent. And when they do, we begin to glimpse the possibility of Great Space.

Great Space is not a new room inside which we relocate ourselves. It is not a refined state to be attained after enough discipline, nor a hidden territory waiting to be discovered if only we push hard enough. Its openness is greatest precisely when it is no longer framed as a "thing that allows." When we stop grasping at Great Space as an "it," as some object to be pinned down, its boundless accommodating quality begins to shine through.

This has profound consequences for how we live. Lower space constantly limits and confines us with partitions: conceptual walls that cast shadows, create echoes, or set up collisions. The result is a kind of psychic bombardment, as though we are trapped in a chamber where the sound of our own thoughts rebounds endlessly, generating new reverberations, feeding back upon themselves until all coherence blurs. It is no wonder that our mental life so often feels cluttered, tense, or overwhelming.

But when these partitions are rendered transparent, the same field becomes luminous rather than confining. Instead of hoarding scraps of clarity or clinging to rare "special" states, we begin to feel that creativity, clarity, even joy are intrinsic to Being itself. We are no longer impoverished by lack, but nourished by an inexhaustible abundance.

One everyday symbol of this shift can be found in generosity. At the surface level, generosity still depends on a giver, a gift, and a recipient. Yet we intuitively sense that the deepest generosity happens when the figure of the "giver" recedes. In those moments, the act itself seems to flow through us rather than from us. That intuition, in its purity, reflects something of Great Space, a kind of infinite providing that is not owned or possessed, but freely given by reality itself.

Language inevitably strains at this point. Great Space is not an object among other objects, nor is it simply the absence of objects. It cannot be contained by concepts, because every attempt to define it risks turning it into yet another "thing." Mystical traditions have sometimes spoken of a *via negativa*, a "way of negation": not this, not that. In a similar way, Great Space is not captured by description, and yet it saturates every moment of ordinary life. What matters for us here is not to solve the puzzle of Great Space with the intellect, but to begin to *feel* its flavor in our own experience. That is why these exercises matter. They are not pointing to a remote beyond, but to a loosening of the fixations of our habitual enclosures so that what we have imagined as the "beyond" can be sensed within the very heart of the here-and-now.

And here is the deeper turn: if the walls of body, mind, and thought are not as solid as they appear, perhaps the "self" we imagine standing behind those walls is also less substantial. What if the supposed bystander, the one we take to be the observer of all this activity, is itself just another echo in the chamber, another construction of lower space? Then the transparency we are cultivating is not only about dissolving partitions in experience, but also about removing the prison bars and unbinding the one who thought it was trapped inside.

Paradoxically, this is not an escape from ordinary life but a deepening of it. Surfaces and structures remain, but a new way of knowing alchemizes. They appear less as rigid barriers and more as flexible membranes: workable, transparent, and responsive. Exercises 7 and 8 are preliminary doorways into this possibility. By following the interplay of body, mind, and thought until their partitions grow translucent, we begin to taste a freedom that does not come from annihilating the ordinary, but from seeing that even the ordinary is already illuminated from within by the extraordinary.

Returning to Spaceland

Square: I've done the exercises, but honestly, I'm not sure what they accomplish. I still feel like me: this solid body, this stream of thoughts. Maybe I just imagined the translucence.

Sphere: Imagination is not trivial. Why assume imagination is only make-believe? In Flatland, remember, imagination was the only hint of a higher dimension. To dismiss it is to miss the doorway it offers.

Square: But the exercises don't stick. I feel something for a few moments, then it fades. I go back to the same old me.

Sphere: Perhaps what returns is not the same old you, but the habit of thinking of yourself that way. Wasn't there even a brief moment when thought, sensation, and feeling mingled without sharp boundaries? That moment was not an illusion. It was a glimpse of Spaceland.

Square: Spaceland? That sounds like another world I can't reach. Isn't this just setting up some mystical realm beyond my grasp?

Sphere: Not higher, not elsewhere. Spaceland is not another world; it is this very life when seen without frozen partitions. It is the openness already here, when you stop insisting that 'I' must stand apart from what arises.

Square: Still, it feels so far away. Why can't I hold onto it?

Sphere: Because holding on is a wall. The tighter the grasp, the thicker the partitions. The invitation is not to seize but to notice, to soften, to return again and again until even the observer becomes transparent.

Square: But what if I feel nothing? What if it's just boring? I sit there trying, and all I get is the same stream of chatter in my head.

Sphere: Boredom is itself a teacher. It shows how quickly the mind craves stimulation. Instead of rejecting it, notice how boredom feels in the body. Where does it land? Is it heaviness in the chest, restlessness in the legs, a tightening in the jaw? Even boredom is part of the interplay. And even boredom has edges that can soften.

Square: Sometimes I just think this is mystical fluff. Where's the proof? Where's the evidence? Isn't this just wordplay dressed as philosophy?

Sphere: Proof is another wall. You are used to proof as something external, a stamp of authority. But what proof is more intimate than your own direct sensing? Look: when you loosen the attachment of thought, do you not breathe more easily? When the walls open a little, is there not a fresh spaciousness? That is evidence enough.

Square: I get it in theory. But when I leave the page, when I go back to my day—email, errands, conversations—it vanishes. It feels impractical.

Sphere: Impractical only if you think practice must be separate from life. These exercises are not techniques to master in isolation. They are experiments in perception, meant to seep into the ordinary. You can notice translucence in a breath between emails, or in the way light falls across a sidewalk. You can sense Spaceland even in traffic, if you listen differently.

Square: You make it sound easy. But it isn't. My thoughts are relentless. My anxieties keep me locked inside.

Sphere: Relentless thoughts are not the enemy. They are the echo of the chamber. Notice the echo, and you are already loosening its hold. Anxiety, too, has translucence; it is not solid, it flickers. To see that flicker is to glimpse the openness in which it plays.

Square: So you're saying Spaceland isn't somewhere else, but right here, already woven into what I am?

Sphere: Exactly. Spaceland is not attained, it is revealed. It is not a place to get to, but the recognition that even the observer, even the self you call 'me,' is part of the field, not a fortress standing apart.

Square: Then maybe the point isn't to escape Flatland at all, but to notice the cracks already in its walls.

Sphere: Yes. The cracks are the openings. What you took as final partitions are outlines waiting to be seen as translucent. The very doubts you voice—'This is too abstract, too mystical, too hard'—are part of the inquiry. They are Square's voice, but they too arise in Spaceland.

Space: To hear them differently is already to begin to live in Spaceland.

Square's struggle is our own. We resist because the walls feel familiar. "Isn't this too abstract? Am I really supposed to believe I am less solid than I appear?" But this is exactly the point of Exercises 7 and 8. They are not there to persuade us, but to let us taste our own patterns and to see those patterns as less final, more translucent. When the chamber of thought stops echoing quite so loudly, when the outlines of body and mind thaw and thin out, when even the observer seems less like a fortress and more like a flicker in space, we are already in Spaceland. This is our inquiry now: to return, urgently and playfully, to the patterns that make us, and to see how even they are spacious.

CHAPTER SEVEN

Seeing Through the Observer

In Chapter Six, we learned to treat body, mind, and thought not as sealed compartments but as a living interplay that could grow translucent merging into space. We began to glimpse how what seemed opaque might, with a shift of attention, be revealed as open. But if walls are not as solid as they appear, what about the one who perceives them? Now the inquiry turns the light around: illuminating not just what is seen, but to the one who is seeing. The "observer" that quietly steers and narrates experience steps into the field of view.

Imagine sitting in a darkened theater. On the screen before you, a story unfolds: seamless, continuous, alive with motion. Yet what you are actually seeing is a rapid flicker of still images, each one fixed, each one separated by a sliver of darkness. The mind edits away the gaps, weaving the stills into a flowing narrative. Continuity is conjured, not given.

Our sense of self works in much the same way. We assume we are continuous beings: one person moving through a stable world, unbroken across time. But what if this, too, is an illusion of editing? What if what we take to be "me" is not a single unbroken line, but a sequence of momentary frames stitched together, each one carrying the trace of "observer" and "observed" arising together?

This is the question that comes into focus here. Exercises 7 and 8 showed how the body, mind, and thought interweave, and how even the partitions between them can become translucent. But we have not yet looked closely at the one who watches, the presumed "self-as-observer." Is this observer truly continuous and independent, or is it another appearance stitched into the film of experience?

Exercises 9 and 10 turn directly toward this point. They are the hinge of this section: moving us from observing contents to questioning the observer who claims to stand apart. Like discovering the dark intervals between film frames, they invite us to notice what has been there all along—space itself, alive and participatory, not exhausted by the appearances that pass through it.

The early exercises trained a sensitivity for how solidity forms. Here we deepen that training by noticing how the sense of "me-as-bystander" takes up a position, freezes that position, and then looks out from it as though from a stable platform. We tend to trust this figure the most: the narrator of our story; we could even say it functions as the movie director: the producer of our moods, the commentator who insists it is "I" who sees, who decides, who endures. Yet the vision being unfolded here suggests something far more unsettling—and liberating. The observer is not outside the field. It too is patterned within the same continuum, it believes, that it surveys. The more a stable platform is presumed, a perch or vantage point from which the observer perceives, the more space is reduced to mere "rooms," locations to move through, rather than the openness that lets anything appear at all.

Chapter 7 asks you to include the observer-position platform inside the experiment. Instead of focusing on body and world, Exercises 9 and 10 turn the lens back on the observer. What happens when the "I" that claims to stand apart is seen as arising within the same interplay of body, mind, and thought?

Exercise 9: Participation as Observer and Person

Return to the interplay examined in Exercise 7, which tracks the body-mind-thought-emotion interaction, but try to remain aware of your own presence as the observer of the patterns. Do this extensively over time before proceeding to the next stage of the exercise.

Open up everything present, rendering all defining regions and surfaces translucent until they finally become 'space'. Exclude nothing from this process: even 'opening up', 'translucence', and 'space' are all opened up until gone. Then, even 'being gone' should be treated in this way. Finally, the subtle locatedness of this final experience as the outcome of a certain process should be opened up, as should its status as an 'experience'.

Be careful not to index the new type of unqualified openness discovered to any standard world order. Let go of the subtle connections that bind this openness to the 'you' of that standard world. Try not to 'come out' of the openness in order to examine 'it'. When you do 'come out', as you will, regardless of your attempts to avoid it, watch that process very carefully. This is important. Finally, release any residual notions of quantity linking the size of this open space to the size of the structures that inhabited it in earlier stages of the exercise.

Reflection

Think of this in two passes.

Pass 1: Notice the perch. Revisit any everyday scene—a meeting, a kitchen conversation, a solitary walk—and track the familiar choreography of body–mind–thought as in Exercise 7. This time, keep part of your attention on the *perch* from which you're seeing: the faint sensation of "me-here-looking." Feel how it quietly positions itself, labels, evaluates, and *stabilizes* experience. (This "position" the self assumes so it can view a world of fixed locations. Noticing that moving to a position is key.)

Pass 2: Include the perch. Now let the observer on a perch image join the field. Give it the same treatment you gave to "body," "mind," and "thought": soften its edges, let its surfaces become translucent, and very gently open even the *sense of opening* itself. The instruction sounds paradoxical ("open up 'opening'"), but it simply means that each time a new boundary appears, even a refined, spiritual-looking one, see if it, too, can thin and become space. Notice the almost irresistible urge to "come out" and examine what just happened. That reflex is part of the pattern; watch it kindly, as instructed.

What to expect:

- You may glimpse how the "observer" is less an entity and more a *moment-by-moment positioning*, a tendency to take up a stance. Seeing this directly unfreezes the compulsion to re-freeze it.
- Periods of openness can feel strikingly *unindexed*—not anchored to your usual reference points. The instruction to avoid sizing or mapping that

openness (e.g., "How big is it?" "Where is it?") helps preserve its quality.

- If the mind protests, "But I need a stable platform!" that's natural. The very need for an "absolutely stable" vantage is part of the freezing effect being challenged; seeing it in action is already a significant shift.

The invitation here is subtle: to see that the observer is not outside the loop. The act of noticing is itself part of the interplay.

Think about being caught in a difficult meeting. Your shoulders tense up, your stomach churns. A thought flashes, "I can't handle this. I don't like what is happening," which sparks embarrassment, then the tension in your gut deepens. You notice the reaction and try to calm yourself, but that very attempt becomes part of the cycle: the observer trying to manage the observed.

The point is not to break free into some imagined vantage point above it all, but to sense how observer and participant co-arise. The "I who notices" and the "I who reacts" are not two separate agents; they are patterns within the same space. This is why Exercise 9 is the hinge of this chapter, marking the transition from observing contents—thoughts, feelings, bodily sensations—to noticing how the observer itself is another content-generated image, another participant in the dance. In this way, the exercise begins to dissolve the frozen picture of "me here feeling my body, in reaction to, a world out there."

Instead of being a spectator in a theater of appearances, you begin to glimpse something more intimate: the entire theater itself is fluid, and the one watching is also part of the play. This shift prepares us for the next stage of inquiry, where we begin to ask not only *what appears* but *how appearance itself originates.*

> **Mind, like space, has no foundation. It is not a palpable or solid thing, and it does not do anything. Rather, the mind is a sign of specific focal setting being taken on Great Space.**

THE MIND AND THE ORIGIN OF APPEARANCE

If the observer is not outside the field, what about "mind" itself? We usually treat mind as a kind of headquarters: the seat of awareness, the inner room where perceptions arrive, where judgments are made. But what if this picture is also misleading?

As we noted earlier, continuity is conjured, not given. The mind sustains the impression of an enduring "me" by stitching discrete moments into a story. What seems like a single, continuous identity is more accurately a consolidation of successive instants, freezing and unfreezing within space. Personhood, in this view, is less an unbroken line than a narrative pattern continually renewed.

Daily experience makes this visible. We assume the "me" who fell asleep last night is the same "me" waking this morning. We look at old photographs and declare: that was me at five, at twenty, at fifty. Yet everything has changed: cells replaced, memories blurred, perspectives altered. Continuity is not found in any substance.

You can also catch a glimpse of this when memory falters. Think of trying to recall a childhood event. The details blur. Were you eight or nine? Did the conversation happen at school or at home? What seemed once like a solid sequence of facts now feels more like a mosaic, assembled on the fly. The continuity of "my past" is something the mind works hard to sustain, yet it is woven together from fragments of memory.

The same is true in the present. Each instant floods with sensations, impressions, micro-feelings, and stray thoughts. To manage this complexity, mind freezes patterns: "this is me, here is my body, these are my thoughts, that is the world out there." In doing so, it erects walls, partitions, and vantage points—stable enough for us to navigate daily life, but very deceptive if we take them as absolute.

UNFREEZING THE ECHO CHAMBER

By returning to the "four views" in Chapter Six, we can now see how each view thaws the frozen picture of "mind in a body, self in a world." Taken together, they begin to suggest something astonishing: what we call "mind" is not a container for thoughts but an arbitrary focal setting on Great Space, yielding a powerful and convincing way of patterning openness. The apparent solidity of mind is also an echo chamber, reverberating with its own constructions.

This realization does not erase our sense of personhood but frees it from absoluteness. What looks frozen can be unfrozen. What seemed like a sealed chamber can be experienced as an aperture opening into space. The danger lies in mistaking the illusion for reality: absolutizing the relative, imagining ourselves trapped inside a mental chamber, when in truth, the activity of mind is inseparable from openness.

Because, "mind, like space, has no foundation," we can begin to see the self in a completely different light—as a constructed meaning—an idea dressed up as something local and solid, supposedly "here" set against an "out there." With clear seeing, a surprising ease becomes possible. Nothing needs to be defended or secured. We can still participate fully in what appears as "the world," but with the recognition that this world is woven from meanings, not bedrock substances.

The self, too, is one of these meanings—an abstraction drawn out of experience, a "coming out" that arrives paired with another abstraction called "the world." Both the "self" and "the world" are horizons of meaning that only seem independent. To take this abstraction as a concrete entity is to fall prey to the fallacy of misplaced concreteness.[19] It is a narrow misappropriation of cognition, resting on the unfounded assumption that mind insists on a foundation, that it is a generative source. This is a delusion; now we can see through it.

As our vision expands and widens, we can see that from this stance, a self-orientation forms, expressed in the primitive label "I." This "I-making" can be seen as a kind of idolatry: a projection mistaken for an independent agent, reinforced for millennia by the momentum of shared meanings.[20] The apparent solidity of the self is not its own proof; it is the shadow of our own vision.

Similarly, thoughts are not prisoners in a skull, nor the private property of an isolated self. They are more like ripples in a larger medium—dynamic appearances of space itself. The knower is not pre-established, outside looking in. The knower arises with what is known, moment by moment, like the image that exists only while the film is projected. This is not a deficiency but a liberation; our deepest knowing is already participatory, woven into openness.

Seen in this way, even the opaque forms of body and mind are not obstacles to space but expressions of it. To see this directly is to begin unfreezing the frozen story and to sense the possibility of a more unbounded participation in reality.

This interlude is not meant to convince by argument but to prepare the ground. Exercise 9 gave you a taste of participation: the observer is not apart. The next step, in Exercise 10, will push this further: what happens when even the sense of "self-as-observer" is opened, when we begin to sense ourselves as embodied participants in space itself?

Exercise 10: Participation and Space

Earlier exercises helped develop an awareness of your presence as the observer of the giant body. Attending to the phenomenon of 'coming out' in Exercise 9 will particularly contribute to this awareness. Now consider again the vision of the dense and opaque form of the giant body. Try to notice if a form of the 'coming out' tendency is also operating in this case. Is the observing self merely a separate entity, temporarily juxtaposed with the giant body, or is the self actually given together with the giant body in an integral relationship that tends, instant by instant, to polarize?

Still working with the opaque form, see if you can minimize or stop 'your' tendency to 'come out'. Very likely you will not have much success. It is sufficient at this stage of investigation to simply remain aware of this tendency, so that the notion of a solid, continuous, and independent self is at least challenged.

Now compare the more sophisticated 'space' vision of Exercise 9 with the opaque form of the body as encountered in Exercise 10. By doing this, you may gain some experiential insight into the possibility that the dense and opaque bodily structures, when seen in the light of your participating role as the observer or the embodied person, could be a kind of open 'space'. Extending the exploration of 'quantity' presented in Exercise 9, consider the possibility that, although the structures of the giant body are finite in size, the new 'space' dimension may be those structures without thereby being finite. Ordinarily, the volume of an object and the volume of the space it occupies are the same, but that does not hold true in this experience of 'space'.

Reflection

This exercise presses directly on a subtle but crucial discovery: the self that "comes out" to observe is not a detached witness standing outside the scene. It is born alongside the very appearances it claims to be observing. The observer and the body, the knower and the known, are not two. They arise together in a constant, flickering dance, polarizing into "self here" and "object there," then dissolving again into the openness that makes both possible.

At first, this can feel frustrating. The instruction to "minimize or stop" the coming-out tendency sounds simple enough, but as soon as you notice it, the observer seems to be already on the scene, watching itself watch. The point here is not to defeat the observer in some contest of will. Each attempt to plant itself as an independent knower can be seen for what it is: not a position outside space, but a move *within* space. This recognition allows for a kind of tracing back: noticing that even the self's habits of withdrawal and reassertion are themselves already occurring within openness.

Something important happens when this tracing back begins. The observer's claim to stand apart dramatically weakens. The dense body once felt as opaque begins to show its translucence. What once seemed a final verdict of solidity now appears porous, shimmering, open to a dimension that is not finite. The very attempt of ordinary knowing to freeze and objectify begins to melt. Like ice giving way to water, the frozen stance of lower space thaws, revealing a more fluid knowing already coursing through our embodiment.

This is why the contrast between the more translucent vision of Exercise 9 and the dense form of the body in Exercise 10 is not trivial. It shows us that opacity itself is not absolute. Even flesh and bone, in their density, are still space appearing in a particular guise. What seemed to cancel openness is now seen as disclosing it. The "space" of this exercise is only an approximation of Great Space, the first taste of what it means for appearances to reveal, rather than obscure, the ground of openness.

> **Great Knowledge is not like a trophy which 'we' can win. We, our space, our awareness are all deriving from a higher space and understanding.**

This taste is fragile, like a sprouting seed that needs protection if it is to ripen. The impulse will be to conceptualize or to try to "get rid of the observer," but that is only the old game of lower space. The invitation here is not struggle but allowing: letting even our presuppositions open into space. The very fact of being embodied and aware already partakes of higher dimensions. Nondual wisdom, higher consciousness, or what the *TSK* vision calls 'Great Knowledge', is not a trophy that the self can win. It arises naturally as the frozen stance of ordinary knowing softens, releasing back into the openness from which it first emerged.

Just as a windowpane can both hold its shape and let light pass through, so too the body, even in its most opaque form, can be experienced as radiant with space. When this recognition dawns, the observer's restless maneuvers no longer need be resisted. It can be traced back, melted, and released into the openness that was never absent.

> **It should now be clear that the new view of reality which is gradually being activated rejects the truth (if not the appearance) of linear connections and causes as accounting for the arising of any particular existent or event. The source of experience is not the self, the mind, some psycho-physiological apparatus, or any other item within the ordinary world view.**

BEYOND PLACE AND POSITION

The exercises we have just explored reveal something subtle yet decisive: the observer is not a hidden sovereign watching from outside but an appearance within the same continuum as the body, thoughts, and sensations. This recognition invites an even deeper question: if observer and observed both arise within openness, what does it mean to say that they "happen" somewhere? Where is this process taking place?

Ordinarily, we equate experience with location. I am here, in this body, looking out at a world over there. The observer feels positioned, anchored to a vantage point, and from that position it measures other things: near or far, inside or outside, self or other. This sense of *whereness* seems unquestionable, and yet the exercises begin to unsettle this certainty. When a thought is opened until it is translucent, where exactly did it go? If sensations dissolve into space, where did they end up?

The very question "where did it go?" misleads us. By an unusual but natural application of a transitive principle, if objects dissolve into space, and if space itself has no location, then the objects do not go anywhere. They are not moved from one place to another; they are seen as never having been bound to 'place' at all. Space accommodates, but not as a container with fixed coordinates; its accommodating quality is non-local, without position.

This reframing unsettles the deepest habits of our embodiment. We are used to treating ourselves as bodies situated at definite points in time and space, as if our existence were another thing among things. But the more we open appearances, whether thoughts, sensations, or even the sense of being a knower, the more we find that our being has no fixed address, no final position from which the self can survey the world. What seemed like solid placement gives way to something closer to groundlessness.

> **An appropriate link exists between the word 'position' as being the same as 'place', and its psychological and philosophical significance as 'orientation', 'point of view', 'disposition', and 'inclination'. Ordinary space in itself has no 'place'. Great Space has no 'position'. All the familiar things constituting phenomenal appearance are Great Space directly, not by some remote or transitive link.**

Here a striking analogy with quantum physics arises. Just as a particle can exist in superposition, showing up as a probability wave rather than a determinate point, so too our psycho-physical presence reveals itself as indeterminate when traced back to space. The body may appear located, the self may feel centered, but their deeper status is more like a shimmering standing wave: definite only from one perspective, already open from another.

This shift is not abstract speculation; it is the felt sense that openness does not need to be reached by going anywhere. The very activity of "opening" exposes that what we thought were positions and fixed points are themselves provisional. Our knowing and our embodiment do not occupy space as tenants in a room; they *are* space showing up in particular guises. In this sense, Great Space is never absent, never diminished, never switched off. Even when appearances seem dense and localized, they have never departed from openness.

To glimpse this is to begin releasing the subtle compulsion to find a secure perch from which to know. Instead, we can begin to sense how every stance, every position, is itself already held in a dimension that has no position. Great Space does not need to be reified as a hidden cause or mysterious source. It is not something "behind" appearances. It is the invariant openness that allows appearances at all: uncompromised, inexhaustible, doing nothing and yet accommodating everything.

When the observer is traced back in this way, its claim to be an independent knower has less and less standing. What remains is not emptiness in the sense of lack, but emptiness as infinite availability: the recognition that appearances and awareness arise together as expressions of Great Space. To fully inhabit this recognition is to let the search for a final position dissolve, and to rest in groundlessness, 'our' natural and innate freedom.

> **If we can allow any presuppositions governing our approach to the exercises to be 'opened up', along with everything else that is 'there', our experience will change. This 'allowing' is both a generous 'sacrifice' and an effective path to higher spaces, since 'allowing' is of the very essence of 'higher space'.**

OPENING TO ALLOWING

The exercises we have practiced so far, moving from body and mind into the subtle play of observer and observed, are not ends in themselves. They are invitations to a new way of being, one that does not force or conquer but allows. We usually think progress comes by striving: breaking through barriers, sharpening focus, gaining control. But the vision we are beginning to touch hints at something very different. What if openness does not need to be achieved, because it is already here? What if Great Space, the inexhaustible capacity to allow, to accommodate, to make room, was never missing?

The difficulty lies not in reaching it, but in releasing our old stance. Lower space trains us to contract, to defend, to calculate, to hold tightly, to identity and certainty. In this posture, everything feels scarce: time, energy, meaning. But as we engage with practices that have a thawing effect, something unexpected appears. The walls and boundaries begin to thin. What once seemed like hard edges become more like outlines; what once felt final now reveals itself as provisional.

This shift is less about gaining new knowledge than about unburdening. In Zen, this is often characterized as "opening the hand of thought."[21] We do not need to add or grasp for more, but to relax the compulsive narrowing that blinds us to the richness already here. Such allowing, however, is not passivity. Rather, it is an active receptivity, a willingness to let appearances come and go without forcing them to fit our old frameworks. In this way, allowing becomes a gateway: a mind that no longer clutches is a mind that can finally receive.

Great Space does not arrive from outside. It shines through the very fabric of our experience once we stop treating it as background. Its openness is radical not because it obliterates the world, but because it enfolds it. Every surface, every thought, every sensation can be translucent when met with this kind of openness.

As we move forward, this open stance of allowing will be essential. Without it, the next stages of inquiry risk becoming another project of management and control. With a receptive attitude of allowing, the path opens not as a straight line toward a destination, but as a widening into dimensions of freedom we have scarcely imagined.

CHAPTER EIGHT

Thoughts Without a Thinker

Where do thoughts come from? It's such a simple question that it almost sounds childlike, like something asked from the backseat of a long car ride. Yet try answering it with any confidence and the ground begins to wobble. We say, "I had a thought," as though thoughts are possessions, objects we own and carry around. But do we really *have* them? Do we *make* them? Or do they arrive, unannounced, already formed?

Notice the everyday strangeness of it. You're walking down the street and suddenly the memory of a high-school classroom flashes across your mind; or you're in a work meeting and, without warning, the taste of a mango from last summer lights up your tongue. Where did that come from? Who sent for it? Most of the time we don't ask. We're too busy following the train: one thought pulling the next like cars on a track, until we forget that the engine itself is missing. If we pause long enough to look, the origin of thought is mysterious, elusive, almost mischievous.

Instead of assuming thoughts are manufactured inside a private chamber of mind, our inquiry asks us to track their arrival more carefully. Just as earlier chapters revealed how body and observer appear within space, we now ask whether "thought" itself may also be an appearance within openness. This shift is subtle but radical: the familiar picture of a thinker generating thoughts begins to loosen. If the self is not the owner or producer of what arises, what is the actual status of a thought? Where does it come from, and how does it appear?

Exercise 11: The Source of Thoughts

Explore the source of your thoughts. Observe them as they arise, without trying to control or suppress them. Ask yourself: Where do they come from? Do they appear out of nowhere, or do they have a definite origin? Are they produced by the mind as a kind of generator, or do they arrive already formed, as if from outside? Can you actually find the point at which a thought begins? Look carefully. Notice whether any thought carries its own credentials of authorship, or whether it simply appears in awareness. Keep returning to the question: What is the source of thought?

Reflection

At first, this exercise may feel slippery, even frustrating. Thoughts appear so quickly that to catch their beginning seems impossible. That impossibility is precisely the point. The ordinary assumption is that "mind" produces thoughts like a factory produces goods. We imagine a conveyor belt inside the head, endlessly spitting out ideas, images, plans, worries. But when we look directly, the belt is nowhere to be found. Thoughts arrive, but their origin remains hidden. This glimpse is destabilizing. It loosens the claim of identity we stitch together every day with the phrase "I think." If thoughts are not authored by a central self, then perhaps "mind" is not the sovereign seat we take it to be. As we explored in the previous chapter, perhaps mind is more like an open and spacious field—porous, receptive, continuous with the space around it.

Don't rush to turn this inquiry into a new belief. Instead, treat it as an experiment. Watch as thoughts arrive like guests at a party: some welcome, some uninvited, some irritating, some puzzling. None of them announces who invited them. This doesn't mean thought has no order or meaning; it means the source is more elusive than our everyday story admits. To live with this awareness is to call into question self-as-knower, the supposed thinker of thoughts. We begin to sense that thoughts arise within a wider openness, not from a private generator. The effect is not nihilism but relief, a releasing of the burden of authorship, the endless pressure to manage the mind.

> **The basic presupposition which will be challenged here is that the mind or some other psychophysical structure is the source of thoughts. Such presuppositions need to be 'opened up' or rendered 'translucent'.**

THE MIRAGE OF THE THINKER

Roughly four centuries ago, in a cold room in France, René Descartes sat at his desk and resolved to doubt everything he could. Perhaps the world was a dream. Perhaps his senses were lying. Perhaps an evil demon was deceiving him. Yet, he concluded, one thing could not be doubted: that he was thinking. *Cogito, ergo sum—I think, therefore I am.* The phrase has echoed through centuries of philosophy, shaping the modern sense of self. To think is to prove I exist; thought is the bedrock of being. But what if Descartes was wrong? Or at least, what if his declaration was premature?

In exploring this vision, we are not so concerned to look at what thoughts say (that is, their content), but at how they arise. Do thoughts prove the existence of a thinker? Or do they simply appear, unbidden, like clouds forming in the sky? When we search for the supposed generator behind them, what we find is more like a disappearing act: the thinker dissolves as we approach.

Here again the metaphor of a film reel helps. Imagine reality as a movie. The ordinary view says that behind the film there *must* be a projector, a machine steadily producing the sequence of frames. That is how we picture the mind: as a projector of thought. But if we are brutally honest, when we look closer, we never find the projector. We only ever see frames—momentary flashes of thought, each one already lit up, already here. The continuity we assume is woven together by habit, by the way our attention strings frames into a narrative.

Descartes mistook the story for the source. He assumed that because the film is playing, there must be a projector; because thoughts are appearing, there must be a thinker. But what if "thinking" is not proof of a stable self but the very mechanism by which a self is conjured? The phrase *I think, therefore I am* might be better rendered, from this perspective, as: *I think, therefore I imagine that I am.*

This is not just wordplay. This new vision of reality challenges the foundation of the modern worldview, which takes mind as the primary generator of experience and self as the primary knower. In truth, thoughts arise within space, not from mind as a sovereign machine. The sense of "I" comes after the fact, spliced into the sequence like subtitles added to a film. When the compulsion to believe the subtitles relaxes, something remarkable opens. It becomes clear that the screen itself, the luminous flickering field in which frames appear, has been here all along. Space does not need a projector. Thoughts do not need a thinker.

This is the deeper promise of Exercise 11. When identification with thoughts as "mine" begins to loosen, the figure of the self as "me" also loses its dominance. What remains is not a void or a fall into nothingness, but broad, panoramic awareness. It is a way of standing within the play of thought without being bound by the assumption that thoughts define who we are.

The Thinker Questions Thought

Thinker: If I don't generate my thoughts, then who does? They come from me. They arise in my head. Surely, I am their source.

Space: Are you sure? Look again. Do you decide when the 'I' arrives? Did you summon the 'me' just now? Or did the 'I' appear on its own, like a bird landing on a branch?

Thinker: But I recognize thoughts. I can trace them. I know their shape and meaning. That must mean 'I' am the one who made them.

Space: Recognition isn't authorship. When you hear an echo in a canyon, do you believe you created the sound? You noticed a 'me', yes. But noticing is not generating.

Thinker: Then where do thoughts come from? From memory? From some unconscious storehouse in the brain? From neurons firing? There must be a mechanism. A projector behind the frames.

Space: If there is, you never see it. You only ever meet a 'me', a frame already lit, already here. And as soon as you try to seize the 'me', it's gone. Another arrives, just as unbidden.

Thinker: So you're saying: I'm just an audience, not the producer?

Space: Not even quite that. You, the 'I' that claims to be the audience, is itself a story constructed after the fact. Like subtitles beneath the film, you appear to explain the action, but the film was already rolling.

Thinker: But without me, how could there be meaning? Without a knower, what is the point of knowing?

Space: Meaning does not require a regulator or some petty official. You and your thoughts arise within me, as waves arise within the sea. You are not outside, looking in. You are part of the play.

Thinker: If that's true, then my whole foundation is shaken. I thought I was the one at the helm.

Space: That is the illusion. You keep trying to prove yourself by pointing to thoughts, as though each one were a certificate of your existence. But what if you are not the captain steering the ship, but the wake left behind? What if the real ground is already here: open, accommodating, never absent?

Thinker: Then "I think, therefore I am." is not the truth?

Space: Closer would be: "Thoughts appear, therefore you imagine you are." And even that is only a provisional pointer. For beyond thinker and thought, what remains is the openness in which both arise. That is not a negation, but a liberation..

Silence follows. The Thinker looks around, uncertain. Thoughts still come, but now each one shimmers differently, less like proof, more like passing clouds.

Contemplative Reflection

Pause for a moment and recall the voices you just overheard: *The Thinker, The Thought, and Space.* Notice how familiar their tones are. Have you not spoken in the voice of the Thinker a thousand times, insisting: "These are my thoughts, I am their source"? And yet, just as often, you've seen thoughts arrive unbidden: in the shower, while driving, as you wake from a dream.

Let yourself feel what the dialogue pointed toward: the Thinker's certainty wavers when questioned. Thoughts seem less like possessions and more like guests who appear and vanish without your consent. And then Space is revealed, not as another thought, but as the silent dimension in which both thinker and thought arise.

Can you sense this now? Close your eyes, if you wish, and wait for the next thought to arrive. Did you make it? Did you know what it would be? Notice how it comes, how it dissolves, and how the openness that receives it remains untouched.

The point is not to banish thoughts or disown them. It is to recognize that "authorship" is not required for meaning. You do not need to generate experience in order to be part of it. The Thought arises, the Thinker narrates, but all along, a more accommodating dimension quietly accommodates both. Rest in that dimension for a breath or two. Let it be enough to know: you are not merely the one who thinks, but the openness in which thinking happens.

> **It is important to investigate whether present experience has to be tied to events, things, or places of origin which are temporally or in some other fashion 'outside' (or different from) that experience.**

IF THERE'S NO SOURCE, WHAT EXACTLY IS THINKING?

We've just run an experiment most of us have never tried: look straight at a thought's point of origin, in real time, without theorizing. If you stayed with it, you probably saw two things. First, thoughts arrive on their own timetable. Second, when you turn to find the workshop where they're supposedly made, you don't find a workshop, you find more thoughts.

That result feels wrong to the part of us that wants a clean causal story. So, two familiar explanations rush in to rescue certainty:

1. **Self-reference and the category trap.** "The mind generates thoughts," we say. "Of course it can't see itself directly, that's just a limitation of introspection." In this view, thoughts are products; "mind" is the invisible factory.
2. **Mind–body identity (reductionism).** "There is no mind anyway, only brain. Thoughts are neural events described in mental language."[22] In this view, the factory is physical; first-person experience is a by-product or re-labeling.[23]

Both are tidy. Both also *decide ahead of experience* what must be true. Each places the source *outside* the domain of what can be directly known: behind the thoughts (a hidden "mind"), or beneath them (an inaccessible neural generator).[24] Either way, immediate observation is demoted before we even begin. But what if we propose something audaciously simple: take your experiment seriously. If, under careful observation, no source is found, that absence counts.

Not as a metaphysical dogma, but as a lived, experiential result: *in the act of thinking, the supposed source is unfindable.*

This proposition seems hard to accept because it's easier to make the body translucent than the mind. With the giant body, we had diagrams, scans, and organs we could name. With "mind," we mostly have assumptions. That's why Exercise II can feel subversive. It doesn't ask you to deny brains or denigrate science; it asks you to notice that first-person evidence does not conform to the picture of a central thinker pulling levers.[25,26]

The skeptical part of you may protest: "So what? Maybe the factory is just off-stage." And here's the turning: the off-stage idea is itself a thought that arrives *on* the stage you're observing now. It doesn't point to an independently accessible elsewhere; it's a move within the current frame. Staying with our film-making metaphor, think of ordinary awareness like a movie. Frames flicker so fast they appear continuous. We then presume a storyline: each frame comes *from* the last and goes *to* the next. Thoughts ride the same illusion: a persuasive, high-frame-rate stream that *seems* to show one idea causing another, producing a sense of an enduring "me" who is doing the producing.

Exercise II slows the projector speed. When the shutter rate drops even briefly, the "continuous stream" reveals itself as discrete appearances with gaps. In those gaps, no source is found, no conveyor belt is visible. There is only openness in which the next frame emerges. The key isn't to freeze the film (no-thought) or analyze each frame to death. It's to recognize the way *continuity is imputed*, tightly woven together by habit and story, and how quickly that weaving hardens into a metaphysics of "mind as maker."[27]

Let's return now to our two go-to rescue 'mind-as-source' theories, re-examining them now within the theatre.

Theory 1: "Mind makes thoughts."

Try to locate that maker *as you think*. What shows up? Thoughts about mind. Images representing mind. Theorizing *as* mind. The "factory" never appears except as product. That's a category error hiding in plain sight: using thoughts to certify a producer distinct from thought.

Theory 2: "Brain makes thoughts."

Brains light up on a fMRI scan when we think—good to know! But the image, the math, the models all appear as *contents of present experience*. They are not "behind" experience; they're *in it*. Correlation remains correlation. Useful, yes. Definitive proof that experience is made elsewhere? Not from inside the only place experience ever occurs: here.

Our point here is not anti-science. It's anti-smuggling: the move where we sneak a hidden cause into the story and then use the story to certify the cause. And a common misstep right here is to turn "no source" into a subtle new object: a kind of mystical blankness we now believe in. That just relocates the factory under a different name. This "no-source way" of looking is not a thing you've found. It's unplugging the reflex that every appearance must be coming from a generator and going to a target. When that reflex ceases to operate, cause-and-effect as an absolute account of experience loses its hypnotic power. Practical causality for cooking dinner? Perfectly useful. Metaphysical causality to explain the existence of the next thought? Not required.

But this goes deeper than a philosophical critique of causality. What's at stake here is how we live our lives. Most of us take for granted that there is a "mind" inside that generates our thoughts and moods, a hidden manager running the show. But when we actually look for this mind, it can't be found. It has no clear location in space, no point of origin in time. What we encounter instead are activities—thoughts, feelings, sensations—appearing and disappearing on their own.

This isn't just wordplay. If there is no inner agent producing thoughts, then there's no need to clutch at them, own them, or manage them. Thoughts arise and dissolve like images on a screen. Their impact comes not from some mental factory churning them out, but from the meanings we attach to them and the momentum those meanings create. Recognizing this shifts the texture of experience: thoughts become lighter, less binding, less freighted with solidity. They no longer demand obedience.

If this seems abstract, consider how the same thing plays out with ordinary appearances. Take a rainbow. To the eye it seems to arch solidly across the sky, yet it has no independent existence apart from a timely alignment of sunlight, raindrops, and observer. What feels like a real, external object is actually a shared construction, one we rarely recognize as dependent on our participation.[28] Now consider something that seems far more solid: a rose. We can see it, touch it, inhale its fragrance. Everything about it persuades us of its reality. But notice how much of this persuasion comes through meanings: "red," "beautiful," "fragrant." Even scientific descriptions—the molecules, the atoms, the particles—are themselves layers of interpretation. We never encounter the particles directly; we encounter roses, wrapped in concepts and associations.

The rainbow and the rose together remind us how readily meanings crystallize into "things." They show how our chamber of interpretation makes the provisional feel solid, turning shimmering appearances into fixtures of a world. What we call reality is already shot through with designation. Seen this way, both rainbow and rose point us back to the same question: if appearances lean so heavily on meanings, what does that say about the "mind" we imagine is producing them?

It is important not to treat "no mind" as a new doctrine about the existence or nonexistence of mind.[29] That only replays the old dualism of "something" versus "nothing." The point here is not metaphysical but experiential: an invitation to see how insubstantial mind is when we stop assuming it must be a source. Trusting this insight experientially, rather than trying to nail it down conceptually, opens the way to a freedom that no proposition could deliver.

> **Once we develop more awareness, we can begin to see that events and thoughts—which we have seen as a continuous surface stream—do not actually have the dynamic connections that we commonly assume and attribute to them. We can then relax and open a bit more; we do not have to keep tidying things up by fitting thoughts together or 'placing' them.**

Thoughts persuade us that they are going somewhere, that they are leading toward understanding, security, or resolution. But when the supposed source is nowhere to be found, their authority wavers. We begin to see them less as carriers of truth and more as appearances—meaningful, yes, but not grounded in a hidden factory of mind.

UN-MANUFACTURING CERTAINTY

In cramped, lower-space mode, the theater is crowded and loud. Events ricochet, meanings multiply, echoes amplify. The sheer density produces the impression of a continuous surface, like a soundtrack that never stops. Inside that pressure, the mind's bookkeeping kicks in: "Place this thought. Link it to that one. Keep the narrative moving." The more we tidy, the more convincing the flow becomes; the more convincing the flow, the more we believe in a flow-maker.

Slowing the shutter shows a different cinema. Frames appear in openness, not out of a constricted tube. Their meaning still functions (you can follow a plot), but the felt need to bind every frame into a perfect chain eases. You don't have to keep the film running by force. But here's the paradox: as the "producer" story relaxes, intelligence doesn't vanish, it becomes *clearer*. What emerges is a more subtle "knowing" that isn't indexed to a personal owner. It doesn't stare outward from a control booth; rather, it pervades the scene. You don't lose agency; you lose unnecessary *tension* around agency.

This is not some hypnotic trance, altered state, or advanced meditative absorption. It's really quite simple, a shift from managing thoughts to noticing how they appear, play, and dissolve inside a wider allowance. Having seen that "mind as source" can't be found, don't now make the error, rushing to enthrone "space as source." Space, in this vision, is not a generator either; it's the non-exclusive openness that doesn't need to generate in order to accommodate. In film terms, it's not a hidden projector in the back of the room; it's the field within which the projector, screen, sound, viewers, and frames all show up together, without exhausting the field. That's why "no source" increases ease and fulfillment rather than inducing tension and nihilism. If nothing must be made to justify showing up, appearances don't have to work so hard to prove themselves. Thought can be vivid without being a verdict. Earlier, we learned to open the body's outlines into space. With Exercise 11, we start opening the subject-pole, the one who supposedly thinks. The result is not vacancy but latitude and flexibility: more room for thinking to be nimble, responsive, and less self-obsessed.

THE WIDE EXPANSE

Reflecting on the "no source" insight, we can see that thoughts are not crafted in a workshop nor emitted by a thinker's command. They appear, echoing in a vast medium of awareness that is vaster than thoughts themselves. The mind, in this sense, is not a source at all. It is an expanse, a canyon wide enough for the sound of thought to appear.

Now, stretch that canyon to cosmic proportions. Imagine the origin of the universe not as a point-struck spark, like a cosmic clap, but as the unfolding of an echo that always was. Recent cosmological thinking leans toward models where the Big Bang is not the first flash of creation, but a turn of cycle, a new chapter in an endless song.

Some physicists now propose that the universe didn't begin; it bounced. One idea (the cyclic model) imagines vast epochs of expansion ending in contraction, then blooming into new beginnings, thus neatly avoiding the need for a final "first cause." Others (like conformal cyclic cosmology) portray the Big Bang as more like a mirror linking one cosmic chapter to the next—the end and beginning folded into one boundaryless continuum. These ideas suggest that the universe may not have a singular hidden cause, but arise perpetually from what already is.

Does this cosmic ambiguity unsettle you? It does many scientists. But it also feels oddly familiar to our "no source" insight. We see that thought, self, mind arise together with the field in which they appear. They don't emerge from a hidden generator. They are part of an open system that itself has no ontological origin. It isn't that nothing is there. Quite the opposite: the openness is blossoming forth in an endless, infinite array.

We began this chapter by asking: *Where do thoughts come from?* We looked for a maker, a thinker, and found none. We tried to trace thoughts to a mind or brain, and the search dissolved into the very flux we were studying. Instead of a factory, we discovered a vast openness: not empty, but unconfined, alive, spacious, and deeply participatory. The insight that mind is not a generator, but a space of appearance, is both unsettling and freeing. It dissolves the pressure to own, manage, or master every thought, replacing it with curiosity, ease, and presence.

In Chapter Nine, we take the "no source" insight further. Exercises 12 and 13 invite you to notice how not only do thoughts emerge without a fixed progenitor behind them, but how thoughts themselves may pose no obstruction to space. Hidden generative sources—whether we label them as mind, brain or some other entities (which we presuppose exist despite our inability to actually see or observe them)—can be opened up further to reveal that all mental contents are also space. Chapter Eight revealed that thoughts echo without a thinker. Chapter Nine extends this discovery: even thoughts themselves can be rendered transparent, seen as part of the same openness that gives rise to everything.

CHAPTER NINE

Mind the Gap

Most of the time, thoughts feel like an unbroken current, a stream that carries us forward without pause. Yet this continuity is more fragile than it appears. If you slow down, you may notice small fissures in the flow: the word on the tip of your tongue that won't quite arrive, the awkward silence when you're asked a simple question and nothing comes, the hovering hesitation before you tap the screen. At night, as you drift toward sleep, one thought dissolves and, for a breathless instant, nothing has yet taken its place.

In Chapter Eight we saw that thoughts echo without a thinker. Here we follow that thread further, not by adding more theory, but by slowing the reel until the splices show. Ordinarily, we skip past these intervals. They are treated as trivial, awkward, or unimportant. But what if they were not blanks at all? What if the very gaps in thought reveal something about the texture of awareness itself? These pauses hint at a dimension that is neither thought nor its absence, a background that is always present but rarely noticed.

Now we are going to precisely attend to these gaps, to the seam where one thought ends and another has not yet begun. These gaps are not just empty silences in the mind's chatter; they are windows onto the openness that allows thought to arise at all. To sense them, even briefly, is to begin appreciating that what is "here" is more than a succession of mental events: it is the presence of space itself, immediately available around and within every thought.

We may not yet be able to fully open to Great Space directly, but we can begin to sense its intimacy through these intervals. Just as light can be glimpsed through a crack in the door, spaciousness shines through the fleeting pause between thoughts. This chapter turns our attention to that crack: the ordinary yet extraordinary openings where the mind's storyline falters, and immediacy stands revealed.

> **We are moving close to an appreciation of what is 'here' as being Great Space. It may not yet be possible to confront 'here' directly, but it is possible for us to be sufficiently sensitive to a 'higher space' dimension that we can apprehend this space as being located immediately round about each thought.**

Exercise 12: Space Between Thoughts

Notice what happens in the 'space' between one thought and the next. If no 'space' seems apparent, notice the endings of thoughts and the beginnings that follow. Attend closely to the last trace of the ending and the first trace of the next. Is there something like a gap that cannot be filled by another thought?

Reflection

At first, this may feel like trying to catch lightning in a jar. Thoughts come too quickly; the space vanishes the moment you look. But even the attempt loosens the sense of continuity. Sometimes the gap shows itself as no more than a whisper, a brief spaciousness, without image or word, without even the sense of a watcher.

If nothing appears, that itself is a discovery. It reveals how deeply the mind is habituated to stitching beginnings and endings together. Patience helps. Each trace of silence, however brief, is a doorway.

CHALLENGING THE STREAM

The philosopher and psychologist William James, often called the father of American psychology, described consciousness as a "stream," a metaphor that has dominated psychology for over a century. Yet he also noted the "flights and perchings," pauses between the drops of thought. What if the mind is not a seamless flow at all, but a rapid fusing of moments, where gaps outnumber contents?

A metaphor from music helps. A melody without pauses collapses into noise. Rhythm depends as much on silence as on sound. Likewise, when we notice the pauses in thinking, we don't find a blank but the condition that makes meaning possible. Or recall a café filled with noise: voices, machines, clatter. Suddenly the power cuts. For a breathless instant, the room falls silent. What fills it is not emptiness but a heightened presence. This is what the space between thoughts can feel like: not a blank but a luminous stillness in which everything seems more immediate. Ordinarily, we rush to fill such silences, afraid of their openness. But if we pause there, even briefly, the quality of the gap changes. It is not vacancy but a lucid, peaceful limpidity. This is why the space between thoughts, though ordinary, may have a tremendously liberating impact.

Think of it this way: when a conversation goes silent, most of us feel compelled to break the pause. But what if we learned to rest in that pause? To hear the room breathe? The exercise trains this sensibility, revealing that openness is not elsewhere, not an esoteric attainment, but already here, surrounding every thought, saturating every moment. When we train in this way, the space between thoughts becomes more than a fleeting interval. We can then directly taste a wider dimension of awareness, a "higher space," a knowing untouched by the noise of meaning-making, not exhausted by the flow of contents. Not being something to cling to as an object, we learn to relax into an atmosphere, always present, waiting to be noticed and appreciated.

Contemplative Reflection
The Silence Between Notes

Listen to a piece of music with pronounced pauses. Notice how each shapes what follows. As you listen, notice how the silence is not separate from the music. Each pause is charged, preparing the ground for what follows. Without the rests, the notes would blur into noise. Then sit quietly and let thoughts arise. Instead of focusing on the thoughts, tune into the spaces that surround them. As in music, the pauses are not empty but alive, already part of the rhythm of mind.

Let thoughts continue to arise as they will. Do not try to stop them. Instead, tune into the spaces that come before and after each thought. Just as in music, the "rests" are already shaping the melody of your mind.

Notice how these pauses are not blank; they carry a clarity, a lucidity, a presence that is not owned by any "thinker." They are not your achievement. They are simply there, surrounding each thought. Stay with this for a few minutes. Let the rhythm of thoughts and silences play like music in your awareness. When you open your eyes or shift your attention, sense how the silence between thoughts is not a rare absence but the very ground of experience.

THE PRESENCE IN THE PAUSE

If the space between thoughts reveals a silent lucidity, what does this suggest about the thoughts themselves? We usually treat them as solid building blocks of experience, the furniture of our inner world. But perhaps they are more like notes in music: arising from silence, fading back into it, never separate from the spaciousness that frames them.

That pause in the darkened café is more than a lack of sound. For those who notice it, the silence is not inert. It is charged, brimming, almost luminous. You realize, if only for a heartbeat, that presence does not depend on the clatter of cups or the hum of machinery. Presence is already there, waiting.

The vision invites us to recognize this presence in the space between thoughts. Our usual way of living makes it hard to appreciate. We are so attuned to how the stream of meaning each thought carries, the way one thought explains the last and prepares the ground for the next, that the gaps vanish from awareness. It feels as though we are riding a train of thought that never stops, every carriage linked to the one before. Yet if we slow down enough, we can see how this sense of continuity is not self-sustaining. It is stitched together by the meanings we project, each thought pointing to the next to keep the story intact.

Let's pause here, to look again. What if thoughts are not beads strung on a single thread? What if the thread itself is an illusion? In the exercise we are not asked to banish thoughts or control their flow, a common mistake most meditators make. We are instead asked to attend to what may lie between them. What we find, if we are patient, is not a blank, not a mindless fog, but rather a quiet spaciousness, vivid and self-sufficient, that does not belong to any "thinker."

Consider how this challenges two powerful stories we carry about mind, two stories related to the two key conventional theories of mind we challenged in Chapter Nine. It's worth returning to them now that we have begun to see the gaps between thoughts not as defects, but as invitations, cracks that reveal something deeper about how mind is framed.

First, there must be a mind, some hidden faculty or entity, behind our thoughts, the "thinker" that produces them. When we search for it, however (as we did in the last chapter), we never find more than another thought. The supposed mind-as-source remains unobserved, only posited as a necessary generator. Our failure to find it is brushed aside: "Of course mind is there," we insist, "this method is flawed." Yet the absence of evidence is not neutral, itself being the evidence. If the mind-as-source cannot be found in experience, perhaps it does not exist in the way we have assumed.

Second is the materialist reduction equating thought with neural activity. On this account, there is no mind at all, just brain. Every flicker of experience corresponds to a neural correlate, and the gaps are merely noise in a system of firings. But here too, the supposed source is out of reach. We do not experience neurons firing; we experience thoughts. The explanatory gap remains, no matter how finely the imaging scans or how sophisticated the neurological models.

> **Ordinarily we consider that there is a mind; and so there are also thoughts, presuppositions, and 'changes of mind'. But through these exercises, we may discover that there is no ordinary mind at all. ...there is neither a mind nor its commonly experienced concomitants—they exist together and are transcended together.**

Earlier we saw that no inner agent can be found producing thoughts, no "mind-as-generative source." Here we press the point further: even the foundation we imagine mind rests on dissolves. No stable ground secures it. Mind and thoughts arise together, but without any base beneath them. This is the significance of 'no mind' as foundational insight. Yet, in both cases, the pattern is the same: we posit something "behind" experience to account for it, either an invisible mind or an inaccessible brain. Both theories refuse to trust what experience itself reveals. Both take the "no source found" result of inquiry and translate it back into a source. One names it "mind," the other names it "matter." Both are attempts to secure the flow of thoughts by anchoring them in a generator.

But in the exercise, we discover that no such anchor is required. What we see instead is that the apparent continuity of thought is like the café's background noise, a layering of echoes, associations, and expectations that creates the impression of unbroken flow. The space between thoughts is like the silence when the power cuts out; suddenly, the assumption of continuity is revealed as fragile, contingent, unnecessary. The space was there all along, waiting for recognition. The interludes of silence matter. They are not empty absences but glimpses of a different, 'higher' dimension of knowing. In these intervals, knowing does not operate through the usual dualism of subject and object. It is not "my" awareness observing a thought-object. It is awareness unmediated, unowned, free of the forward 'from-to' push of meaning. The stillness has a clarity all its own.

In addition to his stream metaphor, William James also once remarked on the "fringe" of consciousness, those subtle intimations at the edges of our attention, often overlooked yet essential to how experience holds together. The space between thoughts can be understood not as a dead zone but as a fringe of presence, a lucidity that frames and sustains whatever arises. Just as the pauses in music make melody possible, the gaps between thoughts are the silent architecture that allows meaning to emerge without collapsing into noise.

When we begin to appreciate this, the quality of our mental atmosphere dramatically shifts. The compulsion to chase every thought, to be at the mercy of its meaning, relaxes. The pause becomes less threatening and more inviting. We may even begin to notice that the so-called gaps are not rare anomalies but constant companions, surrounding each thought "immediately round about." With practice, we can sense that the space between thoughts is always available, even if it is usually obscured.

If the space between thoughts is not a void but a vivid openness, then what does this say about the nature of thoughts themselves? They, too, may be less solid than they appear. Like music notes, they arise and fade, but they do not establish a continuous stream. Because they are not propelled forward by a hidden source, thoughts too emerge within openness and dissolve back into it. The "no source" claim is not a negation but a radical discovery: the origin we were seeking is already here, everywhere, in the very openness of Mind Space.

Seen this way, the space between thoughts is not just an interval. It is an always available, open invitation. We can rely less on the machinations of explanation and more towards immediate, direct experience. By minding the gaps, we do not need to follow every thought to its imagined origin, nor to await some final thought that will deliver certainty. The gaps show us that freedom is not elsewhere, waiting at the end of a chain of causes; it is here, in the lucidity that opens whenever thought falls silent.

We are now invited to turn the inquiry even further inside out. Instead of seeing space as a gap between the "real events" of thought, can we begin to see thoughts themselves as expressions of space? This is the next major pivot. Where Exercise 12 guided us into the interval, Exercise 13 goes further, asking us to look at thought not as content filling space, but as space itself taking shape.

Exercise 13: Thoughts as Space

Settle into a quiet moment. Let thoughts arise naturally: snippets of memory, fragments of planning, stray impressions from the day. As each thought comes into view, notice its texture. Does it feel sharp or vague? Heavy or light? Persuasive or fleeting? Now look more closely. Instead of treating the thought as a solid thing, ask: What is it made of? Does it have weight or substance? Does it stand apart from the openness in which it appears?

Allow yourself to entertain the possibility that each thought is not an intruder entering space but an expression of space itself. Just as a cloud is inseparable from the sky, each thought may be inseparable from the openness that gives it room.

Stay with this for a few minutes. Don't force a conclusion. If the thought dissolves, simply notice: Where did it go? Did it depart into some storage vault of "mind"? Or did it melt back into the same space from which it emerged?

Rather than trying to control or eliminate thoughts, let them show their true character. Each one is translucent; each one is space in motion.

Reflection

Ordinarily, we grant thoughts executive power. They stride onto the stage of awareness as if in charge: You need to check your email. This meeting will be a disaster. She hasn't replied; what did I do wrong? They don't just comment; they dictate, and we nod along. But when we pause, their solidity crumbles. Thoughts do not carry weight in themselves; they only appear convincing because we treat them as more than passing formations. To see a thought as space is to disarm its authority. It is not that thinking stops, but that meanings show up as contingent, temporary, part of an open field of appearance. This recognition reshapes what we call "mind." Instead of a producer hidden backstage, mind is not a generator at all. Thoughts arise inseparably within openness, without needing a source.

> **Mind, even when seen in the ordinary way as an agent, a producer of thoughts, actually does not do anything. Moreover, although the mind may be distributed or structured by a particular physiological embodiment, mind itself is not based on anything else (that would do thoughts).**

WHEN THOUGHTS OPEN

Thoughts can be seen differently, not as possessions, but as weather, passing patterns with no owner. Clouds don't prove the existence of a cloud-maker; they reveal the openness and power of the sky. In the same way, thoughts can be heard as movements of space rather than evidence of a thinker behind them. This shift loosens our grip. Instead of grasping at thoughts, we can let them breathe, allowing them to appear within openness. Meaning still arises, but it no longer dictates our existence. To glimpse thoughts in this way is to recognize their transparency: worries, memories, daydreams already shining through as space itself. What remains is an immediacy both ordinary and astonishing: simply being here, alive, in a world that is not sealed off but is inexhaustibly open.

And yet the paradox remains. Thoughts rise and dissolve, leaving no trace, yet we cling to the sense of a producer, the self, the knower, the thinker. Perhaps the best way to explore this tangle is not with more argument, but through a bit of theater. Imagine a stage. The lights dim. The familiar characters step forward to argue their case.

A Play in the Gap

A short theatrical interlude dramatizes the search for a source behind thought.

Thought: Here I am! Always arriving! Always important!

Space: And always dissolving.

Thought: But I mean things. People rely on me. Without me, how would anyone know what's happening?

Space: Without me, you could not appear at all.

Mind: Order! Let us not forget who runs the show. I am the source. I generate thoughts, I keep things moving.

Thought: Yes, yes, it's true! Without Mind, I'd never arrive.

Space: And yet, when we look for this mighty source—where is it?

Mind falters. Self enters, clutching a mirror.

Self: Don't worry, I'm here to hold it all together. Thoughts, mind, meaning—it all revolves around me. Without me, who would even be reading this play?

Space: And yet, you too are just another shining outline. You come and go like the rest.

Suddenly, a new figure bursts onto the stage, feathered hat in hand. It is Descartes, dramatic and emphatic.

Descartes: Cogito, ergo sum! I think, therefore I am!

The audience gasps. Thought claps wildly. Self bows in agreement. Mind beams with pride.

Space: René, you forgot to ask: Who is this "I" that thinks? And where do thoughts come from when no one is thinking them?

Just then, another figure ambles in: William James, amused.

James: Gentlemen, forgive me, but you're missing the point. Consciousness is more like a stream: flowing, fleeting.

Space: Exactly. A stream appearing within openness. And between the ripples, a silence as fundamental as the water itself.

The lights dim. Thought sputters, fades. Self stares at its mirror, but the reflection has gone translucent. Space remains in the spotlight.

Space: I am not an actor or a source. I am the stage itself: vast, open, always here.

A pause. Curtain begins to fall; but Self suddenly bursts back onto the stage, flustered, waving its mirror like a gavel.

Self: Wait! Enough already! Don't you see I'm trying to meditate here? I've been doing these Exercises, watching for the gaps, hunting for the source of Thoughts. But you won't be quiet! How am I supposed to find silence if everyone keeps chattering?

Thought: Oh, so now I'm the problem? Always blamed, always in the way.

Self: You are the problem! Distractions, intrusions, endless chatter. If I could just stop you, squelch you, hold you down, then maybe I'd reach the space between!

Space: Ah, and so the meditator is born. The one who strains, who tries to capture what cannot be seized. But tell me, Self, who is this "I" that struggles to suppress Thoughts?

Self: Well . . . I am the one in charge. I am the doer. If I don't make the effort, nothing will happen.

Mind: Quite right. Without control, there is only chaos. Effort is essential!

Space: And yet, look closely. Each effort only produces another Thought, another ripple. The more you try to pin down silence, the more noise you create.

Thought: Exactly! Chase me, fight me, fear me—I only grow stronger.

Self: Then what am I supposed to do?

Space: Perhaps nothing. Let go of "trying." No forcing, no special concentration. Just be open. See how awareness is already like light, and consciousness like space. Without space, no light could shine. Without openness, no thought could arise.

Self: So . . . the "space between" isn't something to capture?

Space: Not a hole to be hunted. Not an object at all. We speak of "between" only as a pointer. In truth, there is no gap to guard, no fortress to hold. There is simply openness—silent, luminous—always here.

Thought: In that case, I'm not an enemy?

Space: Not at all, when allowed to arise and dissolve in openness, thoughts are no obstacle. They shimmer like clouds in the sky, already infused with the light of awareness.

Self: Then I don't need to control? I don't need to keep steering?

Space: Control dissolves in openness. The meditator, too, is just another appearance. When you stop clutching at the role of doer, the silence that seemed so elusive reveals itself as the very ground of being.

Silence falls. The stage lights widen, bathing every figure—Self, Mind, Thought—in a warm glow. They all seem less solid, more translucent, as if floating in the light itself.

Space: This is the secret you have all been circling: the source you sought is not hidden behind thoughts, it is the openness in which you already appear.

Everyone is quiet now. The curtain falls, not with finality, but with a sense of vastness still unfolding.

THE MYTH OF FLOW

The inquiry now presses further: what if the movement of thought itself is an illusion? We assume that each thought comes from somewhere, points to something, and leads to the next, as if tracks were laid down in advance. But when we look closely, this continuity is not given; it is constructed. Thoughts flare into appearance without a discoverable source, and they dissolve without a destination. What binds them into a "stream" is our participation in their meanings, the way we automatically link one to another as though they were carriages on a train.

Through our disciplined inquiry, it should be clear that this sense of flow comes less from thoughts themselves than from the persuasive force of meaning. By treating thoughts as if they carry us forward—coming from a mind, pointing to objects—we generate the impression of directed motion. Once this overlay is seen, the "stream of thought" no longer has to be taken as self-sustaining.

The radical implication is that vitality does not come from a hidden producer called "mind." It arises in openness itself. Between thoughts there is no bridge, no traveler, no cargo—only the immediacy of appearance. For lived experience, this means freedom from the compulsion to chase after every thread. Thoughts can be seen as transient, contingent, unestablished—lighter than we imagined. And in that recognition, emptiness ceases to be threatening. It discloses itself as the most intimate ground of all: presence that allows everything without needing to hold anything in place.

STEPPING OFF THE TRACK

To see this clearly is to loosen one of our deepest reflexes: the belief that thought always means forward motion. We imagine ourselves being carried along, pulled from one moment to the next. But if thoughts arise discontinuously, then the sense of a track is added by us. We are the ones laying rails and insisting the train must run.

When that insistence relaxes, thought can be met without the compulsion of direction. A memory does not demand a story. A plan does not require projection into the future. A worry does not prove a disaster is already underway. Each can be acknowledged as a flare in openness, not a carriage in a procession.

This does not leave us inert or blank. Far from it. This transformation shifts the axis from propulsion to presence. Life continues, decisions made, actions taken, but without the drag of an imagined track. In stepping off, we discover that there was never a track to begin with, only the immediacy of appearance.

CHAPTER TEN

When the Mind Rebels

Up to this point, we have moved steadily from giant bodies to translucent walls, from the interplay of body-mind-thought to the gaps between thoughts themselves. Each step has invited us to question what we normally take for granted. Let doubts arise. For skepticism is not the enemy of vision. Exercising our critical intelligence is part of the process. To interrogate these exercises is to test their strength. To push against the frame is to see whether it bends or breaks.

So this chapter is different. It is not about adding new practices or layering on more facets of the vision. It is about clearing the air. About letting our objections and confusions come to the surface. Because if you are anything like me, or like most readers, at times all of this sounds too strange, too subtle, or just too implausible. How could space be alive? How could mind have no foundation? How could thoughts not come from somewhere?

In this chapter those questions get their say. Before moving on, let's give those doubts a voice. It's one thing to outline objections in general terms; it's another to hear them spoken, pressed, argued. What follows is not a script to memorize but a way of staging the questions that inevitably arise. Think of it as an inner dialogue: one voice restless, skeptical, impatient; another steady, probing, responsive. By letting them meet, we test the strength of the vision: not by silencing doubt, but by letting it speak.

Dialogue: Raising Doubts

Scene: A quiet study. The Guide sits across from the Questioner, who is restless, flipping through notes, half-skeptical, half-curious. The air is charged with the sense that something important is at stake.

Questioner: Look, I've followed you this far: the giant body, the translucent outlines, even the space between thoughts. But I still don't get it. Aren't these just elaborate meditations? You sit, you imagine, you watch. How is this different from mindfulness or any other contemplative technique?

Guide: A fair challenge. Most methods ask you to focus, to refine, to control attention. These exercises, by contrast, ask you to loosen control. They are not techniques to master. They are invitations to experiment with perception itself.

Questioner: But isn't that just semantics? Whether you call it a method or an invitation, you're still doing something.

Guide: True. But notice the difference in stance. A method assumes a path and a destination: if you follow the steps correctly, you arrive. An invitation opens the door without promising where it leads. You step through, and sometimes the room rearranges itself entirely.

Questioner: Fine. But here's my real problem. You keep saying the mind has no foundation. That thoughts don't come from anywhere. That just sounds absurd. I have thoughts. They come from my mind. Isn't that obvious?

Guide: Obvious, yes. But only because we've repeated it so often it feels like common sense. Try actually finding this "mind" that generates thoughts. When you look directly, what do you find? A mind producing? Or just thoughts appearing?

Questioner: Still, science tells us thoughts come from the brain. Neuroscience maps the regions that light up. Are you saying they're wrong?

Guide: Not wrong, but partial. We looked at this earlier: the search for a "mind-as-source" comes up empty. Thoughts appear, but no thinker is found producing them. Neuroscience can map correlations, but as we saw, correlation isn't causation. The real question is whether you can see this directly, right now.

Questioner: And what about Buddhism, Vedanta, Dzogchen? All these traditions already talk about mind in profound ways. Are you just reinventing the wheel?

Guide: Not reinventing—not requiring those wheels. This vision doesn't depend on any lineage or belief. It only asks: What do you notice in your own experience? Can you see beyond the assumption that mind is a thing, a source, a controller inside your head pulling levers?

Questioner: That "manager" again? You mean like an inner boss telling thoughts where to go?

Guide: Exactly. The self-as-manager is one of our deepest unquestioned assumptions. But watch carefully: thoughts often appear without orders and vanish without permission. The so-called boss spends most of its time taking credit for things it didn't initiate.

Questioner: So what are you saying: there's no boss, no foundation, no mind? Sounds dangerously close to anarchy and nihilism. If nothing is at the root, then what's left? Doesn't everything just collapse?

Guide: Not collapse—but the emergence of freedom. Removing a false foundation doesn't leave us with nothing; it leaves us with openness. What remains is not emptiness in the sense of lack, but a freedom from the compulsive need to prop up a fictional floor.

Questioner: But without some foundation, how do we function? How do we live, make decisions, get through a day?

Guide: That's the paradox. You already live this way. Right now, countless thoughts, sensations, and perceptions are arising without an overseer orchestrating them. Your liver is cleansing blood without your commands. Breathing happens. Seeing happens. Decisions emerge. Life continues, not because of a hidden foundation, but because openness itself is functional.

Questioner: Hmmm....Maybe. But doesn't this just sound mystical? Like you're smuggling in some airy spirituality under the cover of philosophy?

Guide: It might sound mystical, but it's actually practical. You don't have to believe anything. You just have to look—directly, honestly, repeatedly. If you find a foundation, great, hold it up, let's see it. But if you don't, perhaps it's time to trust the evidence of your own experience.

Questioner: You make it sound simple. Too simple.

Guide: Sometimes the hardest truths are the simplest. The difficulty isn't in seeing it. The difficulty is in letting go of the need for a ground.

The Questioner leans back, arms crossed, not convinced but not dismissive either. The seed of doubt—in both directions—has been planted. The stage is set for the inquiry to deepen.

THREE THINGS THIS DIALOGUE JUST SHOWED

This search for a hidden ground may itself be the problem. It sets up the illusion of an "inner manager" who must supervise, direct, and guarantee the flow of experience. Yet when we look for this manager's office, its location, its authority, we find nothing but more thoughts announcing its role: a PR department for a non-existent company.

- No mind-as-source: When you look for the producer, you find another thought. Absence of evidence is not neutral; here it is the evidence.
- Openness is functional: breathing, sensing, deciding are all already happening without a boss-self running them.
- The "manager" is a role, not a ruler: It narrates after the fact, claims credit, and stirs anxiety, but it doesn't manufacture experience.

These arguments are not meant to be taken on trust. They can be tested in the texture of your own awareness. One of the Manager's main tricks narrows vision into a forward beam, as if experience must always stream "ahead." But what if awareness is not a tunnel at all? What if it can open in every direction at once? The following reflection offers a way to sense this directly.

Contemplative Reflection
360-Degree Mind Space

1. Start with an image of a familiar cone.

Sit or stand comfortably. Notice how thoughts usually stream in a single direction, as though awareness were a narrow cone shining forward. Even when you remember the past or imagine the future, it often feels as if your mind is pointing somewhere "ahead."

2. Widen the angle.

Now, without strain, imagine awareness spreading to the sides. As though you had eyes in your temples; sense what it's like to include the periphery, the faint sounds, the edges of vision, the unnoticed textures brushing your skin.

3. Complete the circle.

Let awareness arc further, behind you. Sense the room at your back, the unseen presence of space cradling you. Without needing to visualize anything, simply allow the sense that experience is not one-directional but spherical. Awareness is all around, 360 degrees.

4. Notice what's included.

In this widened panorama, even the "manager" who once felt like the one steering, choosing, planning, controlling, is just another appearance within the circle. The effort to point forward is itself part of the circle.

5. Rest in the openness.

There is no need to maintain this view, no need to lock it in. The point is not to perfect a new mystical vision but to allow the directional bias of thought fall away. Let awareness taste what it's like when there is no front or back, no privileged point of control.

At first, this exercise may feel odd, like trying to see with eyes in the back of your head. The point is not to conjure new perceptions, but rather to notice how awareness has long leaned forward, as if strapped into a cockpit fixed on the next task, the next demand, the next proof of existence.

When the circle is widened, that forward thrust begins to ease. Awareness can rest in all directions at once: left and right, above and below, even behind. In this wider balance, the seat of control, once so central, shows itself as just another point within the field. A quiet shift may occur. Experience is no longer organized around a single driver. Presence becomes ambient: surrounding, supporting, allowing. The urge to steer and secure a foundation beneath the mind drops away. Such openness can feel liberating, like breaking into a space far more generous than expected; or it can feel unsettling, like standing in a landscape with no landmarks. Both responses matter. Discomfort only reveals how much we have relied on boundaries to feel safe.

This is the spirit of panoramic awareness. The exercise is not about perfecting a technique but about letting presence breathe in all directions. With practice, it becomes clearer that the mind needs no hidden foundation. What once seemed like "nothing" reveals itself as the quiet spaciousness that has always allowed everything.

Even a short taste of this shift reveals how unnecessary the Manager's grip really is. What once seemed like its vital oversight begins to look more like a narrowing habit. With the circle opened, the Manager shows itself as just one figure among many: not the ruler, only a character in the play. The next section puts that figure on trial, so we can see its claims tested in full daylight.

THE TRIAL OF THE INNER MANAGER

The habit of treating this figure as a kind of boss-self runs deep. To question its authority feels risky, even destabilizing. But is this manager truly in charge or only a story we've been telling ourselves? To test this, let us imagine a tribunal, a courtroom of inquiry where the inner manager is called to account. Here, the familiar authority that claims to run our lives must answer questions under cross-examination. What evidence can it provide? Who empowered it in the first place? And what happens if its authority begins to unravel? Let's put the Manager on trial.

Scene: A Courtroom of the Mind

The atmosphere is solemn, though tinged with humor. A jury of ordinary experiences—breath, sensation, thought, and emotion—sits ready. Space itself presides as judge, vast and impartial.

Prosecutor: We are here to determine whether the so-called Inner Manager has rightful authority over mind-space. Manager, do you understand the charges?

Manager: Charges? Absurd! I am the one keeping order. Without me, this entire operation would collapse. Who pays the bills, remembers deadlines, plans the meditation retreats? Me. Without me, it would be chaos.

Awareness: So you claim. Yet witnesses report that your constant control has left them anxious, restless, and exhausted. Breath, please take the stand.

Breath: For ages I have moved in and out, unbidden. The Manager insists it is in charge, yet I continue whether it is paying attention or not. Sometimes it tries to control me, forcing me shallow or deep, but the truth is: I do not need it.

Manager: Without me reminding you, you'd be forgotten!

Breath: And yet, in sleep, in surrender, I carry on unmanaged.

Awareness: Thank you. Next witness: Thought.

Thought: Yes, I admit it, I come and go constantly. The Manager claims to order me, but often I arrive uninvited, sometimes in flocks, sometimes as flashes. I've even shown up in the middle of meditation when being begged for silence. If anything, the Manager chases me, not the other way around.

Manager: You're unruly! Without me, you'd scatter into madness.

Thought: Or perhaps without you, I'd be free, lighter, less burdened.

Awareness: Next witness: Emotion.

Emotion: I surge like tides. The Manager tries to suppress me when I'm inconvenient or exploit me when it needs motivation. But I am not created by him. I rise from deeper waters. When the Manager clutches me, I twist into resentment or fear. Left alone, I move, swell and dissolve.

Manager: But I must regulate you, or else you'd drown the whole system!

Emotion: You mistake my intensity for danger. In truth, I only become overwhelming when resisted.

Awareness: The testimony is clear: Breath, Thought, and Emotion do not confirm your authority. They describe your interference, not your governance.

Space: Manager, how do you plead?

Manager: I only wanted stability. Without me, what holds the self together? Who ensures continuity? I am the guarantor of identity!

Awareness: Identity is precisely your fabrication. You claim to be the conductor of the orchestra, yet every instrument plays of its own accord. You are more like a self-appointed narrator, stitching stories after the fact.

Manager: If I am not in charge . . . then what am I?

Space: A habit. A useful tool at times, but not the sovereign you believe yourself to be. You are part of the play, not its director.

Silence fills the courtroom. The Manager slumps, no longer swaggering, now revealed as a frightened figure propping up illusions of order.

Judge/Space: Let it be recorded: The Manager is not banished, only unmasked. It may serve when needed, but it shall no longer claim dominion. Its role is provisional, not absolute.

The jury—Breath, Thought, and Emotion—exhale together, a sigh of relief that ripples through the whole matrix of awareness.

Narrator's Voice: To put the Manager on trial is not to destroy it, but to see through it. When it is exposed as a function rather than a ruler, a new freedom appears. Thoughts, emotions, and sensations can rise and fall without being policed. Space itself accommodates them all. In that court of awareness, the verdict is always the same: there is no single agent, no boss-self. There is only the vast openness in which everything comes and goes. The dialogue leaves us with a question: how do we test the Manager's authority in real time, not just in theory? The simplest way is to put its claims on trial within our own awareness.

Contemplative Reflection
Cross-Examining the Inner Manager

The "Inner Manager" thrives on making claims: I am the thinker of my thoughts. I must hold this together. Without me, everything will fall apart. These sound persuasive only because they are rarely tested. Here is a way to test them directly:

1. **Spot the claim.** When the Manager's voice arises, pause. Label it as a claim rather than a fact.
2. **Search for the agent.** Ask: Where is the "I" that is speaking? Look in sensation, in thought, in awareness itself. What do you actually find?
3. **Stage the trial.** Imagine a small courtroom of awareness. Call witnesses:
   - **Breath:** Does it really need managing, or does it continue regardless?
   - **Thoughts:** Do they arrive because the Manager summons them, or do they appear on their own schedule—sometimes unruly, sometimes quiet?
   - **Emotions:** Are they manufactured by the Manager, or do they surge and ebb from deeper currents?
4. **Let Space preside.** Picture Space itself as the judge: vast, impartial, allowing all testimony without condemnation. Notice what happens when the Manager's supposed authority is weighed against the evidence.

5. **Rest in openness.** For 10–15 seconds, let awareness remain without trying to confirm or deny the Manager's claims. Experience stands on its own, already moving, already whole.

And yet, the Manager is persistent. Even when its sovereignty has been unmasked, it sneaks back in subtle ways: tightening attention, narrowing awareness into a forward beam. That's the next trick we need to examine.

> **Focal settings range over the capacity to apprehend things as involving a space-dimension, instead of over the degree to which this dimension has been truly screened out. So, we do not need to change what 'we' see to make it appear more space-like. The ultimately open focal setting is one which opens fully to Great Space's 'allowing', and this is sufficient to accommodate ordinary things, as they are, as being 'O.K.'**

THE MANAGER'S NARROW BEAM

Have you ever caught yourself rereading the same email three times because you're convinced you'll miss something if you don't stay hyper-focused? That tight, forward-leaning effort, the sense that "I must stay in charge," is the Inner Manager at work. The Inner Manager survives by narrowing awareness into a contracted focal setting: subject here, object there, a beam aimed forward at the next task. (For how these settings are structured and why they feel inevitable, see Chapter Six, Field Guide to Focal Settings, especially the Lower Space and Bystander patterns.) This two-term machinery feels natural, even necessary, but it is only one setting among many. From within its narrow gaze, life becomes a ceaseless struggle to maintain order and control.

But what if this structure is only the artifact of biased framing? The "self-as-knower" and the "world-as-known" are not fixed poles but positions held in place by habit. When the aperture widens, that subject–object split begins to blur. What we took to be "support" turns out not to be a hidden floor but the absence of floor, openness that already accommodates everything that appears.

Great Space is this wider expanse, its quality not control but allowing. Even the most ordinary or difficult situations are already included, already 'O.K.' When awareness relaxes into this balance, the Manager no longer claims the throne. It becomes a tool, sometimes useful, but never sovereign.

This recognition is not achieved by banishing thoughts or conquering emotions, but by loosening the grip that insists on direction and supervision. The Inner Manager can no longer pose as ruler because its authority is revealed as derivative, a PR department for a non-existent company. What remains is not a void but a radiance: mind itself seen as transparent, arising and dissolving in openness without the need for a foundation. But the Manager's narrowing doesn't just appear in daily tasks, it shows up even in the very practices we trust to set us free.

THE LIMITS OF MEDITATION

The practice of meditation in the West is a relatively recent phenomenon. Yet almost from the start, it was cast in a familiar mold as yet another project for self-improvement. It promises calm, clarity, even enlightenment, if only we log the hours, focus harder, refine the method. For many, the cushion has become a workstation: silence a resource to harvest, stillness a product to achieve. The posture looks dignified, but the subtle message is familiar: an inner manager is at work. It times the session, judges progress, measures success or failure. The very dualism we have been loosening, subject here, object there, is smuggled back in.

This is not to dismiss meditation. For centuries, across many disparate cultures, it has been a powerful doorway. But when it is cast as a causal method—"do this, and you will get that"—it mirrors the productivity mindset of modern life. You sit, striving to control distraction, rehearsing the effort to get somewhere else. Even when calm arises, it is claimed as an achievement: I did it. The boss-self has won another round.

Real life then compounds the split. We finish meditating and step back into traffic, emails, family duties, as if there were two worlds: the cushion and the street, the sacred and the ordinary. Practice becomes a compartment; the walls remain intact.

The Time, Space and Knowledge vision invites another possibility. What if awareness is not something to be performed, but the very field in which all performance unfolds? What if the striver who counts breaths, the critic who scolds, the seeker who longs for peace are all just figures within the same openness they pretend to manage?

Seen this way, meditation is liberated from being a project. It can dissolve into life itself: as attention that does not depend on posture, as openness that does not depend on ritual. Walking the dog, washing dishes, or pausing in a difficult conversation can all disclose the same field. The question shifts from How well did I do? to What is already here, when no one is doing? This is meditation without the meditator: not a technique to master, but a recognition that openness has never been absent.

CHAPTER ELEVEN

When Nothing Stands Apart

We've been tracking the presence of an "inner manager," an internal authority that edits and regulates our experience. Earlier, we likened it to a petty governing official, a minor bureaucrat who presides over the corridors of the mind. The manager's function is not flashy, but it is constant: issuing permits for what may appear, stamping disapproval on what doesn't fit, and ensuring that everything stays in order. It thrives in what we have called lower space, a narrowed and serviceable sense of space that organizes life into familiar compartments.

Lower space is practical enough. It gives us orientation: "I am here, now; objects and others are over there, then." Within this framework, the petty official appears indispensable. Without it, how would we know where we stand, or what belongs to us, or what we can control? Yet this arrangement also hides something important. The more we inhabit its confines, the more convincing it becomes, until it hardens into common sense: of course there's a world "out there," of course I'm a subject "in here," of course reality is what stands apart and must be measured against.

This entire regime is built on taking the position that we function as bystanders to life. We watch. We observe. We take up a position, and in so doing we generate a perspective that seems to make everything else appear. Alongside the bystander comes its counterpart: the outside-stander. If

I am "here," then something else must be "there." If I am the witness, then there must be what is witnessed, often granted greater weight, authority, or permanence than the one doing the observing.

Look closely and you'll see that this stance always splits in two:

- *Bystanders* are all the ways we silently install ourselves as the onlooker: the sense of occupying "here," the reassurance of "now," the notion of being a "self" who stands apart from what unfolds. Even the conviction that "this is my body" functions as a bystander move. I mark a place on the map, I anchor myself in the claim that "my" body is here, belonging to me.
- *Outside-standers* are whatever we take to exist beyond or above us: the world of objects, the natural order, society, God, Nature, the brain, the market, the Big Bang, Buddha-nature, universal awareness. They stand apart, seemingly independent of us, often taken as more real or more fundamental than our particular lives.

The two appear together, locked in mutual reinforcement. The very act of establishing myself as bystander automatically produces an outside that outstrips me. A bystander requires an outside-stander; an outside-stander confirms the bystander. This scheme involves bondage, as the self is always set against something other and elsewhere, an established world order "out there" that it belongs to. In some respects, the "I" is no more than a creative after-thought, ignorant of its own origin. Yet despite this ignorance, the self insists on occupying the driver's seat of experience. This is the architecture of lower space.[30]

Notice how deeply this structure saturates everyday life. I glance down and see my hands. The thought arises, "These are mine. I am here." It feels like absolute proof. But that proof is produced by a stance already taken: the observer installed in advance, then validated by the sight of the body it claims. In this way, even my own body can be rendered an outside-stander, something "there" to be owned, observed, and managed by the bystander "here."

This split is not just philosophical. It seeps into how we live. Once reality seems to stand over and against us, our options narrow to managing, defending, and striving. We cling to identity to maintain balance against what feels larger, more real, or more permanent. We organize life around measuring up to what stands outside us. And the inner overseer thrives here, because the whole setting requires management.

How does the self-as-bystander keep itself at the center of experience, even when nothing in our actual experience warrants such privilege? Much is at stake in asking this. The comfortable positions that have long felt like safe enclosures may have no real ground beneath them. The real invitation begins when we question this stance. What if there were no need for bystanders or outside-standers at all? What if the very posture of standing apart is what narrows experience in the first place? And what if "here/now" and "there/then" were not divided sides of a fence, but expressions of a wider openness that requires no observer to hold them together?

> **The point of challenging first causes is not to urge that there is no beginning, and thus only an endless process. Rather, these challenges focus on the idea that a**

particular world has been set up and perpetuated by a defining or locating causal sequence.

We've seen how the bystander and outside-stander reinforce each other: "I am here, witnessing" and "the real cause is out there." This dynamic plays out not only in ordinary life but also in the stories we tell about existence itself. Whenever discomfort or confusion arises, our reflex is to ask: What started this? Where did it come from? In daily life, that might sound like, "Why did this happen to me?" or "Who caused this problem?" The same reflex, magnified, gives rise to grand origin stories. Religions answer with creator myths or tales of a fall and eventual return. Secular science answers with the Big Bang, the evolution of species, or the neural correlates of consciousness. Even contemporary seekers often imagine a Universal Mind, a pure witness, or an absolute non-dual awareness that stands apart from life.

But notice what unites these answers. To look for an origin is to assume a stance: there must be a source "out there" explaining "me in here." Whether it is God, a cosmic explosion, or a universal awareness, the effect is the same: the outside-stander is granted ultimate authority, and the bystander shrinks in comparison. The split is preserved.

The point is not to dismiss these stories; they may carry deep meaning, inspiration, or beauty. The point is to see how they rest on a stance that may itself be optional. What if we questioned not only the answers, but the very need for a source apart from what is unfolding here and now?

When we let go of the bystander position, experience begins to feel participatory and whole rather than divided and fragmented. Sensations, thoughts, and the world around us are no longer delivered to a bystander; they unfold as a single movement, textured and alive. In this setting, openness is not a backdrop but an active quality: roomy, permeable, hospitable to whatever shows up. The "two-term," dualistic arrangement of subject here, object there, begins to thin. Space is no longer the box that contains us; it is the openness of relating, in which the lines that divide "in here" from "out there" can soften or even dissolve.

From this angle, the petty official loses its authority. There is less to defend, less to certify, less to control. What opens instead is energy for curiosity, care, and creative action within the very world that a moment ago seemed alien or superior. "No bystanders, no outside-standers" is not a clever phrase; it is a practice in reconfiguring the focal setting of experience itself.

This chapter begins with that simple act: watching the inner manager as it narrows and assigns, and then asking, what if I don't take up the bystander's seat at all? The answer cannot be given conceptually. It is felt as relief, as roominess, as permeability, lived as a healing of the split between self and world. From there, a more spacious and responsive knowing can unfold, a way of being that is not just open but wise and compassionate, because it no longer divides what is seen from the one who sees.

Having traced how the stance of the bystander generates its counterpart, the outside-stander, we can now turn this inquiry into lived experience. It's one thing to grasp the argument in words; it's another to feel what happens when the stance itself gives way. The following practice is not about "getting somewhere" or "achieving a state." It is about experimenting with how experience shows itself when we no longer occupy the seat of the watcher, and when we no longer seek for something to stand outside and validate us.

Contemplative Reflection
Dissolving the Stance—
No Bystanders, No Outside-standers

Begin by settling into stillness. Let the body rest, uncoiling from its tasks, as if it were gently held by the invisible hands of space, with no need to direct or shape the breath. Simply allow it to come and go, arriving without effort. In this quieting, notice how easily a subtle watcher appears: the sense of "someone" monitoring the moment.

Pause. Ask gently, almost wordlessly: *Where is this watcher? Can it be found?* And then let the question dissolve like salt in water. What if you don't take the seat of the one who watches? Let this not be a problem to solve, but a stance to soften.

Now, include everything. The sensations of the body, the ambient sounds, the breath, the thoughts drifting through—let them all be present. Let go of the habit of placing yourself "here" and everything else "out there." Allow the scene to unfold without needing a center, without needing to be for anyone. This moment is not being delivered to a bystander. It is *self-unfolding*. Perhaps you even sense your own body not as "mine," but as something subtly "watched." As if the body itself were placed across a divide. Let this noticing deepen. No need to fix it; just let the observation open the possibility that even this form might be space-appearing, not owned or overseen.

Gently bring to mind any story that anchors your sense of what is real: "I am here," "this is the world," "this is awareness," "this is God," "this is energy." Without rejecting the story, ask: *Is this standing apart from me? Am I giving it the authority of an outside-stander?* Feel what it's like to let go of that need for ground. What if nothing needs to be explained, referenced, or proved? What if this unfolding doesn't need to be validated by a witness, a source, or a stance? Let this mystery breathe, without wrapping it in meaning.

Notice now if you are subtly positioned as a seeker, a knower, an experiencer. Gently ask: *What if I don't need to be the one who knows? What if knowing is already happening, without a knower?* Sense how even the act of seeking softens, like a wave spreading out and losing its crest. No grasping, no holding. Just this: fluid, participatory, without edge or center. Let it all unfold now, not in awareness, but as the field in which awareness appears. No bystander. No outside-stander. Just the intimacy of immediacy. Space not as backdrop, but as the aliveness of relation itself. Nothing stands apart. Nothing needs to be managed. The manager, too, falls away.

If the eyes were closed, now let them open, not to resume the stance, but to witness the world without a watcher. Objects appear, but no one stands apart to own them. Forms arise, but they do not imply a position. The play continues, but the stage is boundaryless. And now, simply let this new seeing settle. Not as an achievement, but as a quiet shift in how things show themselves. *What is it like when no one is watching? What opens when the stance dissolves?*

Let these questions remain, not to answer, but to live.

RELAXING OUR HOLD

When we return from this experiment, the world may look much the same: the same body, the same room, the same tasks awaiting us. And yet, something subtle has shifted. The watcher's seat feels less compulsory, the outside world less authoritative. What once seemed like an ironclad division, me here, reality out there, may show its seams.

This is not a state to preserve or a new stance to cling to. It is more like discovering a hidden pliability in the fabric of experience, a pliancy that does not require defense or explanation. Life continues, but with more room. The petty official of the mind may still rise to stamp its approvals and denials, but its rulings no longer feel absolute.

The point is not to rid ourselves of bystanders or outside-standers once and for all, but to glimpse how optional they are. Each time we recognize their appearance, we also recognize the possibility of letting them dissolve. That recognition itself opens a new kind of participation where immediacy is no longer fenced off, but lived as the aliveness of relation.

> **In our approach to Great Space, first we must clear away our 'familiar world order' and 'here' orientation. We can relax our hold on these notions as constituting our point of departure and a contrasting condition of Great Space.**

THE PARTICIPATORY FIELD

When the stance of the bystander loosens, something shifts. Experience no longer feels like a stream of impressions shuttled to an observer or a line of objects parading before a witness. Instead, the whole field comes alive. Thoughts, sensations, and perceptions don't need to cross an invisible divide to reach "me, here." They are already unfolding as part of a larger movement that includes me.

Think of a conversation that suddenly clicks. Words move back and forth, but no one is "holding" the exchange; it carries its own rhythm. In the same way, what we divide into "inner" and "outer" can be felt as a single unfolding. The sound of traffic, the ache in the back, the thought about dinner each arises with its own integrity, but none requires a central observer to certify them.

This is what it means to say immediacy is participatory. The "I, here" no longer stands apart to survey what is given; it participates as one expression within the field itself. Everything shows up in mutual presence, co-articulated, given together.

From this angle, "Great Space" is no longer an abstract idea. It names the openness that allows forms to appear without a supervisor keeping them in line. It is not a container that holds things (there is no need for "holding space," a popular New Age cliché), nor a backdrop that frames them. It is openness itself: roomy, permeable, already welcoming.

The difference is subtle but profound. Lower space insists that subjects and objects are separate and that every event must be tallied, owned, explained. Great Space lets appearances arise without that burden. A tree need not be an object "out there," but can be seen as part of the same continuum that breathes through one's own body. The breeze on the face, the shifting leaves, the noticing itself all belong together.

In this way, the bystander stance unravels, with no permits to stamp, no borders to defend. Life flows without validation from an outside authority. The familiar split between "in here" and "out there" shows itself as optional, not necessary.

To call this participatory is not to collapse into vague oneness but rather to experience the texture of relation itself: each event arising with its own clarity while also belonging to the whole. A sound does not need to become a thought; a thought does not need to be claimed as "mine." They appear as movements within the same openness. In this participatory field, freedom is not escape but intimacy, a way of being in the world without standing apart from it.

DISSOLVING HIERARCHIES OF REALITY

When we imagine outside-standers, we rarely leave them neutral. We place them on pedestals. They become the great authorities of existence: God, Nirvana, Nature, Science, Society, the Brain, the Market, the Cosmos. Each stands apart and above, more real than we are, more fundamental, more lasting. Against these towering presences, our own lives can feel small, provisional, derivative. Consider how often these hierarchies shape our sense of worth. If the outside-stander is God, then we are cast as creatures struggling to prove ourselves worthy. If the outside-stander is Nature, then we are late arrivals, fragile participants in a vast process that dwarfs us. If the outside-stander is Science, then we are little more than epiphenomena of chemistry and physics. If it is the Brain, then consciousness itself is reduced to firing neurons. If it is the Market, then human value is measured by productivity, price, or purchasing power.

Each of these frameworks has its insight, its validity. But notice what they share: they cast authority outside ourselves. Meaning comes from elsewhere, from what stands beyond or above. The bystander stance then shrinks into dependence, always measuring itself against a source it cannot touch. This is not an abstract problem. It shows up in how we live. Students feel anxious about whether their achievements measure up to the standards of "Science" or "Academia." Workers compare their worth against the impersonal authority of "the Market." Believers gauge their souls by the demands of a divine lawgiver. Seekers measure their spiritual progress against an imagined universal awareness that stands infinitely beyond them.

No matter which story we choose, the structure is the same: the outside-stander becomes the gold standard, and the bystander measures itself in relation to it. The more elevated the outside-stander, the more diminished the bystander feels. This explains why even the most noble visions—God, Nirvana, Enlightenment—can become sources of subtle bondage. They set the terms of value at a distance, and we are left striving to bridge the gap.

> **the themes of an eternal deity and of this deity's having created the world may be seen in a different light. This is true also for the Buddhist themes of a primordial Buddha and primordial and infinite perfection pure from the beginning, as well as for the general religious theme of a salvation 'in the end', following a quest for self-perfection.**

But what if this gap is not inherent? What if the authority we grant to outside-standers is the echo of our own stance-taking? The very act of imagining ourselves as bystanders already manufactures what appears as more fundamental, more real. In other words, the hierarchy is self-installed. In a way, the outside-stander Emperor has no clothes.

To see this is not to reject God, Nature, Science, or any of the frameworks that give meaning to our lives. It is to notice that their authority depends on the stance from which we view them. Loosen the stance, and the hierarchy loosens. God may still inspire awe, Nature may still evoke reverence, Science may still reveal extraordinary patterns, but none of them need to stand outside and above, dictating our worth. They can be participants in the same reality we are already part of.

This is what it means to dissolve hierarchies of reality. It is not iconoclasm, but immanence. The divine is not "up there," it is woven through the moment. Nature is not an external backdrop we observe, but the living tissue we are made of. Science is not an external arbiter, but one way of patterning our shared inquiry. Even the Market, when stripped of its authority as the ultimate benchmark, can be seen as a provisional human construct, not the measure of reality itself.

When outside-standers lose their pedestal, immediacy regains its authority. We no longer live in a world divided into higher and lower, ultimate and derivative. We live in a participatory universe where nothing needs to stand above or apart in order to be real.

> **The way to bridge this apparent gulf is to develop an orientation which does not reinforce the 'outside-stander' or 'by-stander' presuppositions—which are what create a gulf in the first place. Goal and progress-orientations need to be deactivated; we can then see that both primordial perfection and the goal of realization or salvation are immediately available to us.**

LIVING WITHOUT BYSTANDERS

If the bystander stance is optional, what might life feel like without it? We don't need to wait for lofty states of consciousness or special retreats to find out. The experiment can unfold in the ordinary pulse of a day: walking down the street, listening to a friend, facing conflict, sitting at work.

Take walking. Normally, we walk as if moving through a pre-existing world "out there." Our body is the vehicle, "I" am the passenger, and the streets, cars, and trees form the scenery. But when the bystander recedes, walking is not "me moving through space." It is the whole scene moving together: the pressure of foot on pavement, the sway of arms, the sound of wind in the leaves, the sight of a passerby, all in concert. There is no one in the stands watching the play; the walk is the play itself.

Or take listening. So often we listen from a position: "I am here, receiving what you say." The other's words come across a divide, and I decide how to respond. But in the participatory awareness, listening is not about *me hearing you.* It is a shared unfolding: voice, tone, breath, expression, the stirrings inside my body are all part of one movement. I don't need to hold a seat as the one who listens; listening is happening in the space we inhabit together.

Consider conflict. A remark cuts deep, or a disagreement flares. The bystander stance leaps in: *I am hurt, they are wrong, the world is against me.* The outside-stander looms as an ideal, an authority that must be appealed to, for justice, fairness, truth. But when the stance dissolves, conflict can be felt as part of the same broadcast message: sharp words, quickened pulse, heat in the chest, silence in the room are all co-arising. Without a watcher to defend or an authority to prove, even the charged moment has space. It doesn't mean passivity or withdrawal; it means responding from within the shared ground rather than fighting from a separate position.

Even at work, where the inner manager often thrives, this shift matters. Deadlines, meetings, emails—everything demands to be managed. Normally, I take my post as the overseer: *I must control this, or it will collapse.* But notice what happens if, even briefly, the overseer is not required. Tasks, thoughts, and actions move by themselves. Some are completed, some delayed, some dropped. The flow is not dictated by an outside tribunal of "shoulds" but by the unfolding of the moment. The petty official may still issue memos, but its rulings no longer have ultimate authority.

This is the everyday miracle of dissolving the stance: nothing grand, nothing dramatic, just the simple relief of not having to sit in the watcher's chair. In that relief, a more natural ease and contact emerges. Life does not need to be delivered to us—it is already here, self-unfolding.

These glimpses are subtle but powerful. They show that living without bystanders is not about leaving life—it is about engaging and participating more fully. Each moment is the aliveness of relation, and we are in it, of it, not standing apart.

DROPPING THE BYSTANDER POSITION

Stepping out of the watcher's chair does not make life vanish. It makes it more immediate: alive, intimate, unmediated by distance or authority. What once seemed like an inner–outer divide softens, and what looked like an overseer proves to be just another part of the flow. This chapter has shown how the stance of "bystander" quietly manufactures a world that feels separate, elevated, or beyond us. When that stance loosens, so do its hierarchies. What emerges is not abstraction but participation: the street as lived terrain, the body as porous and present, the other as co-arising in immediacy.

But loosening the bystander is not the endpoint. As long as observer and observed remain fixed poles, the old architecture reasserts itself. The next step is to let the entire frame, body, mind, even the apparent seat of observation, open into a more generous space.

That is the invitation of Chapter Twelve: to sense both body and mind not as bounded entities, but as translucent forms already opening into Great Space.

CHAPTER TWELVE

The Illusion of Here

We like to believe we know what it means to be "here." The word has a reassuring solidity. I am here, you are there. This room is here, the world is out there. "Here" seems to anchor us, providing a foothold from which everything else can be arranged. Yet if we look more closely, "here" is not so simple. It is bound up with "befores" and "afters," with "elsewheres" and "not-yets." This moment we call "here and now" only makes sense in contrast with the moments that came before and the ones anticipated after. It is stitched into a web of elsewhere and else when, defined by what it is not. Far from being a pure point of presence, "here" is a contraction, a safe setting where the vastness of reality has been toned down to something tolerable for a self.

Think of it like a dimmer switch. The raw light of infinity would overwhelm our ordinary faculties. So "here" functions as a filter, reducing the brilliance to a manageable glow. The nearness of infinity is dimmed down into a local place, a spot on the grid of space and time where a self can plant its flag. "Here" then becomes a kind of staging ground from which a world of particulars can unfurl: this body in this location, those objects arrayed over there, this sequence of events moving forward in time. "Here" isn't a fact we stand on; it's a setting we perform.

'Here' is, both logically and phenomenologically, completely tied up with 'befores', 'not yets', and 'elsewheres'. Here' is a distracting 'by-stander' in a world of 'outside-standers'.

We mistake this dimming for reality itself. Because it is familiar and manageable, it feels true. "Here" becomes the default anchor of our lives, the ground beneath our feet. But this ground is a construction. It is like standing on a platform in the middle of an ocean and forgetting that the platform is not the sea.

This is why simply repeating slogans like "Be here now" or "Stay in the present moment" can be misleading. The phrase sounds liberating, but often it only re-fetishizes the dimmed-down version of reality. It freezes the bystander stance: a self, located in time, making an effort to capture a moment as if it were a thing to hold. The ordinary "present moment" is still trapped within a causal sequence, perched between a past and a future. Far from unveiling infinity, it doubles down on the contraction.

Great Space is 'here' in a sense. But from a certain viewpoint, that nearness of infinity is toned down to a level tolerable for a 'self', a level sufficient for 'here' to 'be someplace'. The infinity of Great Space then unfolds as a particular world, an indefinitely extended field of places and times populated by innumerable particulars.

From the perspective of Great Space, the ordinary "here" is not a final truth but a safety mechanism. It tones down the nearness of infinity to prevent us from being flooded by it. In doing so, it gives us a workable platform for daily life, but it also hides what is most vital. The sheer openness that is closest to us, the boundless dimension that makes every appearance possible, becomes invisible, even irrelevant. We walk around tethered to a narrowed sense of presence, like children playing with shadows on the wall while the sun blazes just outside the room.

If we can sense this toning-down process, we begin to see "here" differently. It is not the anchor of reality but the output of a setting. "Here" is a stance, a point of view we occupy so that the world seems stable. That stance keeps us safe, but it also keeps us small. The irony is that what we are protected from is not a threat at all but the presence of infinity, the very ground of our being. If "here" is a stance rather than the ground, two reflexes immediately arise that keep the stance in place: we double down on doing, and we idolize a point in time.

THE TRAP OF THE DOER

Sensing the narrowness, our first reflex is to fix it: *I will open.* That reflex installs the doer and keeps the stance intact. We want to open to a wider perspective, to access Great Space, to experience reality more directly. But almost without noticing, we translate that longing into a project: *I must open. I must achieve a breakthrough. I must do the practices that will get me there.*

This is the trap of the doer. It seems perfectly logical: if I want to change, then I must be the one to make it happen. Who else could do it? This way of thinking is deeply embedded in our culture. Self-help programs insist that we take responsibility, exert willpower, and generate motivation. Therapies encourage us to shift our attitudes and change our narratives. Even meditation, as often taught today, is framed as a discipline of effort: sit still, maintain vigilance, keep returning to the breath. The unspoken assumption is always the same: a self is here, it is the agent of transformation.

But from the perspective of Great Space, this assumption is precisely what keeps us bound. The very sense of being a self who acts is not a starting point for change; it is an *output* of the focal setting. By taking this output as fundamental and then trying to use it as the instrument of liberation, we perpetuate the setting we are trying to transcend. It is like trying to lift ourselves by our own bootstraps: the more we strain, the more entangled and exhausted we become.

The structure of this entanglement is subtle. The self imagines itself located "here and now," then undertakes techniques (including meditation) to expand or deepen that position. But because "here and now" is itself a contraction, a toned-down stance in which infinity is dimmed, the effort only reinforces the contraction. No matter how sincere or disciplined the attempt, the "I" remains at the center, measuring progress, evaluating results, striving for success. What looks like breakthrough is often just a more refined form of self-maintenance. This is why so many seekers find themselves exhausted by spiritual practice. They may follow instructions with diligence, meditating daily, reciting mantras, engaging in rituals, yet still feel as though they are circling the same ground. Beneath the surface, the doer is still intact, still clutching the reins. Effort becomes another performance of the very stance that blocks openness.

Even traditional religious practices can fall into this pattern. Ascetic disciplines, vows of poverty, elaborate rituals of purification, each can become another project of the doer, another way of reinforcing the self as the one who must overcome itself. These practices may loosen attachments at one level, but if they leave unquestioned the presupposition that "I, here, must be the one to do it," then they reinstall the same focal setting at a subtler level. The form may change, but the stance remains.

We can see the same trap in contemporary mindfulness programs. Participants are instructed to cultivate awareness, to bring the mind back to the present, to let go of distractions. On the surface, these are invitations to openness. But in practice, they often reinforce a regime of self-surveillance: Am I doing this right? Am I focused enough? Am I succeeding at letting go? The "I" remains in charge, monitoring performance, striving to meet the standard of presence. Instead of dissolving the bystander stance, mindfulness can entrench it.

How ironic: the harder we try to open, the more firmly the doer is installed. Every act of effort confirms its own necessity: *See, I am the one making this happen. Without me, nothing would change.* But this claim is circular. The doer is both the problem and the one insisting on its role as solution. The more it tries to let go, the more it proves itself indispensable. Even the act of "not-doing" can be co-opted into the same cycle: the self takes pride in having renounced effort, in "achieving" the state of letting things be.

From the standpoint of the new vision, this is the central paradox of the doer: it cannot bring about the transformation it seeks, because it itself is the very contraction that needs to be undone. To engage the self as the agent of change is to perpetuate the very focal setting that tones down infinity. To discover meditation without the meditator is to find that openness needs no manager, no watcher, no doer; it has always been here, quietly sustaining every breath and thought.

The challenge, then, is to recognize this trap without falling into despair. The point is not that change is impossible, but that it cannot be accomplished through the usual logic of self-effort. Transformation is not another project of the doer. It is a relaxation of the stance that installs the doer in the first place. This relaxation cannot be forced, because forcing is exactly what the doer does. It must be allowed, permitted, even trusted, like unclenching a hand rather than grasping harder.

The path to Great Space can feel so counterintuitive. It requires us to question the very premise that has guided all our striving: the assumption that "I am the one who must achieve." From within the ordinary focal setting, this goal feels impossible. But as the stance is seen clearly as a stance, another possibility comes into view: awakening is not something we accomplish, but something that unfolds when we stop clutching at goals and accomplishment.

Seen in this light, the trap of the doer is not a barrier but an invitation. It shows us exactly where the contraction lies. Every time we catch ourselves striving to make openness happen, we are given a chance to notice the stance itself: the "I" that insists on being in charge. In that noticing, we can relax, allow and let be. The doer need not be overcome; it can simply be seen for what it is: an output of the setting, not its master. When doing becomes the method, the stance stays intact. A second reflex then seals the circle: we shrink immediacy to a point and try to hold it.

> **The popular meditative injunction to 'Be here now' is seen from the Great Space perspective as being probably misleading. On one hand, it might be interpreted as invoking the ordinary sense of 'here' and 'the present'. On the other, it might seem to refer to a kind of**

fleeting, immaculate sensum-like 'here' which must be apprehended. Such orientations are a perpetuation of the restrictive focal setting and its emphasis on locatedness.

IDOLIZING THE NOW

Our second reflex is to shrink immediacy to a point and guard it: the present becomes a prize to hold. If the trap of the doer keeps us locked into effort, then the fetish of the present moment keeps us locked into location. Few spiritual slogans have enjoyed as much popularity as "Be here now." It sounds liberating, even obvious: stop worrying about the past, stop chasing the future, and simply rest in the present. Who could argue with that? Yet this instruction carries hidden assumptions that make it less freeing than it first appears. It presupposes an observing subject, an "I" situated here, tasked with paying attention to something called "the present." The present moment, in this view, becomes a kind of elusive object, an outside-stander that can be reached if the subject focuses hard enough. Mindfulness then becomes a form of mental gymnastics: the subject tries to merge its "here" with the "now," as though two coordinates could be forced into alignment.

This effort may feel profound at first. We notice the breath, the body, the sights and sounds around us. We experience a reprieve from rumination. But beneath the surface, the same structure is being reinforced. The "I" is still on guard, checking whether it is successfully "being present." The present moment itself has been reified, turned into a goal, an achievement, a prize for the diligent. What looks like transcendence is often just another self-project, one more attempt by the bystander to secure its footing.

From the standpoint of Great Space, this entire operation is counterfeit. The "here" we are instructed to inhabit is not the communion with infinity but the toned-down, narrowed version of it. And the "present moment" we are told to capture is not openness itself but a placeholder on a timeline—an instant squeezed between before and after. Instead of dissolving contraction, the injunction to "be here now" doubles down on it, freezing attention into a narrow point.

The result is a subtle but pervasive self-surveillance. Practitioners monitor themselves for signs of distraction, chastise themselves for failing to stay present, congratulate themselves for achieving moments of clarity. The self remains at the center, achieving or failing, proud or ashamed. Even the injunction to "let things be" can become a performance: the self reassures itself that it is doing well at not-doing.

> **There may also be an achievement, a self-orientation involved, to the effect that we are urged to try to 'be here', or to capture something close at hand. Or we might be reassured that everything is fine and that we should just 'let things be'. In either case, the immediate presence 'here' of Great Space, and a true 'opening' to it, are both being missed by clinging to small focal setting counterparts, which are actually *counterfeits*.**

In this sense, the present moment becomes a fetish, idolized, sacralized, invested with healing power, made into an elixir that promises well-being. Mindfulness programs hold it up as the ultimate cure for stress, anxiety, and dissatisfaction. But in practice, the present moment is often little more than a temporal idol, an abstracted instant given authority it does not deserve. We grasp at it as though it were a solid ground, yet it slips away the moment we try to hold it.

The deeper problem is that such practices perpetuate the presuppositions of the old setting. They assume the self must act as the agent of attention and the present is something to be apprehended. The division between subject and object, here and there, now and then, remains unquestioned. Instead of loosening the split, the struggle is simply relocated to a smaller stage, with the self asked to play both actor, referee, and consumer in a drama of presence.

These two habits, doing and localizing, explain why "here" feels safe and small. A different orientation is possible. Instead of treating the present moment as a thing to capture, we can recognize it as an output of the same focal setting that generates self and world. From this perspective, the task is not to seize the now but to loosen the stance that divides time at all. When this shift happens, immediacy is no longer located in a point to grasp. It is spacious ground: the openness in which moments arise, shine and fall away.

> **There are no things stuck in or bound by time. It is important, therefore, not to attend to 'the present' as being a discrete section of an independent grid which 'we are in'.**

True presence is not commanded by the voice that says, "Be here now! Be in the present moment." It comes unbidden when the bystander's seat is dislodged. Then immediacy is already present, not as an object to grasp or an achievement to secure, but as the simple aliveness of relation. On the ground of presence, nothing needs to be held onto, because nothing stands apart. When the doer loosens and the present is no longer a prize, "here" stops being a perch and becomes an opening; meditation reveals itself, without a 'meditator', to be the natural ease of Great Space shining through.

In seeking the mysterious 'presence' and availability of Great Space, we are faced with a subtle challenge. We must not simply resist a directed 'outside-stander' orientation by means of an intensification of our ordinary sense of the 'present' or of clock-time instants. Such an intensification (generating trance states) only reinforces the constrictive focus (or fixation) which leads to bondage to ordinary time. This is exactly what we are attempting to counteract!

THE MYSTERY OF GREAT SPACE

When doing and fixating ease, the horizon changes. Infinity is not far away; it is near—so near we mistake it for nothing. But contraction tones infinity down into a manageable "here," and around that narrowed stance a world begins to arrange itself. From this position, reality appears as an endless tapestry of nested detail: atoms within molecules, cells within bodies, galaxies within clusters. Wherever we look, there is more to parse, more to measure, more to explain.

This infinity of detail, however, rarely fulfills. Each new discovery promises closeness but only pushes the horizon further. Like zooming in on a digital map, the tiles keep loading, but the sense of arrival never comes.

Great Space is closer than close, the most intimate, the very ground of our being, yet it seems inaccessible. We chase infinity in extension, while overlooking the openness that makes extension possible. The result is a paradox: the most immediate dimension feels hidden.

Everywhere and at every level of analysis that we look in this world, we can find an 'infinity' of detail and extent, but it draws us on rather than giving us

> **fulfillment in the moment. 'Here' has a different meaning within this world than it does from the Great Space perspective, and so the availability and primary grounding character of Great Space becomes a mystery, a tantalizing puzzle.**

Much in our culture reinforces this forgetting. Scientific models situate us within a causal grid: neurons firing, species evolving, a universe ignited by a Big Bang. Religious myths often do the same, projecting a first event or divine decree as the source. Whether secular or sacred, both place the ground elsewhere, at a distance.

And yet, religion has also carried forward counter-moves: renunciation, compassion, loosening the grasp of possession and ego. These gestures soften the stance, crack the enclosure, and let openness show through. They prepare the ground not by explaining, but by relaxing the posture that demands explanation. The deeper insight then gradually emerges: the stance and the world arise together. Shift the focal setting, and the world that appears shifts too. Ethical practice and contemplative disciplines matter not only for moral reasons but because they loosen the contraction that makes the world seem fixed.

Still, as long as we cling to the self "in here" and the world "out there," the contraction reasserts itself. Infinity is narrowed to a protective "here," and we settle for a fragile sense of security. The irony is that Great Space is never absent. It is not far away in time or beyond reach in transcendence. It is the most intimate aspect of life itself, overlooked only because it is too near.

RELIGION, ETHICS, AND DISSOLVING THE FOCAL SETTING

If the world that spreads out before us is the projection of a toned-down stance, then shifting that stance requires more than intellectual critique. It calls for practices that can dismantle the self's hold and ease the structures that make the world feel fixed. Across millennia, religious traditions have provided such practices, sometimes more effectively than any philosophical system or scientific worldview. At their heart, the world's religions have offered codes of conduct that counter the narrow orientation of self-concern. Prohibitions against theft, deception, or violence; injunctions to honor parents and elders, serve the community, or care for the poor—these are not arbitrary moral laws. They work to interrupt the tightening spiral of self-orientation. By redirecting attention from the demands of the "me" to the well-being of others, they begin to dissolve the reflexive stance of the bystander who takes its own security as paramount.

Even more transformative are practices of renunciation and service. The act of giving up prized possessions weakens the hold on what we own. The deeper renunciation of personal desires frees us from the pull of what we crave. And the practice of serving others dismantles the illusion of a self set apart. In each case, the focal setting shifts: less fixation on "my world, my needs, my survival," more openness to an inclusive space.

> **All these themes constitute ways and stages of opening up or dissolving a limiting focal setting on the infinity of Great Space. Each stage involves a relaxation of our hold on progressively more fundamental facets of the**

output of a particular setting. We might say that there is a reciprocal dynamic connection between the focal setting and its output.

Many traditions portray this process as a ladder or path. At the lower rungs, the aim is moral discipline: restraining selfish impulses so as not to harm others. At higher rungs, the aim becomes union or transcendence: losing oneself in the presence of the divine or realizing the emptiness of self and phenomena. In Christian mysticism, this might be spoken of as the soul's ascent toward God, seeking to be "perfect as God is perfect." In Buddhist teleology, the aim might be the bodhisattva's vow to extinguish self-clinging for the sake of all beings. However different in form, the function is the same: to progressively relax more fundamental facets of the output produced by the ordinary setting. Such relaxation is not a one-time leap but a process: each loosening prepares the ground for a deeper loosening. At first, we may only be able to let go of superficial attachments: what we own, what we desire, how we defend our image. Later, we may be able to let go of subtler identifications: the roles we play, the stories we tell about ourselves, the beliefs we cling to about the nature of the world. At the deepest level, the invitation is to let go of the stance of self itself, the bystander who claims to be at the center of experience.

We can think of this as a reciprocal process. The focal setting produces a certain output: a world of objects over there, a self over here. But by easing our hold on the output, the setting itself begins to yield. Let go of attachment to possessions, and the "world of mine" starts to dissolve. Relinquish attachment to desires, and the "self who craves" begins to unravel. Set down the habit of separation between self and other, and the whole stage of "me here, world there" opens into something wider. In this sense, religion is not only a system of belief but a technology of non-attachment. Its rituals, codes, and practices can be understood as exercises in relaxing the focal setting. They don't solve the mystery of Great Space, but they help dissolve the thick layers of contraction that prevent us from even experiencing it.

At their best, these practices offer a path of "self-world transcendence" without denigrating the human or idolizing the beyond. When a monk gives up possessions, when a nun renounces desire, when a mystic surrenders to God, when a bodhisattva vows to serve all beings, each is enacting a loosening of the stance that binds appearances into a rigid scheme. The trajectory is toward unveiling: a gradual but steady unveiling of the infinity that had been dimmed.

Exercise caution! As long as certain presuppositions remain untouched, such as the conviction that the world is an accomplished fact "out there," or that the self is a fundamental entity "in here," even the loftiest religious practices risk becoming partial. They can relax many of the bonds, but still leave the central bystander intact. The danger is not that these practices are false or harmful, but that they stop short. They loosen the grip but leave in place the hands that keep gripping.

Still, the value of these traditions should not be underestimated. They remind us that transcendence is possible. They provide models of life that do not revolve entirely around the self. And they testify, across cultures and centuries, that our ordinary stance is not the only way to inhabit reality. Each ethical code, each renunciation, each act of service is a step toward dissolving the focal setting that keeps infinity dimmed.

In this way, religion has preserved a deep truth: revelation is not achieved through accumulating more, but through releasing what binds. Every release is a rehearsal for the ultimate loosening: the letting go of the bystander stance itself.

THE PERILS OF RELEASE

If opening the focal setting were only a matter of renouncing attachments and diminishing self-concern, the path would be simple. But the process is rarely smooth. To dismantle the structures that keep infinity toned down is to disturb the very framework that gives our ordinary life its stability. For this reason, deep releases can feel less like liberation and more like disorientation. At one level, the fear is practical. If I let go of the assumptions that the world is fixed and the self is basic, what will keep me upright? How will I cope? A natural anxiety fears that without these anchors, we will drift into chaos. So, culturally and psychologically, such relaxation and transcendence is often discouraged. Instead, we are taught to strengthen the ego, not to question it; to reinforce reality's solidity, not to see through it.

Yet the disorientation that arises is not due to openness itself. It comes from the half-measures we take when we try to open while still clinging to certain holdouts. If I let go of surface attachments but still take the "world out there" as an accomplished fact, or the "self in here" as a fixed entity, then the new vision collides with the old. The result is conflict: one part of me glimpses a vast openness, while another part insists on the solidity of self and world. The clash between these views produces confusion, anxiety, even fear.

> **When such concepts are not 'opened up', whatever other 'opening' that is done is unbalanced and incomplete. It is still tied to the world and done *by* the self, and these hold-outs tend to conflict in a disorienting way with new visions.**

We can see modern examples of this dynamic in the reports of people who struggle with adverse effects from meditation.[31] In recent decades, clinical research has documented cases where intensive retreat practice has led not to peace but to dissociation, depression, re-traumatization, or panic. Practitioners often report that when the familiar structures of experience began to loosen, they had no framework to integrate the change. Without guidance or a supportive environment, the rupture felt destabilizing, even dangerous.

Traditional religious settings anticipated this danger. Monasteries, cloisters, liturgies, and communities of practice created environments in which loosening could unfold in a balanced way. Ethical codes anchored daily life, while rituals provided rhythm and continuity. Guidance from teachers and the support of fellow practitioners offered reassurance when old certainties dissolved. In such contexts, disorientation could be reinterpreted as a stage on the path rather than a threat to survival.

In modern contexts, where practice is often stripped from its communal and doctrinal frame, we risk confronting the instability without a net. This is why many "spiritual but not religious" seekers, eager to open to wider dimensions of experience, sometimes encounter more turbulence than transformation. The very structures that could hold and contextualize the disorientation have been set aside.

But it is crucial to recognize that the destabilization does not come from Great Space itself. It comes from the persistence of certain unquestioned presuppositions. As long as I insist that the world is ultimately “out there,” fixed and given, and that the self is the one who must manage, navigate, and make sense of it, then any loosening will feel like a contradiction. One part of me says “open,” while another part says “hold on.” That tension produces imbalance.

The challenge is to relax not just the surface features of the focal setting but its very foundations. This does not mean abandoning ordinary life or denying the practical reality of self and world. It means clearly seeing how our insistence that these are absolute, unquestionable facts is not really true. When the fixed frame on “self” and “world” softens, disorientation gives way to a different kind of balance, an equilibrium rooted not in control but in openness.

Seen in this light, disorientation is not a sign of failure but a clue. It shows us where we are still clutching. Every place where anxiety spikes is a place where a presupposition is being defended. If we can allow the clutching to relax, not by force, not by denial, but by gently letting go, then what seemed like chaos becomes a new kind of spaciousness. This is why unbinding has always been described as a path of courage. It asks us to release our foothold on the very ground we thought was keeping us safe, to discover a more fundamental ground that is no ground at all. The safety of the bystander’s “here” gives way to the gentle embrace of infinity. And what once felt like falling reveals itself as being held.

THE COMPLEMENTARITY OF SCIENCE AND RELIGION

If disorientation arises from loosening without support, then where might balance be found? Across history, two great human enterprises, religion and science, have attempted to orient us in relation to the mystery of existence. At first glance they seem to stand opposed, even hostile. One claims revelation, the other evidence; one looks to divine creation, the other to physical law. And yet, when viewed through the lens of Great Space, both can be seen as partial but valuable allies in loosening the focal setting.

Religion's contribution lies not only in its cosmologies but in its codes and disciplines. By teaching renunciation of possessions, curbing of desires, and service beyond the self, religions help break the spell of self-centeredness. Ethical injunctions, whether Buddhist precepts, Jewish commandments, Christian beatitudes, or Islamic pillars, do more than regulate conduct. They decenter the individual. They weaken the stance that insists "I am the axis, here at the center." In doing so, they pry open the possibility of relating to life as more than a bystander peering out at a fixed world.

> **Scientific discoveries can serve as guiding insights which assist in opening the focal setting and thus indirectly complement the religious endeavor.**

Science, for its part, contributes in another way. Although its causal models often reinforce a linear chain of before-and-after, its discoveries can also destabilize the solidity of the ordinary picture. Physics reveals matter to be energy, particles to be probabilities, time itself to be relative. Cosmology reveals an expanding universe without fixed boundaries.

Neuroscience uncovers how our sense of self is constructed by complex networks, not housed in a singular seat. These insights, while often absorbed into the same causal worldview, also carry the potential to dissolve rigid settings and open imagination to wider horizons.

Recognize how both science and religion become problematic only when they are absolutized, when their insights harden into dogmas that reinstall outside-standers. A God enthroned outside creation or a Big Bang posited as a first cause both preserve the same split: a source over there, a self over here. Yet when their insights are held more fluidly, each can function as a counterbalance to the narrowing tendencies of ordinary life. Religions remind us to question the self's centrality. Science reminds us to question the world's solidity. Together, they can help relax the presuppositions that bind both. When taken as complementary rather than antagonistic, they point toward an integrated vision in which ethical decentering and empirical wonder converge.

> **Although contemplation of the discoveries of the physical sciences from a conventional religious vantage point—and in support of conventional religious perspectives—may seem illicit to many scientists, these 'religious' and 'secular' enterprises need not be seen as irreconcilable. Both can be accommodated under the larger, unifying perspectives of the Great Space orientation.**

In fact, the modern notion that science and religion must exist in "separate magisteria," never touching, may itself be an artifact of the narrowed stance.[32] From the vantage of Great Space, both are human strategies for relating to what feels ultimate. Both can inspire humility, awe, and service.

Both can guide us toward seeing through the self-world duality, if we let them. History gives us glimpses of this complementarity. Think of Albert Einstein, who spoke of a "cosmic religious feeling" that infused his scientific work, or Carl Sagan, whose wonder at the universe carried the cadence of a secular liturgy.[33] Both resisted dogma while affirming reverence. They exemplify a mode of inquiry where science and religion are not adversaries but partners in awe.

We might call this stance a kind of "sacred realism." It does not require belief in a supernatural outside-stander, nor does it reduce reality to mechanical causality. Instead, it affirms that openness itself, the vast and mysterious immediacy in which appearances unfold, is worthy of reverence. Science can illuminate aspects of that openness; religion can orient our lives toward it. Neither is complete, but together they hint at a vision larger than either alone. When we allow science and religion to play this complementary role, they cease to be authorities standing above us. They become participants in the same field we inhabit. Their insights are no longer verdicts handed down from on high, but gestures that help us soften our stance and open to what is already nearest.

When religious ethics and scientific inquiry are held lightly, they stop standing above us and join the work at hand. Each becomes a way of undoing the stance that keeps "here" small: ethics loosening the grasping of the self, inquiry loosening the solidity of the world. What they disclose is not a distant source but the nearness we kept dimming: natural morality, a ground that is no ground, openness already sustaining every appearance.

Seen from this angle, "here" is no longer a perch to defend but an opening to be felt. As doing relaxes and the present is no longer a prize to grasp, immediacy stops being scarce. The bystander's platform gives way to a wider participation, and the ordinary room of experience begins to breathe without obstructions or blockages.

The delicate question, "How does this loosening deepen without reinstalling the one who tries to make it happen?" is the threshold of Chapter Thirteen. We now take up the paradox of letting go, why effort quietly rebuilds the doer, how relief differs from transformation, and how release ripens when the meditator steps out of the way.

CHAPTER THIRTEEN

The Paradox of Letting Go

We might be tempted to equate relief with transformation, to sleep better, to have a little less tension, to make the room look brighter. A weekend retreat may calm the nervous system; a new practice could steady attention; the mind might spin a little less. These are genuinely positive. Yet if we look closely, we can feel how easily such benefits plateau. The relief doesn't quite translate into a totally different way of being. Why is this so? Because partial glimpses alleviate symptoms while leaving the stance that generates them largely intact.

Consider how many entry-points are framed: set an intention, observe the breath, notice thoughts, let them pass. None of this is wrong. Yet the tacit architecture remains undisturbed: a centered self stands 'here', monitoring "experience" over 'there'; time unrolls as a sequence the self must keep pace with; the world is still taken as an accomplished fact, independent and already arranged. Yes, the self is more calm but still the bystander, still the manager. Yes, the world is softer yet still "out there," moving through its familiar grooves. We have changed the lighting, not the room.

This is why partial glimpses can feel oddly unstable. Moments of spaciousness arise, then conflict with the old presuppositions: I am the one doing this; the world remains a fixed stage; now is the point I must occupy with discipline. The new glimpse collides with the old ground. That collision is experienced as tension: sometimes as anxiety, sometimes as a sense that we're "almost there" but never quite arriving. The old stance does not know where to file what the glimpse reveals.

Modern mindfulness often sits precisely here. A good mindfulness program reduces stress, improves emotional regulation, refines attention. But when the deeper presuppositions are left unquestioned—self as basic, world as fixed, time as a grid—practice can become an elegant way of maintaining the very stance we hoped to outgrow.[34] We become more skillful bystanders. We perfect our capacity to witness passing phenomena while the architecture of "witness over here, world over there" solidifies. The calm that results is useful, even kind, but not yet liberation.

Something similar happens with spiritual asceticism or moral self-improvement. Renouncing possessions may free us from grasping things, service may free us from seeking status, devotion may free us from fixating on outcomes—all beautiful, necessary moves. Yet, if the presupposition that *I* am the agent of sanctification, *the doer,* is left intact, the renunciant can end up with a subtler project: *I will perfect my letting go*. A holier version of the same stance continues to manage experience, now with sacralized metrics of progress (how many prostrations did I do today?).

Partial glimpses also create a familiar rhythm: expansion, recoil, reorganization. We glimpse a wider horizon; the self reflexively reasserts its place; the system reorganizes around the old coordinates. The expansion is then remembered as "an experience I had," filed on the timeline as a peak that came and went.[35] This chronology is telling. It shows that time is still functioning as a causal nexus—past gain, present loss, future hope—rather than disclosing itself as the ground in which appearance and disappearance are already intimate. When the glimpse becomes an event the self has experienced, the stance has quietly reinstalled itself as archivist and judge.

Another cost to partial glimpses is their unwitting boost to an achievement arc. If a glimpse is treated as a prize, we seek the next one. If calm is treated as the measure, we suppress whatever disturbs it. The result is spiritualized avoidance: staying "present" becomes a way to keep experience within tolerable bounds. The horizon narrows to what the bystander can regulate. Anything that hints at vastness is either domesticated or excluded.

None of this means we should abandon the practices that bring relief, clarity, or kindness. We must recognize their limits when they are carried out from the very stance that contracts reality in the first place. The real question is not whether a method 'works' or how 'efficacious' it is, but what it quietly presupposes. Does it take the self as basic and turn the world into its object? Does it install the present as a point to be grasped? Does it frame change as a project the doer performs on experience? If so, the method may soothe even as it subtly rigidifies the focal setting.

> **As long as we continue to cling to an independent 'self' and subject pole, the observed contrast between mind and thought is perpetuated. The resulting pattern is marked by frustration, because the 'mind' is then an inhibiting factor on our sensitivity to the available fulfillment of Great Space . . . we maintain or even tighten its narrow, restrictive focus.**

What would mark a complete unveiling? Not more intensity, not rapture on demand, not an unbroken stream of pristine attention. A complete opening begins when the *presuppositions* that generate the focal setting are overturned altogether. The self's primacy is decentered, the world's independence is relativized, and the present's fixity is destabilized. Subject, object, and moment cease to function as absolutes and begin to reveal themselves as relational aspects of a single display. The terrain of experience is not arranged around the bystander; it is not presented to an observer; it does not arrive on a linear conveyor belt of moments. Everything is *given together.* In this given togetherness, the calm we once pursued becomes less fragile because it is no longer an achievement. The clarity we admired becomes less precious because it is no longer held by a holder. Even disturbance changes its meaning: what we called distraction is simply another modulation of the same continuum, not a threat to an island of presence. The system does not need the bystander to regulate it, because the very need for a regulator is recognized as part of the veil that has grown transparent.

Practically, this shift is subtle. It is less like acquiring a new power and more like releasing an assignment. The job description that once ran in the background—*be the one who manages reality from here, in time*—is laid down. Attention can still focus, compassion can still move into action, ethical codes can still guide. But they are no longer executed from a perch outside the flow. They operate as expressions within a spacious ground that does not require a center to authorize them. This is the watershed between partial glimpses and fuller openings. Partial openings are valuable and should be honored; they are often the doorway. But if we consecrate the doorway as the destination, the mansion remains unexplored. The invitation now is to step through, not by intensifying effort or perfecting technique, but by relaxing the insistence that *I* must be the one who steps. Which brings us to the next turn: if effort re-installs the enclosure, how does the path proceed without the doer reinstalling itself? How do we relax the outputs, the very feel of self, world, and present, without smuggling them back in as the means of relaxation?

> **By challenging and opening up the output of the setting, working with one aspect or another of this output, we can begin to change the focal setting itself. Strictly speaking, the output is a unitary thing, like a complex image seen through a lens or peep-hole. Everything constituting a particular situation—the output—is 'given together', although usually we only see selected details.**

RELAXING OUTPUTS WITHOUT REINSTALLATION

If partial glimpses leave us circling the same ground, the question sharpens: how do we open without reinstalling the very outputs we are trying to dissolve? How do we soften the self, the world, and the present moment without smuggling them back in as the terms of the practice? Here we encounter the paradox of letting go. For as long as we believe that we, the doer, the bystander, must accomplish the undoing, the undoing remains another act of doing. We unbind with one hand while tightening with the other. The very effort to dismantle the outputs confirms their solidity: *I* am the one unbinding; *the experienced world* is the thing to be undone; *this present* is the moment *I* must be in.

The trap is familiar in everyday life: try to fall asleep, the harder you try, the more alert you become. Try to stop worrying, and worry about your inability to stop takes over. Try to relax, and your eye muscles tighten with the effort of performing relaxation. The intention may be sincere, but the stance silently undermines it. The more we push, the more we prove to ourselves that pushing is required.

The same holds true on subtler levels of practice. When we decide to "let go of the self," the decision itself affirms a self who is in charge of letting go. When we try to dissolve the solidity of the world, the attempt affirms the world as a solid thing that needs dissolving. When we insist on being present, the insistence affirms the present as a discrete object that can be captured. Each maneuver reifies what it seeks to relax.

> **Inasmuch as everything that constitutes our realm and existence is alike in being a function of a focal setting, everything is inseparably related—'given together'. A tempting, but misleading, inference is that this interdependence gives special prominence to the self or mind, that the self has adopted a viewpoint or focal setting but can also change it. Yet, as we have seen, the 'self is only a part of what we are calling the 'output' of the focal setting. It has no special status.**

From the perspective of Great Space, letting go is not something we accomplish, not another product added to the stream of experience, but a shift in how we see: the dawning recognition that self, world, and time never carried the burden we gave them. What feels like a release is less an event than a revelation, an opening in which the supposed absolutes lose their hold.

A useful analogy is waking from a dream. Within the dream, we may struggle to solve problems, escape dangers, or even become lucid enough to direct the story. But awakening does not come from succeeding inside the dream. It comes from seeing that the dream was never the solid reality we believed it to be. The walls that felt immovable, the characters that seemed autonomous, the self that felt imperiled—all of them dissolve the moment their true nature is recognized. So it is with the outputs of the focal setting. Self, world, and reality-as-presented arrive with such conviction that we organize our whole lives around defending or perfecting them.

Yet their apparent solidity comes from the focal setting itself, not from anything that requires fixing. To "let go" in the usual sense only reinforces the claim of reality before withdrawing it. But when the grip of the setting loosens, they show themselves as appearances within openness: never needing to be proved, never needing to be erased.

> **When we can relate to the output as unitary, with all its elements as 'given together', then the perpetuation of an arbitrary setting, due to a fixation or an emphasis on selected details of the output, can be deactivated.**

This is why the paradox can sound almost nonsensical: we must let go without establishing that there was ever anything to let go of. But notice how this already happens in small ways. A child is frightened of shadows on the wall until she sees they are cast by her own hand. The fear evaporates, not because she fought the shadows, but because she realized there was never a monster to fight. The anxiety was real; the premise was not.

The same dynamic applies here. As long as we assume solidity, then try to unfreeze it, we are fighting shadows. True letting go is not a battle but a transformed seeing: recognizing that solidity itself is only a projection of the stance. When this realization dawns, the outputs lose their power, not because we forced them aside, but because their supposed foundation never existed.

The invitation, then, is not to strain for breakthrough, but to notice where effort arises and allow it too to dissolve. Every time the doer insists "I must achieve openness," we can gently acknowledge the stance and let it rest. This resting is not a dismissal, but a clear seeing that the stance itself is unnecessary. In that clarity, the fuel of clinging is extinguished on its own.

This kind of letting go does not leave us blank or inert. On the contrary, it frees energy that was bound in maintaining the mechanism. What emerges is not passivity but a lighter, more fluid participation in experience. Life continues—bodies act, words are spoken, responsibilities are met—but without the heavy overlay of a bystander trying to manage the whole. The world need not be propped up, the self need not be performed, time need not be conquered. They appear, but they no longer dictate.

Self, world, and reality appear with such force that we spend our lives defending and refining them. But this solidity is not inherent; it arises from the way attention is framed. To try to let go of these appearances as if they were real objects only deepens the illusion that they exist in that way. When attention relaxes, however, it becomes clear that they are simply appearances within awareness, requiring no defense and leaving nothing to release.

Here, then, is the quiet but radical truth: letting go is not something we perform, but something we stop insisting must be performed. The outputs never needed to be dissolved; they only needed to be seen through. In that seeing, they are recognized as appearances within openness, not barriers to it.[36] This paradox ushers us to the threshold of a new orientation, one where openness is not an achievement but the ground of all appearances, and where the self's role as conductor can finally be retired.

THE SPIRITUAL DOUBLE-BIND

The difficulty of letting go is not just that we cling too tightly, but that the very stance from which we try to let go is itself the bind. This is the spiritual double-bind: every attempt at release quietly tightens the knot.

Our culture has trained us to approach everything as a project: define the problem, apply a method, track results. Even in spiritual practice, this same logic takes over. We imagine we must "practice letting go" as if unbinding were one more skill to master. But the moment we treat it this way, we reinstall the very structures we are trying to escape: the self as agent, the world as obstacle, the present as stage for success or failure. That is why practice so easily slides into the rhythm of progress and setback. A glimpse of openness is chalked up as achievement; a lapse becomes evidence of failure. Calm and clarity are logged as proof that "I" am advancing. The framework of gain and loss remains intact, while the outputs—self, world, time—go unquestioned.

Seen from the perspective of Great Space, this effort is revealed as unnecessary. Letting go is not about loosening a rope—it is about realizing the rope was smoke all along. The error was never in failing to untie it, but in mistaking it for something solid. The self we strive to perfect, the world we try to master, the time we try to capture—these are not foundations but appearances. Once this is seen, there is nothing left to grasp or release. The project dissolves because its premise was never real.

This is the paradox: letting go is impossible if we think the self is the one who must do it, but inevitable once we see that the self's claim to be the unbinder is only an appearance. In that collapse, openness reveals itself as already present.

Letting go, then, is not something we perform but something we stop insisting must be done. It is not a technique, but a recognition that self, world, and time have never stood apart from immediacy. The paradox does not block the path; it clears it. What remains is not a method to master, but a new vantage: to shift attention from what binds to the openness that has always been here.

That is the invitation of the next exercise: a new focus on space.

Exercise 14: A New Focus on Space

We've reached a threshold. The paradox of letting go cannot be resolved by thought or effort; it can only be felt through another way of inhabiting experience. That is why, at this point, it is helpful to return to the body—not as a possession of the self, but as a living doorway into openness.

Settle into a comfortable posture. Let the body rest as though supported by something vast and unseen, as if space itself were holding you up. There is no need to control the breath or manufacture calm. Let everything be as it is, but notice the quieting that comes when you no longer insist on managing.

Now, bring to mind the sense of "having a body." Feel the weight of it, the way it sits here. Usually we take this as proof of our location: *I am here, inside this body, looking out.* For a moment, let that assumption soften. Instead, imagine the body as translucent, its outlines less rigid, as though every cell were open to space. Organs, bones, tissues, all being gently porous, pervaded by a vitality that belongs not to you but to the openness in which the body appears.

See if you can sense this "giant body," not limited by skin or contained by posture, but expanding beyond your frame. Arms and legs dissolve into the room; the room itself dissolves into a wider atmosphere. It is not that your body extends outward like a balloon, but that boundaries no longer define what is inside and what is outside. The body is appearing within space, and space is alive within the body.

Notice also the observer: that subtle sense of a "someone" registering what is happening. Instead of treating it as the owner of the experience, let it be part of the same field, another shimmering appearance within openness. The watcher is not behind the eyes, directing attention. It too is floating in the vastness, a momentary flicker in the same space that allows breath and sound and sensation.

Allow this recognition to deepen: the mind, like the body, is not a fixed and continuous thing. Thoughts rise and dissolve like currents in water. The "I" that claims them appears and disappears just as fluidly. None of it needs to be held together. Space supports everything without requiring a center.

In this openness, savor the freedom from narrow preconceptions. There is no need to manage what arises, no need to measure success. Even the thought *am I doing this right?* can be welcomed as another ripple in space. The point is not to suppress or transcend, but to notice that everything—body, mind, observer, question—is already appearing within a vastness that is inexhaustible.

Let yourself rest here. Not as someone resting in space, but as the resting that space itself makes possible. This is a new focus, not on the body or the mind, but on the openness that allows them both to appear. The more you taste it, the more you see: space is not a backdrop, not an emptiness, but a living capacity that can host infinitely many perspectives without ever being diminished.

When you are ready, open your eyes. Let the world appear, not as something outside you, not as something to manage or hold, but as part of the same openness in which you too are shimmering. Space supports it all, effortlessly. There is no cave, no barrier, nothing standing apart. Only the play of appearances within an openness that was here all along.

Reflection

This exercise points to a simple but radical shift. Letting go is not a task to perform. It happens when we notice that body, mind, and even the watcher of experience are already appearing within space. Nothing needs to be managed or held together. Seen this way, self and world are no longer fixed poles staring at each other across a divide. They are expressions in the same field, given together. Space is not a backdrop or container but the openness that makes every appearance possible.

The value of this recognition shows up in ordinary life. A conversation, a walk down the street, even the moment before sending an email—each unfolds within the same accommodating space. The sense that "I" must secure, control, or validate the moment begins to ease. Sometimes this feels liberating, sometimes it feels disorienting. Both are signs that the old stance is loosening. What once seemed like a solid foundation is revealed as a projection, unnecessary to carry. Space does the work for us, it always has. The lesson is straightforward: to live as though openness were already the ground of our being, because it is. Having tasted immediacy, notice the old habit that returns almost automatically: the sense that what matters lies behind us or ahead of us on a path.

THE TRAP OF THE PATH

After a taste of immediacy, an old habit reappears: we relocate meaning on a timeline. We picture reality as a line of before and after and then try to place the infinite on that line, either "back there" at an origin or "up ahead" as a goal. Once we do, the present becomes a staging area, never quite it.

This is the quiet logic beneath much spiritual and secular thinking alike. Religious narratives can set perfection in a beginning (creation, fall, lost purity) or an end (salvation, awakening after long discipline). Secular life mirrors this with its ladders of development and achievement. Different stories, same frame: time as a grid; the self as traveler; fulfillment elsewhere.

Seen from Great Space, the gap we're trying to cross is manufactured by that frame. Treat infinity as a point on a line and it will always recede. Intensify effort and you only confirm the premise that completion is not now. (This is the same gain-and-loss rhythm we cautioned against in The Limits of Meditation in Chapter 10)

The alternative is not to abandon practice but to relax the frame that makes practice a commute. Beginnings and endings still appear, but as *appearances within openness*, not containers of it. What some traditions call "primordial purity" or "final liberation" need not be placed behind or ahead; they describe facets of what can be recognized here.

Practically, this changes the meaning of discipline. Renunciation, meditation, and ethical care need not be rungs on a ladder. They can be *expressions* of a fullness *already present*. A kind act is not a down payment on future grace; it is grace showing up as care. A quiet mind is not a trophy; it is the absence of a manager keeping score. When the path is engaged in this way, the pressure to measure progress eases. The self no longer has to be the project manager of reality; time no longer has to serve as a moving walkway toward adequacy. Openings don't need protection or repetition; they are not events to archive but reminders that nothing essential is missing.

The trap of the path, then, is simple: put the infinite on a line and you will never arrive. Step out of the line's logic and the distance collapses. Practice continues, not as a march toward elsewhere, but as life moving freely within openness.

EXERCISES AS DISCLOSURES

If practice is no longer a down payment on a distant goal, what becomes of the exercises we've done? They don't lose value; they shift in meaning. Each exercise can be taken as a disclosure, a way of letting something hidden come into view.

If we treat an exercise as a rung on a ladder, it becomes a means to an end: judged by whether it gets us "higher." In that frame, success is measured by progress, and failure by stagnation. The exercises become installments on a promissory note, payments on a future redemption that never quite arrives.

But viewed from the openness of Great Space, the same exercises are not rungs but windows. Each opens onto what is already present, though previously obscured. Their worth lies not in accumulation but in illumination.

Think of the body practices we began with: the giant body, the translucent body, the body permeated by space. At first they may have seemed like techniques of expansion, attempts to reach beyond ordinary limits. But in hindsight, they revealed something more direct: the body has never been sealed inside "my" skin or "my" space. It has always been appearing in openness. The exercise didn't create that openness, it let us feel it.

The same holds for the mind practices. Rendering the object pole translucent, dissolving the observer, noticing thoughts as space were not rehearsals for some eventual awakening. They enacted what is already the case: the observer is itself an appearance, and "mind" is not a thing but a temporary framing.

Seen this way, repetition takes on a new meaning. Returning to an exercise is not climbing further toward a finish line; it is letting the familiar grow transparent again. Each return discloses the same truth, not because it was absent before but because our stance kept it hidden. This reframing relieves the anxiety of "getting somewhere." The exercises are not milestones to accumulate; they are gestures to inhabit. Each act of loosening, each glimpse of clarity, is not a promissory note toward distant liberation but a disclosure of what has always been here.

The paradox of letting go follows naturally: we discover that nothing essential ever needed to be grasped or released. What felt indispensable—the self, the world, even the ground underfoot—was never ours to hold. The journey resolves not in emptiness but in immediacy: the recognition that space itself is the ground of being.

And yet, much of our ordinary vision is still tethered to default assumptions: that the world is "all in the mind," or wholly "out there"; that perception delivers raw data which we assemble; that the "here" we occupy is the measure of truth. These convictions quietly reinstall the watcher and the watched.

Chapter Fourteen takes this shift further. It asks us to examine these explanations—idealism, objectivism, sense-data stories, the primacy of "here"—and see how each smuggles in bystanders and outside-standers. When these props fall away, life shows itself in a new coherence: no longer split between observer and observed, but shining as a nondual whole.

CHAPTER FOURTEEN

Sky Deep

We have arrived at a natural pause in our journey. The exercises and inquiries of the previous chapters have revealed again and again that what we take to be "fundamental," self, world, time, and body, are in fact outputs of a stance, a focal setting that quietly stages what we take as real. We have already begun loosening these fixtures, glimpsing that they are not unshakable bedrock realities but provisional positions. Yet, even as we open to a wider vision, subtle assumptions continue to reassert themselves. They are like background software running silently in the operating system of the mind: unnoticed but shaping everything we do.

This chapter asks us to bring those hidden assumptions into view and to test their hold on us. The challenge is not abstract philosophy for its own sake. These assumptions matter because they smuggle in dualisms: an observer set apart from the observed, a knower gazing at a known. Unless we see how deeply these habits run, our freedom will always feel conditional, our glimpses of openness, partial.

What follows is an inventory of six familiar outlooks. Each one seems reasonable, even obvious, but each contains a hidden architecture that reinstates the very divisions we are working to challenge and dismantle. By walking through them, we can begin to feel where our vision still narrows and how it might open further.

1. THE WORLD IS ALL IN THE MIND

One response to the mystery of appearance is to say, "Very well, the world must simply be mental. What I see is a construction of my mind." On the surface, this seems aligned with what we have discovered: appearances are not solid, they depend on perspective. But this view quietly reintroduces a hidden anchor: a self with a mind that makes the world. It grants primacy to the observer as ultimate manufacturer, simply replacing "matter" with "mind" as the substance of reality.

But the world is not "in here" any more than it is "out there." Mind is not a cosmic container or artist in which reality is fabricated. To imagine it so is to cling to yet another hidden background, "mind" as an ultimate source, and another hidden agent, the self as possessor of that mind.

2. RELATIVITY AS "HOW THINGS LOOK"

A more modern version says, "The world is just how things appear to a certain kind of observer, from a certain vantage point." This acknowledges that outlook is shaped by where we stand. Yet, if pressed, it still assumes that there is a real, solid "here" from which the observer observes. It turns the bystander into an unquestioned point of reference, as if we can always count on having at least one fixed seat in the theater.

What if there is no unquestionable "here"? What if even the vantage point itself is an appearance, inseparable from what it purports to observe? In that case, we are not spectators peering out from a reliable perch. The perch itself is part of the show.

3. COGNITION AND PERCEPTION "MAKE THE WORLD"

Another popular view insists that our faculties of cognition and perception construct reality. Neuroscience often describes perception as a kind of "controlled hallucination," our brains stitching together signals into a coherent picture. We noted this earlier when critiquing naïve realism. A further refinement emphasizes that perception is not simply invention but an ongoing process of prediction and inference.[37] The brain is constantly making best guesses about what is most likely to be present, testing those guesses against incoming signals, and updating them when they fall short.

There is truth here: our perceptions do filter, shape, and sometimes distort. We do not encounter raw reality; we meet it through layers of anticipation and correction. Yet to say cognition "makes the world" still goes too far. This stance preserves the figure of a sovereign observer, an inner agent manufacturing appearances. In a wider view, perception and thought are not ultimate generators. They, too, are appearances arising inseparably with the world, best guesses that participate in the unfolding but are not its hidden source.

4. THE PRIMACY OF THE "HERE"

We are accustomed to granting special status to "here." This is where I stand, the anchor point from which all else is oriented. From here I reach out toward there, from here I look at what is beyond. But if we grant primacy to "here," we smuggle in the very dualism we have been loosening. "Here" gains its meaning only by contrast to "there." It depends on the structure of inside and outside, observer and observed.

In a more open perspective, "here" is not a privileged position but one expression among many of the unfolding of appearance. It is not a vantage point standing apart but already woven into the whole.

5. ORIGINS AND FIRST CAUSES

Another deep assumption, (explored in Chapter Eleven) is that the world must have an origin. Science points to the Big Bang; religions point to a Creator or a primordial perfection. Both are attempts to explain appearance by positing a starting point. But in doing so, they cast the world order as a finished fact, established once and for all.

From a wider view, this looks like a category mistake. The familiar "once upon a time" stories of cosmic beginnings, whether scientific or religious, rest on shaky ground. If time itself did not yet exist before the Big Bang, how can we speak of a "before" or an "event" that set everything into motion? To say matter suddenly appeared out of nowhere raises the same puzzle: what could "nowhere" mean if space had not yet arisen? Terms like "exist," "before," "from," and "to" make sense only within the framework of space and time. Outside that frame, they collapse.

This suggests that the world order is not an accomplished fact standing apart from openness. It is an output of a focal setting, a way of seeing that stages reality in a certain configuration. Other perspectives are not just possible but actual. They coexist without crowding one another out, because each is a facet of the same openness. The search for a single origin, then, is less a necessity of life than the bystander's demand for ground.

6. SENSE DATA AS THE FOUNDATION OF REALITY

Finally, many theories assume that at rock bottom sit raw sense data from which all else is constructed. Light strikes the eyes, vibrations strike the ears, signals pass along nerves, and voilà, a world appears. This picture reassures us that experience has a solid base. But notice how it quietly preserves the two-term split: a world "out there" emitting stimuli and a perceiver "in here" receiving them.

But even these supposed "raw data" are not unquestionable givens. They too belong to the structuring of a particular stance. They appear only within the frame of a focal setting not as absolute foundations.

> **The capacity of Great Space is never exhausted or compromised by a commitment to one particular trend or world order. Great Space can let anything appear. There is no level or criterion on or by which the various presentations can be compared and judged to be incompatible or inconsistent. Great Space supports infinitely many choices of perspective.**

BEYOND THE OBSERVER AND THE OBSERVED

Each of the frameworks we inherit—idealist, empiricist, constructivist, relativist—tries to explain experience. But in doing so, each smuggles in the same structure: an observer facing a world observed. They differ in content but not in form, and in repeating this form they perpetuate the stance that conceals openness.

To see through these assumptions is not to abandon science, philosophy, or religion. It is to recognize their limits: each is a provisional lens, coherent within its scope but not ultimate. Once acknowledged as outputs, they can be opened; when they open, a wider vision emerges. Observer and observed no longer stand apart as poles; they appear together as facets of one display.

Ordinarily, we don't experience it this way. We divide inner from outer, perceiver from perceived, as if separated by solid walls. But these divisions are more like frosted glass: they blur, yet they do not fully divide. With the right kind of looking, transparency shows through. You can sense this in ordinary moments. Evening cool settles, the air brushes your skin, a bird calls, jasmine drifts on the breeze. Where do you end and the world begin? Is the coolness outside or already in your body? Is the birdcall "out there" or inseparable from hearing? In truth, walker, walking, and world are given together.

> **After we learn to penetrate the partitions of these aspects of the output, we can learn to implement the 'transparentizing' by letting the partitions be as not incompatible with Great Space's openness. 'Letting things be' requires a total and balanced embrace.**

Practice helps us see this. At first, it feels like breaking out of a cave, as though walls have fallen away. But deeper clarity comes when we realize there was no cave.[38] The walls themselves were only projections of stance. To recognize this is not to deny appearances but to see that they were never confining: they are already inseparable from openness. We can let them appear, knowing them to be translucent.

> **Against the claustrophobic view of the feeling of being tied down, blocked off, or backed into a corner or cave by complex layers and levels of strata composed of 'outside-standers' and 'by-standers', even the message "There is no cave!" can have a tremendously liberating force.**

Exercises, then, are not rungs on a ladder but doorways. Each thins the seeming walls, letting openness shine through again. Repetition is not progress but rediscovery: the same truth radiating more freely each time it is seen.

This is what it means to live in a "total and balanced embrace": nothing excluded, not even the structures that once seemed to bind us. Self and world, watcher and watched, thought and perception all appear as facets of a unity, given together. To inhabit this vision is to move beyond the bystander's posture, into a coherence where nothing stands apart.

Contemplative Reflection
Sensing the Field of Togetherness

Settle for a moment, allowing whatever is happening now to come into view. Let the sounds around you, the play of light, the feel of your body, and even the drift of thoughts be included in the same scene. Rather than dividing them into "inside" and "outside," notice how they are already part of one unfolding. The birds chirping outside, the faint movement of air, the pulse in your chest: are these truly separate from you, or are they all expressions of the same continuous presence?

Relax the stance of being a watcher. Instead of holding yourself apart as "the one who experiences," let the moment breathe as a single fabric of immediacy. Breathing, sensing, thinking, and hearing all arrive together, inseparable from the openness that allows them.

Rest here without needing to push anything away or draw anything closer. Nothing stands apart. Self and world arise in the same gesture, given together, allowed by the same space.

SPRING-CLEANING THE PARTITIONS

Once the intimacy of "given together" begins to register, another task becomes urgent: to challenge the hidden scaffolding that still props up our sense of reality. The self and the world may no longer appear as strangers across a divide, yet habits of division remain, partitions so ingrained we mistake them for reality itself.

> **Even 'experience', however, is tied up with presuppositions that are inapplicable to this vision. So a great deal of challenging, in regard to every feature of our existence, must be undertaken as a kind of spring-cleaning. We need to make way for something truly fresh.**

This spring-cleaning does not adopt a new doctrine or cling to mindfulness as a technique. It exercises our full intelligence, arousing the mind without giving it a perch. Each partition we take for granted, "inner versus outer," "self versus world," "here versus there," must be called into question, not once, but repeatedly, in every corner of experience.

To challenge is not to destroy, but to open the opaque windows of perception so that light can move freely again. Each assumption we treat as absolute: "this body is mine," "these thoughts belong to me," "that world is independent out there," can be turned translucent using the clear solvent of inquiry.

> **Challenging is not, in this case, merely a preliminary for more lively explorations. Rather, it can itself be the path to Great Space. Rigid and opaque partitions define, phenomenologically, all the things and orientations of our realm. These same partitions also constitute the doorways to higher spaces.**

The point is not to reach a doctrine of non-duality, but to live questioning itself as a path. Every feature of ordinary life can serve: a conversation, the edge of grief, the pull of desire, the reflex of naming. Each is an invitation to ask: What makes this appear divided? What is insisting that experience be polarized into subject and object? What holds this boundary in place? What if the division is only a habitual stance, not a necessity? Be surprised that these very partitions, once challenged, reveal themselves as thresholds. What looked like walls turn out to be doorways. The solidity of "self" and "world," far from obstacles, become points of access to the openness always shimmering through them.

Challenging, then, is not a preliminary step. It is the path itself. It means treating every appearance—body, thought, sensation, world—as an occasion to question what we assume. Not settling into comfort, not polishing our witness, but rousing intelligence to meet each moment freshly. In this way, the so-called ordinary becomes the very ground of transformation.

DIVING DEEPER INTO THE DEPTH DIMENSION

Thinning partitions, the loosening of inner and outer, self and world, already shifts how reality feels. Yet something still seems to underwrite the whole scene: a tacit ground that assures us there must be a base. We call it "the world," or "my mind," or some primal source. However we phrase it, the effect is the same: stability appears to rest on a floor we assume to be real.

Diving deep into the depth dimension means challenging even this hidden base. At first, it can feel like the last refuge is being stripped away. Yet the discovery is paradoxical: when the supposed ground gives way, there is no collapse into nothingness. What opens is a more reliable support: spaciousness itself, sustaining without needing to be posited.

> **Precisely because Great Space is related to *interaction*, 'width' and 'depth' at a certain point amount to the same thing. At that point it is appropriate to speak of a truly significant change in 'focal setting', a change which penetrates to Great Space by *accommodating* the situation itself, as it is, as Great Space.**

Imagine standing near the edge of a cliff. The body recoils, afraid of the drop. Yet if the cliff itself were to dissolve, not into a void, but into openness, you would not fall. You would find yourself buoyed in a vast medium, weightless in every direction. The terror came not from falling, but from clinging to the ledge. When the ledge is seen as part of the same expanse, the fear of losing ground gives way to a deeper trust. This is the hidden wisdom of insecurity: real support comes not from what lies beneath us, but from the spaciousness that permeates all appearances. Width and depth converge here: reality is not upheld by an origin or destination, a "here" or "there." It abides as openness itself.

TURNING TOWARD THE OPEN SKY

Having tasted the dimension of depth, the inquiry naturally shifts in tone. Words can point and images can hint, but a time comes when description must yield to direct encounter. If the depth is not another stratum beneath appearances but the very openness that sustains them, how do we learn to dwell there? How does that depth surface as awareness?

The answer cannot be found in more explanation. It calls for a different mode of engagement, one in which the body, the senses, and the breath participate fully. Just as earlier exercises invited us to sense our body as porous, translucent, or unbounded, so now we are asked to bring the whole of our being into relation with a more expansive horizon. What horizon could be more fitting than the sky itself?

The open sky has always stirred something in us. Children lying in the grass feel it as infinite play. Travelers look up and sense both their smallness and their belonging. Pilgrims climb mountains to be closer to it, as if altitude thinned not just the air but also the veils that confine perception. The sky is never far, yet rarely truly met. We look at it as a backdrop, weather, light, horizon, but seldom as presence.

The next exercise asks us to do precisely that: to meet the sky not as scenery but as a partner in practice, a retreat, not in the sense of escaping the world, but of entering more deeply into its openness. The exercise is simple, but setting crucial. To taste its depth, one must seek out a place where the sky dominates the field of vision: on the crest of a hill, the slope of a mountain, or any expanse where blue spaciousness surrounds and steadies attention.

This exercise is unlike the others in one respect: it asks for time. A few minutes here and there will not do. It invites immersion, a sustained dwelling in which the body, the breath, and the sky commingle until the sense of separation softens. What results is not an extraordinary vision or peak experience but a recognition: the very space in which the sky shines is the same space that breathes through us, holds us, and sustains all that appears.

Exercise 15: A Mountain Retreat

Find a place high above the world: on a mountain or hill where the sky stretches wide and unobstructed. Let yourself settle there, upright but at ease, eyes open and relaxed, the breath moving smoothly as if it belonged more to the air than to you. At first, you may recall the body explorations from earlier exercises, sensing yourself as immense, even giant, positioned within the sky itself. But soon the giant gives way to a simple openness: your gaze softens, your body quiets, and the great bowl of blue becomes your horizon.

As you breathe, let the sky draw in with each inhalation, as though its clarity and brightness were pouring directly into you. Feel it pervade not just the lungs but the skin, the bones, the subtle layers of thought and memory. With each exhalation, imagine your breath mingling back into the air, until the boundary between "inside" and "outside" begins to blur. The body does not merely inhale space; it breathes space.

Allow this exchange to deepen. Inhaling, the vastness enters you from every side: above, behind, around. Exhaling, the space flows back through every pore, as if body and sky were engaged in a single rhythm, a single commingling. Nothing is withheld, everything participates.

In time, the sense of being a located self, seated here, gazing out there, begins to soften, fade, and dissolve. The position you once called "here" dissolves into the same openness that surrounds it. Even the subtle posture of "I am the one doing this exercise" can be surrendered, as space itself gently touches and transforms those structuring habits. You do not need to hold on to any vantage point. Space is enough.

Even so, radiant moments may arise: a sudden feeling of satiety, as though you had been fed on light; a quiet ecstasy, as if the sky itself had become your bloodstream. Welcome them, but do not cling. These too are currents in the wider expanse, appearances that arise and dissolve within the immeasurable. Eventually, even the sense of "having an experience" can be released. The very idea of an event occurring, of "something happening to me here and now," grows thin and transparent. What remains is not a void but fullness: life freed from the need to be located, openness that is not an object and not an event.

And then, when the mountain practice has ripened, carry this expanded awareness back down into the density of daily life. Step into a crowded street, a noisy café, a hectic meeting and notice how the same vastness is still present, waiting. The sky is no longer only above you; it permeates voices, footsteps, traffic, and thought. What seemed jagged and confining is revealed as porous, a texture of space itself.

The mountain is not a place apart. It is a portal, reminding you that the spaciousness tasted there is never absent. Once glimpsed, it can be felt in the very heart of ordinary life, not as an escape from it, but as the freedom that makes every moment possible.

Reflection

The mountain retreat is not a fantasy of withdrawal, but a revelation of what has been true all along. By breathing sky into the body and letting the body dissolve into sky, we glimpse a dimension of life that is not bound by place or position. What seemed like "me here" and "world out there" softens into participation in a single field.

The importance of this exercise lies not in the grandeur of mountaintops but in the reorientation it seeds. We discover that spaciousness does not depend on altitude or landscape. It threads through the crowded café, the messy kitchen, the tense meeting. Once the illusion of confinement loosens, the same vastness that opens on the ridge can be sensed in the press of ordinary hours. Such is the real retreat: not a place apart, but a shift of ground. The mountain shows that openness is not elsewhere, waiting to be reached; it is already the medium of every moment. To live with this recognition is to breathe differently, to relate differently, to let life itself feel less like something to manage and more like something that arises freely within the field of openness.

CROSSING THE THRESHOLD

The exercises have carried us to a threshold where body, mind, and world no longer appear as separate compartments but as translucent forms, porous to the vastness in which they appear. The sky itself becomes a teacher, reminding us that openness is not elsewhere, not deferred. It is available in every breath, in every glance that dares to linger without grasping.

What we called "here" was never as small as we thought. The ground we feared would give way beneath us was already buoyed by a greater openness. To live this vision is not to chase an experience but to fully participate in the immediacy of this openness. Fulfillment is no longer postponed to some distant goal. Appearances shine in the simple ease of letting things be, in the discovery that what we took as fixed points, boundaries and limits were only made of light.

Each gesture of attention is not a step toward elsewhere, but a revelation into what is already here. We are invited to walk through the world with the same unbounded clarity as the sky itself: immeasurable, inexhaustible, endlessly accommodating.

This is where our exploration of space has brought us: to the revelation that depth and sky are not two, but one. The further we open, the more we see that the true measure of our lives is the uncharted expanse of Sky Deep. And yet, this is not the end of the journey. To cross this threshold is to step into another register of the vision, one where the openness of space begins to unbind time. What happens when we discover that time, too, is not the relentless stream we imagined, but as radiant as the sky itself?

CHAPTER FIFTEEN

Time Unbound

Beautiful awakenings often arise in deep practice. A sudden stillness, a moment of radiance, even a felt fullness as if the body itself were nourished by space can all shimmer through when the sky has been allowed to enter us. Yet the instruction is clear: do not fixate.

Fixation is subtle. It doesn't only show up as clinging to possessions or identities; it can show up as clinging to the very experiences meant to free us. A glimpse of spacious satiety on the mountaintop can quickly become another treasure to hold, another milestone to guard. The more luminous the experience, the more tempting it is to want to repeat it, own it, or make it the new measure of progress. But this "holding on" is itself a contraction. It is another way of stepping outside the openness, trying to anchor ourselves in a fixed point, another "coming out" of the sky into the narrowed confines of "my experience."

What liberates is not the experience but untying the knot we fasten around it. We discover that what appeared as a special state is actually a glimpse of something more fundamental and profound: a dimension that is *not an experience at all, not something that occurs, not a thing that can be located.* Here we begin to sense what it means to live in the register of non-occurrence: not the absence of life, but the presence of a reality that does not need to be measured in moments or located in positions.

We can open to a dimension which is not a doing, an achieving, an experiencing, an occurring, or even a locatable particular. Location, direction, thing, and experience—all are related on many levels. The world of the present is subject to changes through time, to the directedness of time. Any particular position within this world is also subject to this.

Ordinary consciousness ties us to a spatial-temporal grid. "To exist" is to occupy a place "here," to move toward a "there," to mark ourselves in time in a "now" between a past and a future, as if life can only be validated when pegged to coordinates, where every event has its assigned slot. But the openness of Great Space does not conform to this grid, not being parceled into moments or positions. The deep recognition that comes in mountain practice and beyond reveals that the ground we stand on was never confined to a time slot and never circumscribed by coordinates.

This recognition does not remain on the mountaintop. The final movement of the exercise impels us to descend, to carry this spaciousness back into the buzz of ordinary life. We return to the city, where traffic churns, phones beep, and conversations overlap in crowded rooms. Here the texture of experience is jagged, noisy, relentless. The nervous system itself seems to contract under the strain of so much incoming pressure. And yet—*this too is space.* The same openness that filled the high blue sky is available on the morning commute, at the office desk, in the clutter of the kitchen, even throughout social media. The challenge is sharper here because the cues to contact are stronger. But once the taste of openness has been known, it can surface anywhere.

Freedom, then, is not a vacation from life but a radical change of view within it. The mountain practice reveals the nourishment of space in its pure form: the return to ordinary life shows that this nourishment does not vanish when the environment grows dense. Each honk of a horn, each press of obligation, can be met without recoil, without withdrawal into a defended shell. They too are permeated by space, if allowed to.

In this way, practice matures, no longer depending on seclusion, silence, or purity of setting. Its measure is not how high the mountain is, but how fully the openness of space can be felt in the middle of things. The real test is not whether we can relax into the sky on retreat, but whether we can feel the same sky pulsing through the crowded marketplace. To taste that experience is to begin to live beyond occurrence, beyond the narrow confines of "here" and "now," free in a space that is everywhere and nowhere at once.

GREAT TIME

If space first revealed itself as openness, time now shows itself as vitality. What seemed like a vast stillness is not inert or empty; it is alive, resonant, dynamic. The mountain practice hinted at this. Breathing with the sky, one could sense more than bland calmness: an energy coursing through body and mind, a pulse that feels inexhaustible. That pulse is Great Time.

> **The vitality of Great Time is the direct expression or evidence of the openness of Great Space. Great Time plumbs the depths and breadth of Great Space. Just as ordinary sound needs space in which to occur, and in turn gives evidence of the extent of that space, so**

Great Time resounds in, speaks of, and sounds out the infinity of Great Space.

Ordinary time is quite different. We know it as the clock's tick, the forward march of deadlines, the wearing down of our bodies. Time in this frame is a line: past receding, future approaching, present a vanishing point we never manage to hold. Each event seems to cancel the last, each moment displaces what came before. Life becomes a necklace of beads strung in succession, each fragile and fleeting, where we measure our worth by how many remain before the string breaks.

Great Time does not parcel out reality in this way. It does not cut life into pieces; it sings of the wholeness. Imagine listening to music: each note fades even as it sounds, yet the melody carries, overlaps, reverberates. The fullness is not in any single note but in the resonance and harmonies that join them. No moment excludes another; each belongs to the same orchestrating of time: that is how Great Time discloses itself, not as a sequence of vanishing instants, but as an inexhaustible unfolding where nothing and no moment stands apart.

You can sense a taste of this when watching a fire. Flames lick upward, constantly changing, yet their vitality is not carried along by a before and after. Each flicker is already complete, alive in its immediacy, and yet it also participates in the whole. The flame does not need to grasp at continuity in order to exist; its continuity is the very movement of appearing.

This is why the satiety tasted in the mountain retreat could never be an ordinary "experience." To call it an experience would be to locate it at a point in time, to bind it to a "before" and an "after." Great Time is not something that occurs; it is the aliveness that allows occurrence at all. It is not an event but a vitality, present even when unnoticed, resonating through every breath, every step, every thought.

Ordinary knowing struggles with this alternative way of understanding time. Trained to count, compare and distinguish, it translates vitality into a blur of moments and messages, each pointing elsewhere. We chase meanings down the passages of time, hoping fulfillment lies just ahead. Yet in the chase, we miss the vital, pointless point: that nothing needs to occur for fullness to be present; it already reverberates in the simple fact of being.

Great Time reframes even the chatter of ordinary life. The clatter of dishes in a café, the surge of traffic on a busy street, the overlapping voices of a marketplace: each sound seems separate, competing. Yet heard differently, they reveal a polyphony: not fragments in conflict but facets of one resonance. In Great Time, simultaneity is not a problem to be sorted out but a vitality in which events interpenetrate, each sustaining the others. Even dissonance belongs, deepening the texture of the whole. What we mistook for noise was always song.

To glimpse Great Time is to discover that change itself is not loss, but rhythm. Winter storms and spring blossoms, partings and reunions, grief and joy are all movements in the same inexhaustible vitality. They do not cancel each other but belong to a rhythm where nothing is excluded, just as in Great Space.

> **All appearance is Great Space. . . . although all form and partitions are Great Space, the givenness of form and the partitioning or drawing up of form into particular configurations is Great Time.**

Space opened a sense of immeasurable width; Time now reveals the depth that breathes within that width. At a certain point, the two converge: breadth is not just spread, and depth is not hidden ground: both are facets of a single openness. What appears as stillness shows itself to be alive; what moves as change reveals itself to be free. To live in this recognition is to know that life is never diminished by its passing, because nothing ever departs from the resonance that gives rise to it. The flow and the fullness are eternally one.

This shift in how we meet time can be invited into our experience. As you read these words, pause for a moment. Let your awareness open not only to what is happening "now," but to the sense that the present is not a sliver cut off from past and future. Feel how the past murmurs within your memory, how the future leans forward with possibility, and how both are already infused into this very breath. Instead of grasping for a point called "the present," allow yourself to rest in the sense that *all of it*, past, future, and the vivid immediacy of now, is arising together as one interwoven presence.

Great Time discloses the flow we thought was carrying us away, never separate from the fullness of being. Time does not need to be conquered or transcended; it is already the vitality of openness. The anxious sense of moving from here to there, from today toward tomorrow, dissolves into nondual presence, inseparable from what is always here. Like Great Space, Great Time is not another dimension waiting to be reached: it is the pulse of reality already beating and presenting within and as each event.

THE COLLAPSE OF THE LINEAR TIMELINE

If Great Time is the vitality of openness, then its most radical implication is that the timeline itself is not what we thought. We imagine time as a sequence: one thing happening, then another, each locked into position by a before and an after. Our lives are measured against this sequence: childhood, adulthood, old age; birth, life, death. The line of time becomes the axis on which meaning turns. To exist, we believe, is to be carried along that line, each moment replacing the last.

> **Although Great Time embraces everything in a comprehensive, nonextended manner, lower time must conform to the spread out, 'one thing at a time' view encompassed by a limited 'knowledge'.**

But what if this picture is already misleading? What if the so-called line is more like a chalk drawing in air, visible for an instant, yet without substance? Great Time reveals that the segments we cling to as evidence of linearity are themselves appearances within a wider vitality that cannot be parceled out. The past does not vanish, the future does not wait ahead, and the present is not a razor's edge. All are given together in a resonance that does not fluctuate.

This sense of time is difficult to accept because it undermines our most basic security. We trust the timeline to hold our identity together, to assure us that the "I" of yesterday connects with the "I" of today, who will carry on as the same "I" into tomorrow. Without this chain of moments, who would we be? Yet the very restlessness of our lives betrays the fragility of this trust. We are always moving, always planning, always trying to secure a future that immediately slips away and ultimately evaporates like a puff of smoke.

Consider how we speak of our lives: "Where do you see yourself in five years?" "When did it all begin?" "How much time do I have left?" Each of these questions presupposes a line stretched taut across existence, with the self as traveler shuttling from one end toward the other. But this is a picture, not a fact: a story drawn by meanings and by the grammar of language and philosophy that requires beginnings, middles, and ends.

Great Time exposes the artifice, showing how what we call "moments" are not beads on a string but eddies in a stream, swirls that appear distinct only because of the way our knowing divides them. The deeper current does not move from one to the next; it flows as a whole.

Imagine sitting at the seashore, watching waves roll in. Each crest appears to have its own birth and death, but the ocean itself has no such divisions. It is always present, alive in every swell and retreat. So too with time: each experience can appear as if it begins and ends, but the vitality beneath is continuous, seamless, unsegmented. To live within Great Time is to stop counting the waves and to become the ocean.

Or imagine walking through a forest in early spring. Around you, new leaves are unfurling, the sound of water runs beneath the moss, shafts of sunlight pierce the canopy. For a while you may be tempted to think in terms of sequence: this bud opened today, that one will follow tomorrow. Yet as you walk, you begin to sense that all of it is happening at once: the growth, the decay, the turning of the season. The forest is not advancing on a line; it is presenting its fullness in every direction. Each step is not a move forward in time but a deepening presence already complete yet evolving.

This recognition does not deny change. Seasons still turn, bodies still age, days still pass. But these changes no longer need to be interpreted as steps on a vanishing line. They can be received as variations within a spacious ground that never withdraws. "Now" is not a sliver between two voids, it is the fullness in which all change occurs.

The consequences reach further than convenience. Our most persistent anxieties, the sense of not enough time, the fear of death, are fueled by the fiction of serial time. We imagine life as a bounded stretch between two points, birth and death, and we obsess about how many segments remain before the line terminates. From the perspective of Great Time, this construction is an overlay. Life and death are not markers on a track but appearances within openness, neither beginning nor ending in the way we suppose.

> **Great Time and lower time are not contrary conditions. One of the more straightforward ways of picturing this is to consider that the different 'times'—'now', 'then', 'before', 'after', even two billion years from now—may not stand as evidence of any fundamental change in time. Different times do not violate the nondistributive nature of Great Time. They are not linked, in a way that irrevocably separates them, by their respective positions in a temporal series. The 'series' is a fiction.**

Great Time does not abolish lower time but recontextualizes it. Different times, yesterday, today, two billion years hence, are not locked in separate compartments, competing for reality. They are equally present in the non-distributive dimension of Great Time. We are not trapped inside the series; the series itself is floating inside a larger openness.

Now picture a field just before dawn. At first the experience is hushed, indeterminate, waiting. Then, almost at once, a chorus arises: birds calling from every direction, mist lifting, light dawning over leaves. None of these events waits its turn. They unfold together, intensifying one another in a resonance beyond sequence. This is the gesture of Great Time: not a chain of instants, but a simultaneity where nothing is excluded.

Seen in this light, simultaneity is not confusion but coherence. What we call opposites, life and death, gain and loss, stillness and movement, are revealed as facets of one unfolding, held in the same embrace. Continuity no longer depends on stringing moments into a fragile chain; it rests in the openness where all arises together.

To touch even a glimpse of this is to feel the compulsion of "going" begin to ease. The river of time still flows, but we no longer need to chase each ripple as if it were all there is. Beneath the clocks and calendars, the linear fiction softens into a richer intimacy: a simultaneity in which nothing jostles for place, and nothing stands apart.

> **Neither we nor time are getting anywhere 'up ahead'. There is no evolution, no 'from' or 'to', no creation or first instant, and no existence. 'Nonexistence' does appear, but it does so in a fashion that is wondrous—without its wonder deriving from any incongruities within our standard picture of reality (with its doers, experiencers, experience, existence, evidence, and so forth).**

You might try this for yourself. Close your eyes and let the usual markers fall away: clocks, calendars, the inner chatter of "before" and "after." Settle into the simple sense of being here. Notice how time shows itself when you stop pressing it into a line. Can you sense a seam where one moment ends and the next begins or a shimmering continuity, a presence in which all distinctions arise together?

Rest in that for a few breaths. Let time feel less like a narrow corridor you are rushing through and more like the expanse you already belong within: unbroken, unhurried, without edge. This is not a special state to achieve but a recognition; the series was never binding you. It was only ever an overlay on the depth of time, which is already free.

THE GIFT OF TIME

As we have followed the arc from mountain sky to the depths of experience, time itself has begun to unwind. What once seemed like a forward-thrusting series of moments, carrying us along from past to future, now shows another face. Beneath the restless current of succession is a wider flow, an openness in which beginnings and endings lose their finality. This recognition does not dismiss the ordinary clock, nor deny the felt passage of days. Rather, it places these familiar rhythms within a more vast horizon. No markers, the tick of the second hand, the arc of the sun, the milestones of a human life, need be rejected nor imprison us. Each can be appreciated as one dynamic movement in an immeasurable choreography that is never reducible to before and after.

In this light, the drive to measure, to accumulate, to race against time loses its magnitude and urgency. What remains is not a schedule to be mastered, but a vitality that is endlessly available. To live with this recognition is to feel less like a passenger, shuttling along a fixed track that ends in death, and more like a participant in an unfolding that has no fixed direction. Here, time is not a burden but a precious gift, not a series of vanishing instants but an inexhaustible vitality. To sense this is to glimpse a freedom more spacious than any future could promise: a freedom that is present in each breath, in each glance, in each appearance as it arises. But even as this vision opens, the ordinary conventions of time remain. Clocks still tick, calendars still order our days, history still unfolds. The question now becomes: how do we inhabit these conventional structures without being confined by them? Chapter Sixteen takes up this challenge, exploring how time, space, and knowledge present themselves on the conventional level, and how their very ordinariness can be a doorway into the depths of vastness.

CHAPTER SIXTEEN

Time, Space, and Knowledge on the Conventional Level

Looking closely, it becomes clear: nothing ever appears "plain." Every encounter arrives already freighted with meaning. A rose is not just petals and fragrance. It arrives as beauty, as memory, as the echo of a gift, or the ache of a loss. A red light is not only color in a circle but the command *stop*, accompanied by a surge of caution, impatience, or relief. Ordinarily, we take these meanings for granted, as though they were stitched into the fabric of things themselves. But meanings are not properties of objects; they arise within a web of habit and expectation, culture and memory, bodily learning and social code. The "out there" and the "in here" collaborate so seamlessly that the result feels final: this is how the world is.

What encloses us is not that meanings are false, but that they harden. They fix both self and world into recognizable roles: *Here I am, the one who remembers, who longs, who judges. There is the world, full of what must be known, navigated, obtained, or avoided.* These positions reinforce each other until openness narrows into a private enclosure.

This enclosure is highly efficient. It keeps calendars intact and roles functioning, protects us from danger, and makes communication possible. Yet the very efficiency exacts a price. The walls of meaning become invisible, their echoes mistaken for reality itself. We live inside a chamber of interpretations, rarely meeting the freshness of experience unmediated. This chapter takes us inside that chamber. It asks us to notice not only how deeply meanings structure perception, but also the friction they generate. Meanings don't just shape; they scrape and press. They grind against one another, producing tension that we absorb as restlessness, self-judgment, or the sense of being walled in. That grinding, the grating effect of meaning, is where we now focus.

> **Lower space is a very egocentrically oriented womb, a protective enclosure that nevertheless involves a kind of friction or resistance phenomenon. The interaction of the two sets of walls just mentioned is what meanings accomplish. But this interaction is too rigid to be harmonious and satisfying. Meanings are communicative, but in a way that involves a kind of 'grating' effect.**

THE GRATING EFFECT OF MEANINGS

Meanings do not rest quietly. They scrape against one another, each asserting its claim. Every time an event is declared to mean this, another surface hardens. These surfaces partition the mindscape, like walls that narrow the chamber of experience. This grating is not merely metaphorical. It can be felt in the body: a forehead tightening while reading an email, the jaw set in the middle of an argument, the churn of thought circling on itself. Interpretations collide, generating heat without clarity. The felt texture is friction. Why does meaning grate? Because meaning is never neutral. It points and presses. It directs attention outward toward what comes next, toward what is implied, toward what needs to be explained. In that forward momentum, the ground of openness is obscured. Like shoes scuffing across a floor, meaning calls attention to itself by the noise it makes. Language intensifies the pressure. Words carve distinctions: inside/outside, relevant/irrelevant, mine/yours. These distinctions allow navigation, but at a cost. The more finely the lines are drawn, the more stratified the world becomes, and the sturdier the chamber grows.

Yet this irritation is diagnostic. If meanings were intrinsic to things, they would not demand so much upkeep. But they require constant reinforcement: interpretations must be repeated, categories defended, identities rehearsed. The endless labor of maintaining meaning produces the grind. To notice the grating is already to loosen it. For beneath the noise lies something else: the quiet hum of openness that requires no defense. Meaning both reveals and conceals; it shows us the world, but also walls us off from the freshness of what is given. When we slacken the demand to extract meaning, a different register of knowing emerges: lighter, smoother, less tethered to the insistence of "here" against "there."

In this sense, even friction carries a clue. The scrape of meaning points beyond itself, toward a ground that does not scuff or snag. Attend closely and the very irritant becomes a threshold: a doorway into the openness in which meanings come and go without binding.

The same dynamics hold for time. Past, present, and future appear solid only because they have been absorbed into our interpretive habits. We narrate a past to explain who we are, project a future to secure where we're going, and then treat the present as a narrow passage between them. Time itself becomes another chamber: partitioned, directional, grating. Calendars, reminders, and mental notes reinforce this story. A deadline looms, a birthday approaches, a meeting is remembered, all tethering us to a timeline that seems inevitable. But these markers are not givens; they are interpretations, stitched together by the same impulse that insists events and objects must mean something for "me." Seen this way, time is not undone but unburdened. Its familiar rhythms, clocks ticking, seasons turning, can still be followed. But they need not imprison. The compulsion to make every moment a link in a chain begins to relax. Each appearance can arrive whole, without the demand that it be fitted into a before or an after. This recognition sets the stage for practice. The following exercise explores what happens when we let the framework of time, space, and knowledge be felt on their conventional level, not to discard them, but to loosen their grip and glimpse the openness they conceal.

> **All communications and delineations on this level are done by 'time'. But time's chatter, which structures and partitions our egocentrically oriented realm (in a way that remains as an agitating 'grating'), is relieved by a more open 'space'. And such a more open 'space' does not stand as a chamber reflecting someone's personal images and messages.**

Exercise 16: Space–Time–Knowledge on the Conventional Level

Choose a quiet place where settling does not feel like a task. Let the body take its natural posture, not ramrod straight, not slumped, but balanced, like a tree that stands without asking permission. Notice how much the usual stance depends on dividing positions: here and there, inside and outside, self and other. Feel how those divisions are carried in posture and attention, in small anticipations of action. For now, let them soften.

Grant all forms, surfaces, and positions their space. No need to mystify or reimagine objects; simply allow the furniture, the walls, the window frame, the body itself to present as spacious. Space does not block; it accommodates. As this shift settles, there may be a sensation of flowing into what is seen, not by moving, but because the boundary between seer and seen becomes less insistent.

Invite time, but not the familiar time parcelled into past and future. Let every flicker of sensation, every ripple of thought, every change of light be "time." Not a line along which occurrences travel, but like lightning: flickering and flashing, playful and immediate. Nothing freezes. Everything is already in motion, arising and vanishing without residue.

Notice that this play is not "out there." There is no distant spectacle with a watcher apart. The play is here; woven into it is a knowing that is not produced by effort, native to the unfolding. The sense of "your" presence, too, can be felt as one way openness takes form through the dynamism of time. If orientation is helpful, use a simple heuristic. Let objects be understood as *space*. Let the observing presence be *knowledge*. Let the interaction that presents, sounds, thoughts, sensations, be *time*. This is not exhaustive; it is a doorway. Space and Time carry innumerable knowings; they reveal themselves when openness is not clenched. Now relax the familiar markers: here/there, inside/outside, now/later, existence/nonexistence, with no need to abolish them or push them away. Let them recede into the wider vision. As they relax, they dissolve into passages, doorways into a wider expanse.

Gently stay with this. Treat it not as a task but as permission for experience to refract differently. What moments ago was simply "sitting in a room" reveals itself as a seamless play of Space, Time, and Knowledge: fluid, boundless, self-illuminating. Rest in that, not as an achievement, but as a recognition.

Reflection

This exercise does more than adjust attention; it completely reorganizes experience.[39] Ordinarily, features of the world arrive bundled in a way that makes ego the anchor: I am here, the world is there, meaning flows toward it, and time pushes me forward. The package is so familiar that it masquerades as truth. When the play of Space, Time, and Knowledge comes forward, this conventional bundling disentangles itself. Elements that seemed welded, inside/outside, subject/object, before/after, rearrange around a wider openness.

The consequence is decisive: the centrality of ego softens without struggle. The old pattern required effort to maintain the ego's centrality: to guard a boundary, defend a position, and prove its existence against an external world. That effort is exhausting. Day after day it demands vigilance: reinvent and defend the storyline, manage impressions, search for experiences that confirm identity. When Space, Time, and Knowledge are permitted to show themselves, the labor looks unnecessary. Vitality flows without a center needing to contain it.

Picture the body braced against a strong river current: feet dug in, muscles tensed, shoulders rigid. That is ego's posture: standing apart, resisting the stream. Now picture yielding the stance and letting the water carry. Not drowning, not spacing out, just buoyed by the movement itself. The exercise enables that yielding. Fulfillment is no longer pursued "out there" or defended "in here"; it is disclosed as the aliveness of the flow.

Contact with appearances also changes. Under the old regime, contact is mediated by distance: reach for what lies beyond and hope it fills the lack.[40] Fulfillment is perpetually deferred. In the new view, contact is immediate. Space accommodates without resistance, Time presences without delay, and Knowledge illuminates without a separate knower. What is essential was never missing. However, none of this abolishes ordinary life. Forms remain, boundaries function, and meanings still arise. But their weight of ultimacy drops. Boundaries become translucent, and meanings inform without imprisoning. Even ego, once imagined the lonely guarantor of existence, appears simply as another pattern in the play, neither repressed nor enthroned.

This shift is subtle yet far-reaching: from standing apart to participating directly; from grasping to availability; from a private enclosure to an openness shimmering with possibilities. This is not utopia or merely a spiritual fantasy; rather, it is a practical recognition that openness is already the groundless ground. Living from that ground means letting moments be sustained not by self-driven effort but by the inexhaustible capacity of Space, the vivacity of Time, and the quiet sufficiency of Knowledge.

Having touched this loosening directly, you may begin to notice how different "voices" still echo inside: the vigilant manager, the doubting self, the habits of grasping, the quiet spaciousness that simply allows. They are not separate entities but familiar postures that rise and fall within the same openness you've just tasted. The following dialogue gives those postures a voice so they can be seen clearly rather than acted out automatically. Think of it not as a play to watch, but as a way of listening to your own inner council—Space, Time, Knowledge, Ego, and even Death—speaking within you in real time.

The Inner Council

Knowledge: Let's use a simple orientation:

- Let all objects be Space.
- Let the observing presence be Knowledge.
- Let the presenting, the subtle "happening" between sounds, interactions, thoughts, images, and sensation be Time.

Ego: So, you're telling me, everything is "Space"? And all this buzzing of thoughts and feelings is "Time"? If that's granted, where am I? Who holds it all together?

Space: There is no need to hold it together. "You" are already being held. Breath enters without your command; the ground supports without being asked. You have never been outside me.

Inner Manager: One moment. If letting go is the plan, something has to stay on duty. Someone must check whether this is being done correctly. Otherwise things will fall apart.

Knowledge: Manager, your care is understood and appreciated. You have protected and kept Ego from overwhelm for years. But look closely: knowing is happening even when you are not at the controls. Awareness does not require your stamp of approval.

Time: And look at me: arriving already! This word, that sensation, a sound outside, a memory, a whisper of an idea. You do not have to chase me, Ego. I keep showing up all the time (pun alert).

Ego: Yea, but if I don't keep up with this movement, won't something essential be missed? Won't life pass me by?

Time: Life is not passing you by; it is passing through you. Each flicker is complete. What slips away is your attempt to freeze me.

Inner Manager: Oh come on now! But what if Ego drifts? What if all this "letting go" business means losing a grip on reality?

Space: Grip? Even your grip floats in me. You have been buoyed all along.

Knowledge: Your vigilance can become a deep listening. You can still be present without guarding. In fact, you would be more fully present beyond what you can now imagine.

Ego: I am still not so sure: If my grasping stops, does the self vanish? Is there just . . . nothing? I can't allow that to happen.

Knowledge: No, not nothing: less than fixation, more than absence. Transparent to what is here.

Time: The moment grasping and fixations release, you are with me—lighter, freer and more fluid and spontaneous. No counting and keeping track is needed; simply ride the shimmering and appreciate the flickering.

Ego: That's a surprising discovery. When I stop insisting on being the owner of knowing, I don't disappear. There's lightness: as if floating in Space, presenting by Time.

Inner Manager: Ok, I get it. Perhaps the job is not to control and micro-manage every event. Perhaps keeping an eye out is enough.

Space: Rest is possible even for your vigilance. Time, Space and Knowledge are self-managing.

Knowledge: Every voice, Ego, Manager, even doubt, already speaks within this wider knowing. Nothing has to be erased or censured.

Ego: I feel relieved! So this "experiment" is not about losing myself. It reveals I was never standing apart from the play of appearances to begin with.

Time: Exactly. Stop trying to keep pace and notice you are already moving.

Space: Your belonging or legitimacy has never been in question. There is no need for you to feel estranged from your parentage: Space (yours truly), Time, and Knowledge.

Ego: I can't believe that this now feels like home.

A new presence enters: calm, unhurried, undeniable.

Death: Home, yes. And remember, this acquaintance is old. I have walked with you since your first breath. Each inhalation is already my whisper; each exhalation carries me too. You have always known me, though you push me to the edges of thought.

Ego: What the heck! Death? This was an exercise, an experiment we were engaged in. You are not on the agenda! I didn't see your presence in the instructions! Who invited you? Why are you here?

Inner Manager: Just slam that door. Death only means loss, annihilation, the end. You're not welcome 'here'!

Death: That is the rumor. Look again. Nothing you cling to has ever been yours in the way you imagine. What you fear me taking has never belonged to you; it was always passing. I do not come to erase what you are; I come to show that you were never what you thought.

Space: Everyone can stay calm. Notice how naturally Death belongs here. Without partitions, Death is not an intruder but one of vastness's ways of presenting.

Time: Yes, I have always carried Death within me: every flicker, every passing. Not an interruption, not impermanence, but the rhythm itself. There is no real passing in me. I allow the appearance of passage and passing away.

Death: Exactly. I am not the end of life but its teacher. I remind you that each moment is complete, that nothing can be secured. Without me, the fantasy of permanence would never crack. Without me, you would cling forever, and never glimpse the openness that is you.

Knowledge: Ego, Manager: feel this. Death is not standing against you. It reveals that what seemed solid was already transparent. In knowing, nothing is lost.

Ego: Still, I am afraid. If I stop resisting, don't I vanish? Isn't Death a void swallowing everything?

Death: No. I am not the void you imagine, but a threshold. I am the soft collapse of boundaries, the loosening of what never held firm. I show you that the "self" you defend has no fixed core and that this is not loss, but a great release. I am the opening through which your grasping and clinging dissolves into freedom. I am the reminder that all appearances are gestures of openness.

Inner Manager: You mean that even my vigilance, even fear, belongs?

Death: Yes. Even your fear is part of my teaching. Fear says, "Hold on." I say, "See through." Both voices belong, both dissolve in the same openness.

Space: All belongs.

Time: All passes.

Knowledge: And in the apparent passing, everything is known without being owned.

Ego: Then Death is not outside life? It is part of living?

Death: More than part. I am woven into every breath, every heartbeat, every change. When you stop running, you discover: I was never here to end you. I was here to remind you that you were never apart. I am the echo of your own openness, not its opposite.

Silence follows; not heavy, not fearful. The voices soften into the openness that held them from the start.

LESSONS FROM THE COUNCIL

What has played out is not foreign. The voices are familiar: the manager who tightens control at the first hint of uncertainty, the ego that places itself in the center, the subtler currents—Space's permissiveness, Time's liveliness, Knowledge's clarity—that keep showing through despite resistance. And the twist in the plot, Death's arrival, is not melodrama. Mortality shapes daily choices even when banished from conscious plans. It stands at the threshold of each moment's passing.

The lesson is plain. Practice is never abstract. It is the rearrangement of these voices as they move through a day: sometimes braided, sometimes at odds, sometimes surprising by undoing certainty in a single sentence; even protest belongs. Nothing stands outside the field: not fear, not resistance, not the unspoken calculus of loss.

> **Such an understanding does not itself involve meanings. Paradoxically, this understanding may be more available to us—more near at hand—once we have shown that understanding does not have to be other or elsewhere than meanings. That is, it does not have to be an "understanding that is delineated by the special characteristic that it is beyond meanings."**

The exercise reframes familiar features, objects, meanings, the sense of self, not as barriers to be overcome but as expressions within a wider play. The voices do not need to be silenced or refined; they only need to be heard as arising together within the same accommodating space, the same living time, the same native knowing. When this recognition begins to settle, the machinery of meaning eases. The forward pressure slackens. Boundaries turn translucent. Life reveals itself not as a contest to be managed or survived, but as a participation already underway. The stage, vast, permissive openness, was never absent.

From here, a quieter confidence becomes possible. Schedules can still be kept, projects pursued, relationships tended. Yet underneath runs a different current: less of a stance to be defended and more of a readiness to respond. The guiding question shifts from, "How do I secure the self in a resistant world?" to "How does availability meet what appears?" The answer is not abstract but practical: by letting Space show its capacity, Time its liveliness, and Knowledge its unowned clarity, each functions within the ordinary course of a day.

This intimacy requires no manufacture. It does not arrive as a mood to be chased but as the natural disclosure of how appearances are already related when the aperture of the focal setting loosens. Standing in a kitchen, taking out the trash, waiting in a line, speaking with a stranger, nothing extra is needed. Effort relaxes, and intimacy reveals itself as the shape of experience all along.

Meaning still matters. Language still designates. Plans can still be made. But they need not harden into the world's walls. The chamber of interpretation can be used without being mistaken for the whole. When the scrape of its boundaries is heard as a cue rather than a command, another register of reality becomes audible.

This chapter began with the weight of interpretation and the drag of linear time. It unfolded a practice that treats ordinary experience as the very ground where Space, Time, and Knowledge are already in play. It staged a dialogue in which familiar voices found rest within a larger coherence and even Death was welcomed as part of life rather than its opposite. It closes by returning us not to retreat but to the street, the desk, the marketplace, the sink: the ordinary stage of daily life. What remains is openness. Even the most entrenched patterns form within it and dissolve back into it. The invitation is not to perfect the self or to escape the world, but to recognize the nearness of vastness, in rooms and streets and conversations, and to let that recognition guide how attention meets what appears. Where rigidity melts, participation becomes simple. Where participation is simple, intimacy is uncontrived.

Here the path turns. Having seen how interpretation softens within openness, we are ready to explore how vastness itself comes near, not as a distant goal but as the very texture of immediacy.

CHAPTER SEVENTEEN

The Nearness of Vastness

A pattern has begun to emerge. Touch the body, and it opens. Examine the mind, and it dissolves into movement. Question the inner manager, and its authority weakens. What looks rigid becomes flexible, what looks private reveals its transparency. These changes do not come from altering the world, but from a shift in vantage, the focal setting through which experience appears.

It is tempting to think of a focal setting as something small: a tweak of attention, a choice of lens. But in truth, our whole world order is nothing other than a particular focal setting. We rarely notice this, because the apparatus is so pervasive. Like a pair of glasses worn since childhood, the lenses feel indistinguishable from vision itself. Yet what we call "the world," streets and sky, calendars and currencies, all the furnishings of daily life, is a local limitation on something greater. The ordinary realm is not outside of Great Space; it is Great Space seen through a narrow aperture.

This is the focal trick. When the aperture is closed tight, reality seems to consist of solid things in definite places, each distinct, each taking up room that excludes the others. I am here; you are over there. Events line up in sequence, like beads on a string. The world feels distributed across a grid that has been set once and for all. From this vantage, Great Space seems remote, hypothetical, perhaps mystical. We imagine it as a realm beyond or above.

But the humility clause must be honored: even the phrase "Great Space" is a concession to our present limitations. To name it is already to draw a boundary around what cannot be bounded. At best, "Great Space" serves as a working hypothesis, a scaffold we can lean on as we dispense with the default frame. The words are provisional; the reality they point toward is closer than the thought that tries to name it.

Or take a morning commute on a crowded expressway. Cars bumper to bumper in a traffic jam, each vehicle jostling for position. The conventional reading is one of scarcity: limited space, limited time, limited patience. The focal trick presents this as absolute. Yet even here, am "I in a traffic jam" or is the traffic jam appearing within an openness that easily accommodates every car, every driver, every beep of the horn? In the midst of congestion, openness is not absent, it is the condition for any of it to occur at all.

This is what it means to say that our ordinary world is only a narrowed slice of Great Space. Take the same rush hour commute: it can feel claustrophobic, each car a rival for limited ground, or it can open into a sense of vastness, the sky spanning above and the motion of thousands moving together. Nothing in the physical setup changes. What changes is the aperture of attention.

The significance of this cannot be overstated. If even the most everyday scenes are saturated with openness, then fulfillment is never elsewhere. We don't need mountaintops or altered states to taste it, nor a deity outside the world to bestow it. The task is more simple and more subtle: to recognize that what looks like a fixed, confining world is actually a narrowed lens on something immeasurably wide.

This chapter introduces a progression of views, described in the TSK vision as three "levels" of space. These levels aren't steps on a ladder or stations on a spiritual map, but teaching devices, ways of noticing how experience can open. We begin with *level one space*, the ordinary sense of reality as fixed and external, and see how even this view already contains cracks in its rigidity. From there we move to *level two space*, where loosening the focal grasp allows new sensitivities, luminosities, and freedoms to emerge, though even here, the old habit of self-appropriation can creep back in. Finally, we arrive at *level three space*, where the very scaffolding of levels dissolves, and what remains is a direct intimacy with whatever appears.

The risk, of course, is to mistake these "levels" for a hierarchy, as though Great Space waited at the top like a prize. That is not the point. The levels are provisional, as tentative as the word "Great Space" itself. They are not destinations but aids for challenging our taken-for-granted presuppositions, until we recognize that what seemed "beyond" was never apart from this moment at all.

SPACE, LEVEL ONE: OUR ORDINARY REALM SEEN ANEW

When we hear that our ordinary world is only a "local limitation" on Great Space, it can sound abstract, even mystical. But what is being pointed to is not remote. It asks us to look more carefully at the familiar. Most of us treat space as the backdrop: a neutral container, the stretch between here and there, the emptiness that lets things exist. From this angle, space is a kind of nothingness, a stage on which events play out. Yet the very fact that anything at all can occur—a conversation, a storm, a birth—already points to something more. Space is not an add-on. It is the open condition that makes every happening possible.

> **Great Space is not a thing and cannot be said to 'exist'. Ordinary space is a derivative but distorted expression of Great Space. The difference is that 'being something' and 'existing' are considered as small focal setting manifestations and as rather deadening in comparison to the infinite fulfillment of Great Space.**

Seen in this light, the ordinary world does not disappear. Rooms, streets, and landscapes remain what they are, but they are not sealed compartments. They are saturated with an openness that is neither inside them nor somewhere else. This is why "distance" itself begins to lose its finality. Conventionally, we organize life around distances: home versus work, here versus there, birth versus death. But when space is recognized as an accommodating openness, separation is less rigid. Near and far reveal themselves as relational, not absolute.

> **While all familiar things are separate and distributed over ordinary space, delineated partly by differences in position, they are all intimately connected insofar as their Great Space dimension is considered. 'Distance between' becomes meaningless.**

The same holds for finitude. What looks like a fixed and bounded thing is, in its very presence, already a window into something immeasurable. The point is not to deny limits, but to see that limits themselves disclose a larger possibility.

> **. . . nothing has been set up in only one way, with one history of interconnected events. Great Space is not a creator that has created a particular universe. Great**

Space is not committed or bound by one standard world order.

This is perhaps the most radical implication. We tend to assume reality is settled: history unfolded as it did, the rules are fixed, the story is already written. But Great Space resists this closure. It is not bound to one version of events. What we take to be "the world order" is only a focal perspective—partial, provisional, subject to shift.

To glimpse even a hint of this is significant. It loosens the sense that life is locked into a single track or a single destiny. What appears as final may be nothing more than a narrowing of view. What we seek is not elsewhere—it is breaking through here, in the very space we inhabit.

SPACE, LEVEL TWO: DOORWAYS AND DETOURS

Relaxing and opening the ordinary focal setting often brings palpable relief. The pressure of self-orientation lightens. Tensions held in the body soften. Vision brightens, sounds become vivid, small details feel alive. For some, this may show up as a sense of weight falling away during a retreat or a walk in nature: the mind no longer fixates around what needs fixing, and everything appears more fluid, more available.

This relationship can manifest in infinitely many ways. Typical examples include an increase in personal freedom, less psychological pressure, greater physical relaxation, a heightening of the senses, and even parapsychological capacities, such as telepathy and clairvoyance.

From the standpoint of ordinary space, such phenomena appear anomalous, even impossible.[41] But from within a more open setting, the assumptions that made them unthinkable, "locatedness," "separation," and "intervening distance," are no longer binding. When those restrictions loosen, it is not surprising that new forms of knowing emerge. What once looked like paranormal anomalies may instead be understood as disclosures of a deeper spatial coherence.

Yet even here, a subtle bias remains. The shift into Space Level Two is often experienced from the subject pole, as if the self were a bystander enjoying greater freedom, clarity, and perhaps unusual abilities while still standing apart from the world. This lingering dualism—self as knower, world as known—means that the new opening is still a doorway rather than a destination.

The risk, then, is appropriation. Relief, clarity, or even clairvoyance can be seized as personal property. Ego rushes in to claim ownership: *my clarity, my stillness, my openness.* In wellness culture, the pattern is amplified: yoga becomes "my self-care routine," meditation becomes "my edge in business," even silence becomes "my productivity hack." Freedom is folded back into the orbit of self-improvement.

The pattern is clear. A collective hush on a subway platform, a wave of unity at a concert, even the release of a digital detox can all be shared doorways into spaciousness. But quickly the appropriation sets in: "my chance to meditate," "my best night," "my new productivity tool." Openness collapses back into ownership. Seen this way, the danger of Level Two is not its gifts but their misreading. Openness shows itself, but the gravitational pull of the self-centered frame reclaims it. Spirituality, too, is not immune: seekers talk of "my awakening," "my higher state," "my enlightenment." The covering may be thinner, but the pattern remains. This is not failure, it is instruction. The speed with which freedom becomes property shows how deeply the reflex of self-centeredness is ingrained. That reflex cannot be dispelled by adding more experiences; it requires a more radical shift, which turn belongs to the next level.

SPACE, LEVEL THREE: BEYOND THE SCAFFOLDING

Level Three Space takes the final step: the recognition that even the idea of "levels" was a scaffold, useful only up to a point. The notion of progression dissolves, and with it the last vestiges of a project of attainment. First, we need the image of levels. They reassure us that progress is possible, that we are headed somewhere beyond the confines of ordinary space. But when the scaffolding has done its work, the structure it supports is revealed to be nothing other than what was here all along.

The very idea of breakthrough itself lapses. There are no lower spaces; no ascent, no descent, no elsewhere to arrive at. What we call "Great Space" is not higher than ordinary space; it is the same reality, recognized without frame. The ordinary focal setting and the expansive vision are not two realms but two readings of the same text: one cramped, the other laid bare.

What follows is not the annihilation of experience but its transfiguration. Self and world, inner and outer, subject and object, no longer need to be held apart. They show themselves as facets of one unfolding, as if the glass panes that once divided reality have gone transparent. The result is not emptiness but intimacy, a closeness so complete that the need for ownership evaporates.

At this level we completely transcend a self-centered orientation and become fully with everyone and everything else. Locations and attitudes, problems and confusions, no longer bind us.

This intimacy has lived consequences. When the self-center drops away, one is no longer set over against the world, anxiously defending territory. Instead, being-with arises, fully with others, with situations, with the flow of appearance. Problems and attitudes still arise, but they no longer feel like enemies or insurmountable obstacles. Even birth and death are seen differently: not endpoints in a linear series, but episodes in the play of appearance.

We have no improvement orientation, and yet are fully available to help other people—or to improve things—by phrasing and exemplifying our appreciation of perfection in terms of others' improvement-oriented views.

The improvement orientation drops away most decisively. The drive to become better, more advanced, more accomplished loses its grip, yet without breeding passivity; it generates availability. Attention is freed from "How am I doing?" and released into responsiveness: to console a friend, to act with clarity, to let presence itself be the reassurance. Availability becomes the teaching. In this light, the ordinary is not a stepping stone to the extraordinary. It is already lit from within. Washing dishes, answering email, listening to a child's question—none of these need to be elevated into "practice." They disclose the intimacy of Great Space without adornment.

The danger of Level Two was appropriation: turning freedom into property. The promise of Level Three is recognition: discovering that freedom was never owned in the first place. The sense of *my calm, my clarity, my openness* is replaced by the recognition that clarity, calm, and openness are not possessions but dimensions of reality itself. The cage was never locked; it had paper walls.

Here the language of levels falters. To call this stage "higher" misleads, as if we were climbing a mountain to reach a summit. It is more like standing still until the mountain itself becomes transparent, revealing that height and base were never separate. The journey was never toward a distant peak but toward the ground that has been here all along. What remains is an uncontrived intimacy with all that appears. Life does not need to be edited or improved; it only needs to be met. The narrow and the vast, the trivial and the momentous, the beautiful and the painful are all gestures of the same openness. The intimacy is not something we generate; it generates us.

FROM CLIMBING TO RECOGNIZING

The metaphor of levels has served its purpose. Like scaffolding around a building, it gave us a way to imagine progress, to orient ourselves in unfamiliar terrain. Level one reassured us that even the ordinary realm is not as opaque as it seems. Level two encouraged us to lean into the cracks, to taste the relief of loosening. Level three reminded us that the ladder itself dissolves, revealing no separation between narrow setting and vast openness. Scaffolding is meant to be temporary. If left standing, it obstructs the very structure it helped to raise. To remain preoccupied with levels is to miss the intimacy they were pointing toward. Great Space does not need our designations: it is not waiting at the top of a ladder, nor resting on the far side of an accomplishment. It gives rise to ladders in the first place.

The language of levels can be helpful, but only if we hold it lightly. These designations, first, second, third, are not steps on a hierarchy so much as provisional perspectives that help us notice habits. Their purpose is not to generate Great Space as a result but to loosen the assumptions that obscure what is already here.

This unraveling is rarely linear. It moves in spirals and returns, more like the ripening of fruit than a march forward. Reading, studying, reflecting, meditating, practicing—the boundaries between them blur. A close reading can destabilize as much as a formal exercise; an exercise can illuminate as much as a passage of text. Taken together, they form a single mode of cultivation, a training of perception into what can be called *cognitive non-dualism*: the capacity to notice how appearances and meanings, self and world, inquiry and insight, all arise together without requiring a fixed foundation.[42]

Sudden glimpses may come—a taste of openness, a flash of intimacy—but they tend to fade. The deeper transformation comes not from holding onto these moments but from staying with the process itself, allowing old orientations to soften and new spaciousness to take root. What looks like a path is really a way of letting go of the need for a path at all. The real shift is from acquisition to participation. Instead of striving to accumulate more clarity, more openness, more experience, we recognize that openness was never absent. Instead of progress measured against a future goal, we find availability to what is present now. The play of life does not need to be harnessed into self-improvement. It calls only for presence, for the willingness to let appearances shine without trying to own them. This turn is subtle but decisive. The seeker's stance, always climbing, always looking ahead, relaxes into intimacy. Not intimacy with an object "out there," but intimacy with reality itself, in which self and world are no longer divided poles but facets of one unfolding. Here the language of levels finally collapses and with it the illusion of distance.

The journey that began with cracks in the familiar and methods of approach ends in something more natural: an ease that asks nothing, an availability that does not strain to improve or possess. The name is not important, but the feeling is unmistakable: the taste of being wholly with, the discovery that appearance itself is radiant, that nothing needs to be elsewhere.

The promise of this chapter is fulfilled not by adding something new, but by clearing space for what was already here. What remains is the nearness of vastness, the recognition that depth is not hidden beyond the horizon but saturates even the most ordinary moment. To stand in this recognition is to discover a groundless confidence: nothing needs to be secured, because nothing was ever at risk. The scaffolding can be set aside; the building stands on its own. We realize the building is not a structure at all, but the open sky, endlessly supporting, endlessly accommodating, endlessly free.

CHAPTER EIGHTEEN

The Mandala of Being

When we step back to consider the arc traced across the previous chapters, a subtle pattern becomes visible. Each inquiry into Space has carried us beyond the familiar outlines of our lives, loosening the stranglehold of the "inner manager," opening the sense of enclosure, and exposing a wider horizon. Time has occasionally appeared at the edges of these explorations, flickering as something more mysterious than the ticking of clocks or the turning of calendars. Knowledge, too, has come into view, not as possession or expertise, but as the clear luminosity that makes experience possible at all.

What gathers these three strands together? What holds openness, dynamism, and clarity in a single embrace? The answer is not an abstract doctrine but an invitation to turn attention toward *Being*. To speak of Being is to walk on the thinnest of ice. The word has been used so often, by philosophers, mystics, and psychologists alike, that it risks sounding either overblown or hollow, like a grand declaration shouted in an empty hall. The culmination of our inquiry in *Mind Space* and the heart of the *Time, Space, and Knowledge* vision is a turn toward Being, a quiet gathering of all the strands that came before: the openness of Space, the dynamism of Time, and the radiance of Knowledge. Without Being, these three facets remain like windows without a house. With Being, they reveal themselves as dimensions of a single dwelling: our dwelling.

Living the Space-Time-Knowledge vision, discovering more of the resource which these three represent, we can find the way to our Being. So far we have been concentrating on Space, Time, and Knowledge, but only to comprehend—through a triple-faceted vision—the unity of *Being*.

In ordinary thought, Being often appears distant, lofty, abstract, perhaps even inaccessible. We ask whether Being exists, or what its essence might be, or whether it is the same as "reality." But these questions already miss the mark. Being here does not mean a metaphysical essence or a cosmic ground lurking behind appearances, waiting to be discovered. Nor is it an object to be located or a principle to be proven. In fact, the first move requires disarming the reflex to treat Being as an "it." To speak of Being is not to point to something hidden out there; it is to notice the way appearance itself shines. Being is the intimacy of presence, what makes this word, this breath, this very instant already complete. What a startlingly different perspective: Being is not behind the play of Space, Time, and Knowledge; it is the play itself!

Consider a simple example: the act of turning a doorknob. Ordinarily, this is the most forgettable of gestures, merely a means to get from one room to another. But if attention slows, something else is disclosed. The cool brass against the skin, the weight of the latch, the slight creak of hinges—none of these can be reduced to a neutral mechanism. Each is a pulse of aliveness, a revelation that anything at all is here. The turning is not simply functional; it is an event in Being. To appreciate this requires a shift in stance.

Instead of peering past appearances, hoping to pierce a veil, we begin to see appearances themselves as radiant with significance.

The point is not to romanticize the everyday but to recognize its depth. We often imagine that Being must lie elsewhere, in extraordinary moments or transcendent revelations. Yet the more radical claim of the vision is that Being is never elsewhere. Being saturates the ordinary so completely that we fail to see it, like fish failing to notice water.

One temptation, when we broach the subject of Being, is to elevate it into abstraction. Philosophical traditions from Aristotle to Heidegger have sought to define or decode it: as substance, as ground, as the "to be" that underwrites existence. Religious traditions have aligned it with God, spirit, or the divine essence of the world. In both cases, Being becomes an answer to the question of why there is something rather than nothing. But what if the question itself is misplaced? What if Being is not an answer at all, but the refusal of the question? To ask "why is there something rather than nothing?" assumes that "something" and "nothing" are ultimate categories, opposed and mutually exclusive. Yet the vision invites us to see that these categories are themselves provisional, arising within the larger play of Space, Time, and Knowledge. From that vantage, "something" and "nothing" are not opposites at war but aspects of a more subtle openness. Existence and nonexistence shimmer like waves on the surface of a sea, neither exhausts the sea.

This is why Being, in this vision, cannot be stabilized as a concept. The more tightly we try to grasp 'it', the more it slips away. The invitation is not to define but to appreciate. To appreciate Being is to let presence present itself, without reducing it to a mental category or a theological placeholder.

BEING AND HUMAN BEING

The inquiry becomes sharper when we ask not only what Being is, but what it means to be a *human being* in its light. For the question of Being is never abstract; it implicates us directly. The time of our lives, the space of our bodies, the knowledge that flows through perception and thought are not separate from Being, they are its enactments. To ask about Being is to ask about ourselves, not as psychological profiles or social roles, but as presencings of openness.

This is why the vision speaks of the inseparability of Being and human being. The mystery is not far away. It pulses through the rhythm of breath, through the eyes of the newborn that open to light, through the word spoken and the silence between. The miracle is not that we might one day ascend to Being, but that we are already its living expression.

Imagine sitting in meditation, attention gathered around the breath. At first, there is the familiar sense of "me" doing the practice: the watcher who counts inhalations, the evaluator who measures progress, the striver who wants calm. The posture seems dignified, but beneath it runs the quiet tension of management. Now let attention soften. Instead of focusing on the breath as an object, notice the whole field of arising: sounds, sensations, thoughts, even the flicker of self-awareness. All of it comes and goes without needing to be secured. The "meditator" who seemed to sit apart is also appearing, no more or less substantial than the play of light on the eyelids. In this shift, Being is not an abstraction. It is the immediacy of the meditation itself—the breath and the thought of the breath, the watcher and the watched—already inseparable, already sustained within openness. Calm and distraction, presence and mind wandering, are facets of the same display. The effort to become dissolves into the natural ease of Being.

BEING: VAST AND NEAR

One of the paradoxes of Being is that it is both utterly vast and utterly near. Philosophical traditions often tilt toward the vast: Being as cosmic backdrop, infinite horizon, or transcendent ground. Everyday awareness tilts toward the near: being as my existence, my life, my consciousness. The vision dissolves this split. Vastness and nearness are not opposed but inseparable. Vastness is what makes nearness possible, and nearness is how vastness is lived.

Think of standing under a night sky. The stars stretch out across unimaginable distances, the Milky Way spilling its river of light. The mind reels at the vastness: billions of years, countless galaxies, the silence of an unfathomable expanse. And yet, at the same time, the gaze itself is intimate. The starlight touches the eye, the body shivers in the cool air, a breath condenses in the dark. Vastness is not elsewhere; it is here, in the touch, the breath, the seeing. To be human is to stand at this intersection: where the infinite and the intimate are one gesture.

BEING AND VALUE

A further twist is that Being is not neutral, an empty backdrop against which values must be constructed or imposed. Being is intrinsically valuable, though not in the sense of utility or morality. Being's value is its radiance, its beauty, its sheer givenness, the fact that anything appears at all. This is why even the most ordinary occurrence can strike with quiet beauty: the way sunlight falls across a table, the way a child's laugh rings out, the way rain streaks a windowpane. Each is not merely something happening, but the appearance of value, the shimmering of Being.

> **The search for Being is not one which can be based on egoistic purposes and values. Our being has a primordial value that is continually being worked out within its sphere, and our fulfillment requires that we attend to this value.**

Recognizing this intrinsic value undermines the ceaseless drive to measure, to compare, to evaluate according to external standards. It is a powerful antidote to utilitarian thinking, the sense that worth must always be justified by function or result. Instead, we begin to see that worth is woven into presence itself. The world does not need to prove itself; it is already radiant.

TOWARD A QUADRINITY

At this juncture, it becomes possible to introduce a subtle but important expansion of the vision. Up to now, the teaching has unfolded as a trinity: Space, Time, and Knowledge. Space has been explored in depth, along with some preliminary peeks at Time and Knowledge, each reframed as more than an abstract category: openness, dynamism, and clarity. But this trinity is not complete; it is enfolded in something larger that does not stand apart but shines through them all. Being enters as the fourth, not as an addition, but as a *recognition*: Space, Time, and Knowledge are not separate strands waiting to be tied together; they are already woven as Being. To name this weaving a "quadrinity" is not to introduce a hierarchy but to acknowledge wholeness. Being is not above the three but permeates, within and through them. Without

Being, they would not be; with Being, they are luminous facets of one mystery.

This quadrinity can be pictured in many ways. One image is the mandala: four gates opening into a center, four directions that are not divided but integrated. Another is the labyrinth: a path that winds through turns and thresholds, yet always circles back to the same center. In both images, the fourth is not outside the three but their natural completion. To walk the mandala or the labyrinth is to realize that what seemed separate was always already whole.

THE INVITATION

This is not a preface to theory but invites non-conceptual knowingness. To speak of Being is not to pile concepts upon concepts, but to knowingly see the way appearance shines as presence, the way presence reveals value, the way value dissolves separation. The task is not to grasp at Being, but to let Being reveal us, to let the vastness show itself as nearness, to let the ordinary glow with radiance, to let the trinity of Space, Time, and Knowledge unfold and shine as the quadrinity of Being. This is not an achievement or an attainment; it is a direct recognition. Like recognition, it does not add anything new, it simply allows what is to be intimately seen, fully appreciated.

In this sense, the inquiry that has unfolded through Mind Space now bends toward its culmination. We are no longer exploring techniques for dissolving the confinement of lower space, or exercises for tasting time differently. We are beginning to glimpse what these explorations have been pointing toward all along: the intimate presencing of Being. Not as an idea, but as the fabric of our lives. Not as a conclusion, but as a dawning of wonder, of value, of the radiant immediacy of what is.

THE RADICAL GESTURE OF WONDER

To speak of Being as radiant presence is to already stand at the threshold of wonder. Wonder is not an extra response layered on top of experience; it is the way reality first greets us before habit and explanation dull the encounter. A newborn opening its eyes does not classify or interpret; it is immersed in wonder. A child playfully chasing fireflies in the summer dusk does not analyze light refraction; it marvels. Even an adult, despite decades of habit, can still be disarmed by a sudden glimpse that cracks the veneer of the ordinary: the sweep of clouds lit by evening sun, the quiet dignity of an elderly relative's face.

The vision insists that such wonder is not decorative, not a fleeting mood, nor a sentimental overlay. Wonder is how reality discloses itself when our defenses melt, the felt register of Being's inexhaustibility. Recognizing this shifts the axis of our lives: from treating wonder as a rare exception to seeing it as the undercurrent of every moment, hidden only by our inattention and lack of appreciation.

In our cultural inheritance, wonder often gets downplayed. Modernity equates maturity with disenchantment, as though to grow up is to shed amazement.[43] The Enlightenment taught us to seek explanation, not astonishment. Science, in its triumphalist mood, portrays the world as a puzzle to be solved rather than a miracle to be inhabited. Religion, too, sometimes domesticates wonder, packaging mystery into doctrine so that awe can be directed into orderly channels.

But what happens when we take wonder itself as foundational? When we allow it not to be explained away, but to stand as the most accurate response to reality? From the standpoint of the vision, this is not naïveté. It is precision. For what else could possibly match the impossibility of appearance itself: the sheer fact that anything at all shows up, presence rather than absence, light rather than void?

Philosophy often phrases this as the question: why is there something rather than nothing? Yet the issue can be seen differently. Being is not a "something" that fends off "nothing." Both existence and nonexistence are latecomers, conceptual filters placed on top of a more primordial openness. When this openness shines, the question "why something?" dissolves. There is no answer because there is no need for one: only wonder.

THE MAGICAL WORLD

We live in a magical world. Yet magic here does not mean superstition or trickery. Not a sleight of hand performed by an unseen magician, it is the recognition that appearance itself is magic: arising without cause, persisting without substance, shimmering without support. Ordinarily we domesticate this magic. We translate it into the law-like regularities of physics, the rational order of categories, the predictable march of clock time. Of course, these frameworks serve their purposes. They allow us to build bridges, cure disease, navigate daily life. But if we mistake these devices for reality itself, we lose sight of what they are resting upon: the fathomless spontaneity of appearance.

> **Nothing performs anything, and this is itself an unlimited, centerless, boundaryless performance. Everything is included within this performance, yet there are no things 'there'. What there is is entirely open in a way that remains an undimmed radiance, an infinitely textured radiance that is magic.**

Time provides the clearest example. In our usual stance, time is conceived as a line: a series of points extending from past to future, with the present a narrow slice between. This picture feels inevitable, unquestionable: built into our clocks, calendars, and very grammar. Yet the vision reveals that time is not distributed like beads on a string, not distributed across an infinite grid. Instead, Time is luminous immediacy: the flash of presence that never departs. When we glimpse this, we realize that both "time as passage" and "time as non-passage" are simultaneously true. Ordinary chronology unfolds: meetings are held, seasons change, children grow, and yet from another register, nothing moves at all. The wonder is that these two are not in contradiction; they both express Time as Being's play.

Neither we nor time are going anywhere "up ahead," no first instant, no final culmination, no teleological arrow stretching toward a hidden goal. Living with this recognition casts off the anxiety of arrival. Life is no longer a project of getting somewhere; it is the magic of presence, endlessly self-arriving.

DOING WITHOUT A DOER

Another layer of this magicality lies in the absence of a central agent. In our habitual imagination, there must be a doer behind every doing, a performer who enacts the show, a self who causes thought, a God who launches the cosmos. But in the vision, Space, Time, and Knowledge simply do themselves. They are not functions of something else, nor caused by an external source. Space spaces. Time times. Knowledge knows.

This may sound strange, but it is actually the most natural thing. We constantly misread reality by positing hidden actors. We assume that for every phenomenon there must be an underlying entity holding it up: self behind thought, substance behind appearance, cause behind each event. Yet the radical disclosure of Great Knowledge reveals that these posits are unnecessary: appearance itself is sufficient. The magic needs no magician. To live in this way is not to deny causality or agency in practical terms; we still navigate the world of reasons and responsibilities. At the most fundamental level, the compulsion to anchor appearance in a hidden substrate is misguided. What appears is self-sufficient; this sufficiency is wonder itself.

WONDER AS PARTICIPATION

Wonder here is not some detached observation; it is participatory. We are not spectators of a cosmic magic show, marveling or cheering from the sidelines. We *are* the magic. The very capacity to notice, to feel, to think, to act, these too are Space, Time, and Knowledge at play, with no outside.

Think of sitting on a high ledge, gazing across a valley. The sweep of sky, the drift of clouds, the scent of pines, all unfolding with effortless majesty. Equally the body breathing, the eyes widening, the mind settling are also part of the scene. The wonder is not out there in the panorama but here, in the indivisibility of panorama and perceiver. The mountain practice reveals this most vividly: not as a special state to be attained, but as a disclosure of what has always been the case.

In this light, even the partitions that seem to limit us, inside versus outside, past versus future, are revealed as porous. They are not barriers but doorways. The categories themselves, the very devices that appear to tame magic into order, are also magic. Language, logic, measurement: each is an appearance within the same openness. Far from obstructing wonder, they can be seen as its playful expressions.

If reality is so magical, why does it rarely feel that way? The answer lies in our taming of wonder. We have trained ourselves to flatten what appears into predictable frameworks. We treat the sunrise as routine, the body as a mechanism, the mind as software running in the background on the hardware of the brain. We translate vitality into information, presence into productivity. In doing so, we have muted the very resonance that makes life luminous.

Yet this taming is never complete. A sudden illness, an unexpected kindness, the glance of a stranger can pierce the veneer and restore the rawness of reality. The task is not to manufacture wonder but to stop suppressing it. Wonder requires no addition. It is the natural fragrance of Being. Our role is simply to allow it, to give it room to breathe.

> **Wonderment is the presence, the presenting, the appreciation of reality as Being. All appearance is sheer art, beautiful beyond all enduring, appealing beyond all possibility of possession. It cannot be possessed but it is entirely accessible.**

THE ETHICAL EDGE OF WONDER

An ethical consequence also lives here, wonder disarmed of possession. What appears cannot be owned, because it is perpetually given freely. Beauty resists capture; its very nature is to be shared. Thus the vision of Being undermines possessive individualism. When we see that "all appearance is sheer art," appealing "beyond all possibility of possession," we lay down the impulse to seize. We stop treating the world as a resource, as an object for exploitation. Instead, we begin to participate in its radiance. This does not mean retreating into passivity. On the contrary, wonder ignites care. When the world is recognized as magical, each gesture becomes more precious. A word spoken carries weight; a touch is suffused with meaning; even the most mundane tasks, washing dishes, answering emails, walking the dog, are revealed as opportunities for presence. Wonder roots ethics not in obligation, but in appreciation. We care because we cannot not care, once value shines through.

The recognition of wonder and magic is not the endpoint of this inquiry, but its deepening. To sense the magicality of reality is to stand at the edge of another turn: the realization that Being is not merely vast and wondrous but inherently intimate. Wonder, left unintegrated, can drift toward passivity or reverie. The next step is to see how wonder folds into participation, how the openness of Space, the dynamism of Time, and the clarity of Knowledge are not distant marvels but the very tissue of our own existence. This is where the vision communes in wonderment. From seeing the world as magical to realizing: we are the magic and the magic is us.

BEING AS INTIMACY

Intimacy carries the force of this vision into the marrow of our lives, not the intimacy of romance alone, nor even the closeness of friendship, but a deeper nearness: the sense that nothing stands apart, nothing is held at a distance, nothing requires a bridge to be reached. When Being is allowed to shine through the interplay of Space, Time, and Knowledge, reality itself is revealed as intimacy.

Ordinarily, we move through the world in a posture of separation. The body appears here, the world over there, linked by moves to reach and grasp. We imagine that closeness must be cultivated through effort, as when we strive to understand another person, push through obstacles to get closer, or strive to communicate our point of view. Intimacy is imagined as the exception rather than the rule, a fragile achievement rather than a natural condition. But what if this assumption is upside down? What if the very fabric of experience is already uncontrived intimacy and only our insistence on distance makes us feel estranged?

The vision hints at precisely this: to appreciate Being is to sense that nearness is not something earned or constructed, it is given from the outset. The same openness that allows a tree to appear on a hillside, or a thought to flicker in the mind, allows us to be present in relation to one another. We do not have to generate or reach for intimacy; we only need to stop insisting on separation.

> **And once we have become more vigorously appreciative of our inner potential and value, the same appreciative commitment to the value of all humanity naturally emerges. It is impossible for this not to happen, because it is so clear that we are all very**

intimately related. We all have the same parents—Space and Time.

In not being sentimental, such intimacy has a peculiar quality: it does not collapse differences or dissolve boundaries into a featureless unity. Like light, it can illuminate a thousand shapes without erasing their contours. In the same way, intimacy radiates through distinctions. My face is not your face, my memories are not your memories, and yet they shine with the same clarity of Being: each is distinct, but not divided.

This recognition can feel disorienting at first. We are so accustomed to organizing our lives around the posture of an imagined self: the one who must secure closeness, defend boundaries, and navigate a world of obstacles. To discover how intimacy is already present seems like stepping onto a floor we thought was missing. It removes the drama of distance, with no outside to be conquered, no inside to be fortified. Everything participates in the same, immediate presence.

Herein the language of value enters. For if Being is intimacy, then everything that appears shares in value; not value in the sense of utility or worth measured against a standard, but value as radiance: each thing shining with the significance of being here at all. The rose is not valuable because it decorates the garden, smells divine, or inspires poetry, but because its very blooming is inseparable from the openness that allows blooming to happen. The barista handing over the freshly brewed espresso is not valuable because of the service performed but because their presence is a manifestation of the same intimacy that bares the universe.

Seen in this way, value is no longer something we assign, being intrinsic, woven into Being itself, with profound ethical implications. If each appearance radiates with value, compassion is not a moral duty imposed from outside, above, or after the fact. Ethical, loving responsiveness is the natural recognition of what is already so. To see another as valuable is not to grant them dignity out of benevolence, but to awaken the fact that they are already shining with intrinsic worth.

This overturns many of the assumptions upon which our culture is built. We live in a world where value is constantly negotiated, ranked, and distributed: through markets, through politics, through systems of status and recognition, even in intimate relationships. Value seems fragile, contingent, bestowed by forces beyond our control. One job is "worth" more than another. One life is treated as expendable while another is safeguarded. But if Being is intimacy and value, this entire edifice begins to crumble. What we call injustice is not simply a failure of fairness, it is blindness to the radiance of Being. The cure is not redistribution alone, but a profound recognition of equality. This recognition strikes close to home, in the body itself. When awareness rests in the openness of Space and the liveliness of Time, the body is no longer a possession to be managed or improved, nor a tool to be worn down in service of the self's projects. It is recognized as an expression of Being: radiant, sufficient, inexhaustible. In this light, even the tensions and limitations of the body are not signs of deficiency, but aspects of its intimacy with life. Pain is not an enemy; fatigue is not a flaw. They, too, are value shining through.

The same holds true in the sphere of relationships. To live within an unmediated presence is to meet others without the secret calculation of distance: What can I gain? What must I protect? Instead, each encounter becomes a meeting of value with value, radiance with radiance. This does not make relationships effortless; conflicts still arise, misunderstandings still sting, but the ground shifts. We are no longer confronting obstacles to our selfhood. Together we are participating in Being's unfolding. Even disagreement can become a form of communion, a way of being drawn into the shared fabric of existence.

Perhaps the most startling implication of this view is how it reframes death. Ordinarily, death appears as the negation of intimacy, the ultimate separation, the vanishing of a presence we once held close, or the looming prospect of our own transition. Yet when intimacy is recognized as the very nature of Being, death itself is transfigured. What disappears does not fall into nothingness, for nothingness itself is already suffused with intimacy. The absence is not outside the weave; it is one more way it shows itself. Death is not the end of intimacy but its deepening, a reminder that nothing ever stood apart.

To name this is to come close to what earlier passages called wonder or magic. The wonder is not an added gloss on reality, but the direct recognition of its intimacy and value, the amazement that there is something rather than nothing, and that this something is inseparable from knowing. In this sense, Being is not a static condition or hidden ground, being instead wonder itself, a wonder that cannot be possessed but is always accessible, always near, always radiant. Here lies the invitation of this chapter: not to treat intimacy and value as abstract concepts, but to live them. To sit at a desk, answer an email, take out the trash, or pause on a street corner, and sense that every gesture is already saturated with intimacy, already radiant with value. No act is too small, no moment too ordinary, each is an expression of Being. To recognize this expression is to invite wonder back into the fabric of life.

This does not mean living in a constant state of exaltation or awe. The wonder of Being is more subtle than that: quiet, like the way light fills a room without asking to be noticed, not demanding intensity; it merely asks for availability. When we relax the fixation of the self and its anxious projects, intimacy and value are simply present, like air, like gravity, like breath. They do not need to be manufactured, they only need to be trusted.

In this way, the vision of Being as intimacy and value prepares us for the culmination to come. For intimacy is not only between self and world, nor value only in the particularities of things. They are the resonances of a deeper wholeness, one that gathers Space, Time, Knowledge, and Being into a single luminous field: the Quadrinity is not a theory to be dissected, but a mystique to be entered. Toward the mystique of Being we now turn, as the arc of the chapter spirals toward its center.

THE QUADRINITY AND THE MANDALA OF BEING

If the earlier movements of this chapter have felt like a circling, around intimacy, around value, around the luminous presence of Space, Time, and Knowledge, this final section brings us to the center. The center, though, is not a destination reached after a long approach. It is more like the heart of a mandala: already present, always waiting to be recognized. What we have been circling is nothing other than Being itself.

In the traditional mandala, the eye is drawn from the outer gates inward through successive thresholds, each layer more refined, more concentrated, until finally the gaze rests on the still point at the center. But the mandala is not a picture of hierarchy, where the outer is lower and the inner higher. It is a geometry of wholeness, a way of showing that each part belongs, that the path inward is also the path outward, that center and circumference mirror and depend upon each other. The same holds true for the mandala of Being that emerges from the vision. Space, Time, and Knowledge are not rungs on a ladder to be climbed toward some hidden summit; they are gateways, each one already complete, each one an entry into the whole.

When we bring these three into relation with Being, the vision becomes fourfold. A quadrinity emerges: Space, Time, Knowledge, and Being, not as four separate substances, but as four resonances of the same radiance. The image of a mandala captures this better than any linear model could. The fourfold symmetry is not mechanical; it's alive, dynamic, self-generating. Each facet shines with its own clarity, yet reflects the others, and the whole only appears through their interplay.

This quadrinity invites us to see Being not as something behind or beyond the three, but as intimate co-arising. Space is openness, the endless generosity that allows anything at all to appear; Time is expressiveness, the movement and unfolding of appearance; Knowledge is clarity, the luminous knowing through which appearances register as meaningful; and Being is the intimacy of all three: their indivisible presence, their value, their wonder.

It helps to imagine the quadrinity as a mandala in motion. At one moment, openness shines most strongly, and we recognize Being as spaciousness, as freedom from confinement. At another, expressiveness surges, and we sense Being as creativity, as ceaseless becoming. At another, clarity dominates, and Being appears as insight, transparency, recognition. Yet in each case, the other dimensions are not absent. They infuse and sustain the one that stands out. Like colors blending in light, the colors of a rainbow, or the magic of a prism, they are never separable. What shifts is our attunement, our emphasis, our mode of participation.

This fourfold vision also helps dissolve one of the most subtle traps in spiritual or philosophical inquiry: the tendency to elevate Being into a hidden ground, an ultimate that towers above its manifestations. In the quadrinity, no such hierarchy abides. Being does not stand apart as a fourth term reigning over the other three. It is simply their interpenetrating intimacy, their resonance, their luminous weave. The mandala metaphor prevents us from sliding back into dualism, where appearances are one thing and Being another. It shows that Being is the radiance of appearances themselves, inseparable from their openness, expressiveness, and clarity.

Why speak of a quadrinity at all, then? Because it makes explicit what might otherwise remain implicit: that Being is not a concept behind the three, but their ever-present unity. Naming it gives us permission to trust the closeness we already sense. And the mandala form reminds us that this unity is not static, not a frozen totality. It is dynamic balance, a play of resonances endlessly unfolding.

To live within this mandala is to discover a new sense of orientation. No longer do we move through the world as isolated selves navigating an indifferent backdrop. We move as participants in an ever-present mystique that is at once spacious, expressive, clear, and intimate. Every perception, every gesture, every relationship becomes an enactment of the quadrinity. The shifting colors of the evening sky are not just atmosphere, they are openness appearing, time flowing, knowledge clarifying, Being radiating. The way a conversation unfolds is not just words, it's the mandala in motion, intimacy taking form as exchange.

This way of seeing is what earlier passages called wonder or magic. Magical not because it suspends the laws of nature or introduces supernatural agents, but because it reveals how the ordinary itself is inexhaustible. To say that Great Space does Space, Great Time does Time, and Great Knowledge does Knowledge is to recognize that there is no hidden doer, no machinery behind the scene. Reality performs itself. The mandala dances itself. To participate in this dance is to live the magic of Being.

Such a vision also reconfigures how we imagine the path of human life. Ordinarily, we conceive of growth as a linear progression: a line moving from ignorance to wisdom, from immaturity to maturity, from birth to death. But the mandala offers another image: a labyrinth. Not the maze of dead ends and confusions, but the ancient labyrinth whose winding path always leads toward the center, even when it seems to stray. The labyrinth does not ask us to solve it, but to walk it. Each step, however circuitous, is already part of the journey inward. And yet, paradoxically, the center is never absent. It is implicit in every turn.

To envision life as a labyrinth within the mandala of Being is to relax the anxiety of progress. There is no race to win, no final destination to reach. Each moment is already enfolded in the whole. Even when we feel lost, we are not outside the pattern. The labyrinth reassures us that our wandering is itself participation in Being's unfolding. Magic is not waiting at the end; it saturates the path.

This perspective also carries ethical force. For if 'one point is all points', as the vision insists, then every step in the labyrinth is the center. Every life, every moment, every gesture is a complete expression of the mandala. This means that value is not deferred to some ultimate beyond. It is right here, in the immediacy of appearance. To act with care, to respond with compassion, to live with attentiveness is not to approximate a distant ideal. It is to honor the intimacy of Being as it already shines through this moment, this place, this relationship.

The quadrinity also suggests a new way of thinking about freedom. In the ordinary view, freedom means the ability to choose among options, to assert one's will against constraints. But in the mandala of Being, freedom is something deeper: the spontaneous unfolding of openness, expressiveness, clarity, and intimacy. When we align with this unfolding, we are not limited by the narrow dictates of self-interest. We act with "complete propriety and utter spontaneity." Freedom is not the absence of limits, but the presence of resonance, our capacity to move in harmony with the whole.

> **Wealth is intrinsic to our Being. When this is recognized—without there being a recognizer—there can be no bondage, fear, or worry, and no ugliness or imperfection, for the presence of these is itself**

incomparable beauty. Everything is the embodiment of Being and a totality.

To describe this is to come close to the experience of beauty. For beauty, too, is not something added to reality, nor a quality possessed by certain privileged objects. Beauty is the radiance of the mandala itself, the way intimacy shines through form. When we call a landscape beautiful, or a piece of music harmonious, or a human gesture a majestic embrace, what we are recognizing is not a property but a participation. We are glimpsing the quadrinity in action: openness, expressiveness, clarity, and intimacy woven into a form that awakens our own resonance. Beauty is Being reminding itself of its own radiance.

Unless we recognize and live out this opportunity, it would seem that we are going to stay trapped. For if Space-Time-Knowledge's direct elicitation of Being does not inspire us to wake up, what will? Only active commitment to our own Being (through Space, Time, and Knowledge) is essential to a joyous and liberating life.

And so, we arrive at the culmination. The mandala of Being is not a model to be believed, nor a theory to be defended. It is a symbol of living, a way of attuning to what is already here. Space, Time, Knowledge, and Being are not four parts of reality. They are four ways of saying what cannot be said: that reality is radiant, intimate, inexhaustible, ever-present. The quadrinity does not close the inquiry; it opens it infinitely.

This is why the chapter ends not with conclusions but with invitations. To see the mandala is to be invited into participation. To sense the quadrinity is to be invited into wonder. To live the intimacy of Being is to be invited into a life that is at once ordinary and magical, finite and infinite, particular and whole. Nothing needs to be added; nothing needs to be removed. The mandala already shines. The labyrinth already guides. The quadrinity already supports us. All that remains is to walk, to see, to trust. In this trust, life itself becomes a mandala: ever unfolding, ever centered, ever radiant with the nearness of vastness and the wonder of uncontrived intimacy.

NOTES

1. *Time, Space, and Knowledge* has been translated into German, Italian, Dutch, and French.

2. Six major sequels include *Love of Knowledge* (1987), *Knowledge of Time and Space* (1990), *Visions of Knowledge* (1993), *Dynamics of Time and Space* (1994), *Sacred Dimensions of Time and Space* (1997), and *Gesture of Great Love* (2022). In addition, several edited books have been published in a different series as compendiums of reflections and essays on the TSK vision, authored by a wide array of professionals, students, educators, teachers, and practitioners. The first of these edited volumes was called "Perspectives on Time, Space and Knowledge," titled *Dimensions of Thought: Volumes 1 & 2* (1980). Volume 1 included an in-depth interview with Tarthang Tulku that elaborated on the vision. A little over a decade later, a new series manifested with the publication of *Mastery of Mind* (1993), *Light of Knowledge* (1997), *A New Kind of Knowledge* (2004), and *A New Way of Being* (2004). An original essay by Tarthang Tulku "Geographies of Knowledge" appears in *Light of Knowledge*. In addition, *Inside Knowledge* (2015) also contains a number of original TSK related essays by Tarthang Tulku, as well as a helpful and informative orientation by Jack Petranker to the reprint of the "Oceans of Knowledge" interview that originally appeared in *Dimensions of Thought (Volume 1). Inside Knowledge* also contains a number of contributions by long-term students of TSK. A comprehensive and systematic study guide to the TSK series of books, *When It Rains Does Space Get Wet?* (2006) was also authored by Jack Petranker. All these sequels and compendiums were released by Dharma Publishing.

3. For a lively history of this period, see David Kaiser's *How the Hippies Saved Physics* (New York: W. W. Norton, 2011). Kaiser recounts how a small group of young physicists at UC Berkeley formed the Fundamental Fysiks Group in 1975 to reopen foundational debates in quantum mechanics once waged by Einstein, Bohr, Schrödinger, and others. Among its founders was George Weismann, an early student of *Time, Space, and Knowledge* and a friend of Tarthang Tulku, who, along with Elizabeth Rauscher, explored the implications of John Bell's then-obscure paper on quantum nonlocality.

4. Regarding the idea that TSK is a "disguised form of Buddhism or mysticism," see Tarthang Tulku's statement in *Dynamics of Time and Space*, ". . . I have no special quarrels with readers who insist the

TSK vision is really a form of mysticism or meditative practice or disguised Buddhism. This is not my understanding, but others can offer their own interpretations. The vision itself is not affected by characterizations. Only when such interpretations turn into dogma will they restrict the benefits that the vision has to offer." (p. xxi).

5. Several related remarks differentiating TSK from Buddhism can be found in the interview with Tarthang Tulku, "Oceans of Knowledge," where he states "I'm not offering the Time-Space-Knowledge Vision as an extension of Buddhism or Buddhist goals, although I think it's fully compatible with those goals" (p. xlvii). The interviewer goes on to ask Tarthang Tulku, "You weren't trying to restate Buddhism or Nyingma thought?" to which Rinpoche responds, "No, I had no conscious idea or desire of that sort. Buddhism is vast, almost beyond my ability to fathom it all; I wouldn't attempt such a restatement. Time, Space and Knowledge suggests an independent path. It's similar or parallel to Buddhism in some way, fine, but that's not so important" (p.xlviii). This interview was originally published in the *Dimensions of Thought (Volume 1),* Ralph H. Moon and Steve Randall (Eds.), Dharma Publishing, 1980, (p.xlvii). It was later reprinted in Jack Petranker's edited volume, *Inside Knowledge*, Dharma Publishing, 2006, pp. 67-68.

6. In the introduction to *Love of Knowledge*, Tarthang Tulku reflects on the unusual process of ideas that came to him, which led to the TSK vision. In his recollection he states, "The course of investigation and research that I was carrying out seemed to me rather unusual. Although I had been raised in a tradition where inquiry into the workings of mind was an integral part of education, the specific approach I now found myself adopting had no direct connection to this tradition, or any other path of inquiry that I was familiar with."

7. This quote is from an informal essay "Yes, We Have No Bananas" which Tarthang Tulku contributed to the 1995 Compuserve TSK-email listserv group. The essay was delivered to the group on June 6, 1995, via an email from Jack Petranker. The title of the essay is based on the old song "Yes, We Have No Bananas".

8. For a brief and coherent description of naïve realism see: https://thedecisionlab.com/biases/naive-realism

9. For an in-depth treatment of naïve realism, or what the cognitive neuroscientist Anil Seth refers to as "the how things seem view," see

his excellent and highly readable book, *Being You: A New Science of Consciousness,* (New York: Dutton, 2021).

10. Tracing from the ancient Greek, phenomena literally means "appearance" or "representation." See Landon Loftin and Max Leyf, *What Barfield Thought: An Introduction to the Work of Owen Barfield,* (Eugene, OR: Cascade Books. 2023), 74. Any "phenomenon," that is, any appearance, is never *not* perceived or *not* re-presented. Our minds are always actively participating in the formation of appearances.

11. According to Loftin and Lefy's read on Barfield's concept of *figuration*, they state: "Hence, far from the image of the Cartesian theater in which objects utterly heterogeneous to the mind succeed, by a sort of conjuring trick, in becoming perceptions for it, Barfield offers a view in which the mind is already latent in every object of perception. He called this function 'figuration' (p.79)."

12. The nucleus of an atom is virtually 100% of the entire atom's mass. If you were to enlarge a single atom to 500 square feet, the size of the nucleus would still be like a speck of dust. The space between it and the outer bands of electrons is merely empty space. For further details see the following articles:

https://owlcation.com/stem/outer-space-the-final-frontier
https://www.forbes.com/sites/startswithabang/2020/04/16/you-are-not-mostly-empty-space/?sh=67992b72c2b0
https://factmyth.com/factoids/the-universe-is-mostly-empty-space/

13. I have adapted this flat-earth parable and analogy from Steve Hagen's excellent book, *The Grand Delusion: What We Know But Don't Believe,* (Summerville, MA: Wisdom Publications, 2020) 17-19.

14. The familiar phrase "monkey mind" usually refers to restlessness: the way thoughts leap from one branch to another like a hungry monkey swinging through trees. But as Steven Tainer (editor of the first *Time, Space, and Knowledge* book) points out, the issue is deeper than distraction. The monkey's vision is confined to its small canopy; it has no awareness of the ground that supports the forest. In the same way, our ordinary mind misses the wider ground of experience. For a vivid description of this metaphor, see Charles Belyea and Steven Tainer, *Dragon's Play: A New Taoist Transmission of the Complete Experience of Human Life* (Berkeley: Great Circle Lifeworks, 1991), Chapter One, "Discovering Monkey," 42–47.

15. At issue here is not just survival but the evolution of consciousness. Human awareness reaches beyond reacting to stimuli; it carries innate capacities that connect us with a deeper unity. When life is reduced to survival alone, fragmentation and conflict dominate, and we lose touch with this more participatory vision of wholeness.

16. The homunculus argument pertains to a folk psychology theory of vision based on recursive loops and a fallacy that leads to an infinite regress. See https://en.wikipedia.org/wiki/Homunculus_argument

17. An excellent treatment of Edwin A. Abbot's classic book, *Flatland*, is an edited edition by William F. Lindgren and Thomas F. Banchoff, *Flatland: An Edition with Notes and Commentary.* (New York: The Mathematical Association of America and Cambridge University Press, 2010).

18. An animated depiction of Flatland and how different dimensional spaces appear can be found in this YouTube video: https://www.youtube.com/watch?v=4TI1onWI_IM

19. In *Process and Reality* (New York: Harper, 1929), Alfred North Whitehead warned against what he called "the fallacy of misplaced concreteness": mistaking abstractions for reality itself. A "location in space," for example, is never absolute but always relative, yet we often treat such abstractions as if they were concrete facts. The same mistake happens when we treat consciousness as something separable from the flow of reality.

20. Owen Barfield described idolatry as our habit of mistaking abstractions for solid realities. In *Saving the Appearances: A Study in Idolatry* (New York: Harcourt, Brace & World, 1957, 142), he argued that modern consciousness treats objects as if they existed on their own, forgetting that meanings are representations. This stance fueled science and technology, but also narrowed vision: space itself became an idol, "simply the absence of phenomena" (ibid., 149), a neutral container observed from outside. Barfield held that we cannot return to premodern "original participation," but we can rediscover a participatory way of knowing. In the idiom of *Time, Space, and Knowledge*, this means loosening the stance of the bystander and recognizing space and time as alive, generative, and inseparable from awareness.

21. See, for example, Kōshō Uchiyama, *Opening the Hand of Thought: Foundations of Zen Buddhist Practice*. (Trans. Shohaku Okumara & Tom Wright. New York: Arkana Penguin Books, 1993).

22. The contemporary Western Zen teacher, Steve Hagen, in his book *The Grand Delusion*, states that, "The 'hard problem' isn't actually hard. It's impossible. It's just another FEQ (Flat-Earth Question) based on groundless assumptions. Physical processes in the brain have *never* been demonstrated to give rise to subjective experience. We only *assume* that they do—because there *seems* to be a correlation." (New York: Wisdom Publications, 2020), 218.

23. David Chalmers called this the "hard problem" of consciousness: even if every neural correlate were mapped, it would not explain why experience exists at all. See *"Facing Up to the Problem of Consciousness," Journal of Consciousness Studies* 2, no. 3 (1995): 200–19. Neuroscience can show correlations, but the causal leap from brain activity to subjective experience remains an "explanatory gap." From a reductionist view, "mind" is dismissed as an imputed construct, with only the brain deemed real. Evan Thompson contrasts this stance with Tibetan Buddhist views of consciousness in *Waking, Dreaming, Being: Self and Consciousness in Neuroscience, Meditation, and Philosophy*, (New York: Columbia University Press, 2017), chap. 3.

24. For more on this point, see the philosopher Evan Thompson, who states, "Consciousness itself has not been and cannot be observed through the scientific method, because the scientific method gives us no direct and independent access to consciousness itself. So the scientific method cannot have the final say on matters concerning consciousness." *Waking, Dreaming and Being: Self and Consciousness in Neuroscience, Meditation, and Philosophy*, (New York: Columbia University Press, 2017).

25. In the late nineteenth century, psychologists like William James used *introspection*, trained attention turned inward, as a method for studying the mind. But as experimental psychology developed in the early twentieth century, the practice was dismissed as too subjective and difficult to replicate. For a fuller history, see B. Alan Wallace, *Fathoming the Mind: Inquiry and Insight in Dudjom Lingpa's Vajra Essence* (Somerville, MA: Wisdom Publications, 2018), chap. "The Nature of Mind."

26. William James's radical empiricism emphasized methodological neutrality toward religious experience: he sought to honor first-

person accounts without imposing preconceptions. In *Varieties of Religious Experience* (New York: Longman's Green & Co.,1902) James resisted reducing mystical or spiritual phenomena to a fixed theory or framework. Instead, he allowed the experience to dictate its own terms, treating it as worthy of inquiry rather than forcing it into existing categories.

27. The image of a fixed observer, "the one who thinks thoughts," is why gaps between thoughts are rarely noticed. Mu Seong, in *Trust in Mind: The Rebellion of Chinese Zen* (Somerville, MA: Wisdom Publications, 2004, 30–34), reframes this: thought and thinker are not separate, but an inseparable process of "thinker-in-thoughting." His description states, "A thought, for example, is not a simple event happening statically to a thinker. It is changing the thinker by its impact and since the thinker has thought the thought in the first place, the thinker (being) *is* the thought (becoming) itself, and thought itself is the thinker. The two are an inseparable process rather than two distinct entities. A proper designation perhaps is "thinker-in-thoughting." This view of *being-in-becoming* loosens the sense of a static thinker and resonates with Exercise 11, which points to a spacious trust in first-person insight beyond conceptual support.

28. The rainbow analogy comes from Owen Barfield's *Saving the Appearances: A Study in Idolatry* (New York: Harcourt, Brace & World, 1957, 15–20). Barfield argued that what we take as "real" is shaped by a system of collective representations. Often overlooked, he showed how shifts in consciousness—and even in language—have continually reshaped how humans experience themselves and their world. His work challenges the standard scientific view by insisting that consciousness itself plays a decisive role in the phenomenal world.

29. In *The Grand Delusion*, Steve Hagen warns against imagining some hidden "supra-substance" behind nonsubstantiality. There is nothing lurking behind appearances. Yet our habitual bias is to assume there must be something—an essence, a ground—that explanations, theories, or labels can capture. The same danger applies if we treat Great Space as a reified "something" beyond appearances. Even awareness itself is easily objectified: when we speak of "me," we turn subjectivity into yet another thing .

30. The stance of a "bystander" rests on a hidden dualism: if there is someone standing inside, there must also be something standing outside. Together, these poles harden into the ordinary picture of

separate selves inhabiting a stable world of objects. This focal-setting is persuasive enough to generate a shared consensus reality, an "out there" that feels unquestionable. Yet even these roles of by-standers and outside-standers are not fundamental; they are habits of perception, not essences. For a striking parallel, see Kennard Lipman's translation of Klong-chen rab-'byams-pa, in yid bzhin mdzod, "How Samsara is Fabricated from the Ground of Being," *Crystal Mirror V*, Tarthang Tulku, ed. (Berkeley: Dharma Publishing, 1977) 336–356.

31. Adverse effects of meditation and mindfulness practices can take the form of either hyperarousal or hypoarousal. See Willoughby B. Britton et al. "Defining and Measuring Meditation-Related Adverse Effects in Mindfulness-Based Programs," *Clinical Psychological Science,* Volume 9, Issue 6, (2021), https://journals.sagepub.com/doi/full/10.1177/2167702621996340?casa_token=QieW-knGe57AAAAAA%3A3jaGdx4dH6GnHwHUh96aJ2xJRkWwHopE-UFa5Nc9SMHSKlxVYdL1_RXr3DgckaHVSjlr7sYJO2JgzQw

32. The paleontologist Stephen Jay Gould proposed that the knowledge domains of science and religion are worlds apart, each having dominion over their own special domains of inquiry, what he referred to as "non-overlapping magisterial." For his original essay, see: https://caspar.bgsu.edu/~courses/4510/Classes/48A078B0-8402-4995-9161-A2C418612C75_files/Gould_97.pdf

33. Kieran Fox, *I Am a Part of Infinity: Albert Einstein's Search for the Sacred* (New York: Basic Books, 2025). Fox offers a beautifully written spiritual biography of Einstein, tracing how his sense of the "cosmic religious feeling" informed both his science and his ethics. Drawing on newly uncovered letters and archival materials, Fox reveals Einstein's lifelong effort to reconcile mysticism and mathematics, a vision of reality where mind itself participates in the infinite.

34. Scott Barry Kaufman reviews psychological research showing how practices such as meditation and yoga, rather than diminishing egoic concerns, can sometimes be co-opted by the self as tools of self-enhancement, reinforcing tendencies toward self-centeredness and narcissism. Scott Barry Kaufman, "The Science of Spiritual Narcissism," *Scientific American*, January 28, 2021, https://www.scientificamerican.com/article/the-science-of-spiritual-narcissism/.

35. Richard Dixey and Ronald Purser analyze how contemporary mindfulness practices can reinforce the very structures of self they

claim to loosen, leading to cycles of achievement-seeking, avoidance, and subtle forms of self-entanglement. See Richard Dixey and Ronald E. Purser, "Mindfulness Traps and the Entanglement of Self: An Inquiry into the Regime of Mind," *International Journal of Transpersonal Studies* (Advance online publication, 2023), https://digitalcommons.ciis.edu/advance-archive/57

36. In Christian mysticism, "uncreated grace" describes an indwelling presence of the divine, immediate, uncaused, and available here and now. Karl Rahner framed this as a "grace-centric" vision of human existence in *Concerning the Relationship between Nature and Grace in Theological Investigations*, Volume 1, translated by Cornelius Ernst (London: Darton, Longman & Todd, 1961) 297-317; see also Andrew Prevot, *The Mysticism of Ordinary Life* (New York: Oxford, 2023) 31-62. Parallel insights appear in Dzogchen's non-doing and Daoism's *wu-wei*: not passivity, but a reminder that spaciousness is intrinsic and does not need to be manufactured. See Dylan Esler, *Effortless Spontaneity*, (Leiden: E.J. Brill, 2023).

The paradox, of course, is how one can "try not to try." Edward Slingerland in *Effortless Action*, (New York: Oxford, 2003, 6), shows how striving contaminates its own goal. This points to a deeper issue: the self's compulsion to emerge as agent and doer. Effortlessness unsettles this "coming out" tendency, loosening the grip of the focal setting that insists there must always be a manager behind experience.

37. Neuroscientist Anil Seth describes perception not as passive reception but as active prediction. The brain continually generates models of what is most likely present, testing them against incoming signals. What we perceive is the brain's "best guess," constantly revised to minimize error between expectation and input. See Anil Seth, *Being You: A New Science of Consciousness* (Dutton, New York, 2021).

38. The German notion of *Lebenswelt* ("lifeworld") points to how our experience is always framed by interests and concerns, leaving much unseen. Plato's famous cave allegory captures this confinement: prisoners mistake shadows for reality until one escapes, glimpses the light, and struggles to describe it to those still imprisoned. The story remains a vivid reminder of how hard it is to step outside our inherited frames of perception. See Plato, *Republic*, trans. C.D.C. Reeve (Indianapolis: Hackett, 2004).

39. A pithy observation from Dr. Richard Dixey, Dean of Dharma College, highlights the radical shift in Exercise 16:

"Exercise 16 represents the reformulation of the view inherent in the metaphor of the 'field' of time. Instead of seeing ourselves as moving through space to the beat of the three times, which is the narrative staging we all inhabit as a heroic actor in a world of things, we can learn to abandon that recognitive map and awaken to find ourselves as the still point, the center of the mandala, effortlessly held in the complete openness of space, with the dance of appearance presenting itself to us as time. We are, as it is. Suchness becomes the fourth time, the time out of time."

40. The term 'regime' is a more recent metaphor that Tarthang Tulku has used in describing the walled-in enclosure of the meaning-making mechanisms of ordinary knowing as a "Regime of Mind." See Tarthang Tulku, *Revelations of Mind,* (Berkeley: Dharma Publishing, 2013),13-15.

41. Religious studies scholar Jeffrey Kripal argues for what he calls *superhumanism*, a new cultural imaginary that recovers humanity's long quest for transcendence. Across history, the source of meaning has often been tied to extraordinary figures and anomalous events: saints, yogis, prophets, and founders of religions whose lives were marked by miracles, visions, levitation, prophecy, or other forms of "high strangeness." Kripal suggests that we were "superhuman before we were human," and that acknowledging these dimensions remains essential for reimagining the future. See Jeffrey J. Kripal, *The Superhumanities: Historical Precedents, Moral Objections, New Realities* (Chicago: University of Chicago Press, 2022).

42. Gregory Fueges uses the phrase *"cognitive nondualism"* in his book *Radical Nonduality: Ju Mipham Namgyal Gyatso's Discourse on Reality* (Wien: Arbeitskreis fur Tibetische und Buhddhistischen Studien, Universität Wien, 2024) 14. Ju Mipham (1846–1912), a major Nyingma scholar of the Rime movement, argued that no conceptual view, whether framed as "two truths" or "buddha nature," can capture reality itself. Such teachings are provisional, useful only as support for practice. For Mipham, the unmediated realization of non-duality comes not through doctrine but through practices grounded in what Fueges calls *cognitive nondualism,* an approach strikingly resonant with the TSK vision.

43. For a full account of disenchantment and secularization, see Charles Taylor's *A Secular Age* (Cambridge, MA: Belknap Press, 2018). A shorter overview is available in this essay: "Enchantment and Disenchantment in Taylor's Essay on Western Secularity"

LIST OF EXERCISES

AFTERWORD
Tarthang Tulku

ONE

I would like to express my way of understanding of Time, Space, and Knowledge and share with you some thoughts. At one level, time is *measured*, in points, rhythms, actions. And space is *emptiness*, appearing to contain planets, particles, and chemical structures. We are taught to distinguish times and treat space as empty of characteristics; yet this understanding itself is a point made by way of space, by virtue of time's interconnections. If objects and events seem substantial and measurable at first glance, at another level, it is possible that all these manifestations are a matter of light: shining, showing, sharing space and time. With no clear 'from' or 'to', this magical arising nevertheless appears, a situation we could call *samsara*. Just as stages of enlightened embodiment are inherent in samsara, the unending cycles of karma may harbor deeper potentials of mind. Studying the meanings of time, space, and knowledge can show us how the *contacts* we call *contents* appear in ways we understand. The understood of the understander forms a vault of compelled conclusions called *alaya*; through these banked findings, occlusion informs patterns of meaning. The meanings of knowledge are caught in nets of identity cast in prehistory; yet knowledge has many means to communicate the rhythms of time, the openness of space.

Level 1: What permits points to appear?

Level 2: How do contents communicate?

Level 3: What does understanding matter?

TWO

Time is irreducible to units of measure, yet it permits marks to be made. Tallying marks set up rhythms; rhythms appear to show relations. This play cannot play out without space. Bottomless, borderless, baseless, space may appear different from things, with their physical limits and chemical structures. But if space were absent, mind and senses could not identify points, thoughts could not arise in response to feedback, and we could not capture conclusions. Suppose, then, that space and manifestation are inseparable; that space permeates and permits points known as observer and observed. With the help of time, space could be staging both seeing and seen in a globe theater; what we take as tangible may be frozen light. Could these apparent points of contact be twin illusions, reflections mutually mirrored in space? Light itself may be ray and radiance. According to a perceiver, it shines from and to, questing here and there, appearing to illuminate; but light might be completely open, its journey perfectly and profoundly accomplished.

Level 1: What is marked?

Level 2: What is reflected?

Level 3: What is permeated?

THREE

Mind, it appears, has a capacity for light; without it, there could be no knowing, no realization. We point to see and to understand; yet these light-body presentations may not support a regime of 'from' and 'to'. Can knowing transcend aim and intention, subjects and objects? Our present tools are party to divisions on which they depend; the cloven basis of logic and truth allows us to distinguish relative from absolute. 'Beyond' itself is a tag that depends on duality, imposing a vehicle and a path to reach the sought-for fruit. But in deeper knowing, perhaps no reliable reporter stands ready with descriptions; measuring may not leave marks. In response, we might say, "Beyond, neither subjects nor objects appear." But not-delineating, through this careful cut of 'neither nor', may not transmit realization.

Yet perhaps it could be achieved, by virtue of the qualities of light. Shining, it shares space and time. Its showing is sharing. Like wetness does for water, its characters can communicate. Knowledge could be transmitted if we knew how to embody it without subjects, objects, or presentations. Perhaps a very subtle way exists: in early times, some made that magical journey without vehicles. The light of their embodiment is ever-available in knowing: journeying still.

Level 1: What is the point of understanding?

Level 2: What is beyond duality?

Level 3: What is the question?

You are invited to read this text slowly. Meanings open layer by layer as understanding deepens. Every level can liberate, and every level communicates, from relative realities to the great play known as magical arising. Masters of manifestation know the way to open the points of arising, revealing realms of unimaginable beauty, flawless expressions of the openness of space, treasures of knowledge freely offered to all.

Study the words; contemplate the appearance; meditate the meanings. May understanding blossom.

Tarthang Tulku
Head Lama, TNMC
Odiyan Copper Mountain Mandala
July 23, 2024

ACKNOWLEDGEMENTS

No words can adequately convey my gratitude to Tarthang Tulku Rinpoche, who bestowed the extraordinary gift of the *Time, Space, and Knowledge* (TSK) vision. Whenever a TSK retreat began and participants introduced themselves, sharing their intentions, I often found myself overcome with tears of joy. That joy has remained with me for nearly forty years, inspiring and sustaining this work. My hope is that *Mind Space* offers readers glimpses of that same inspiration and of the immeasurable benefits of Rinpoche's creative genius.

This book could not have been written without the support of Wangmo Dixey, Executive Director of Dharma College, and Dr. Richard Dixey, its Dean. Their invitation to join the faculty gave me the opportunity to bring TSK to wider audiences. Their tireless dedication has nurtured the conditions for these teachings to flourish. I am also deeply indebted to Jack Petranker, whose support, mentoring, and friendship across my thirty-five-year academic career have profoundly shaped my understanding of TSK. His close collaboration with Rinpoche, especially in his editorial work, has been indispensable to keeping this vision alive. Without Jack's dedication, this book would not exist.

My TSK journey began in the early 1980s, when I enrolled in the ten-month program at the Nyingma Institute, where I met Robert Pasternak, who, along with the late Tom Morse, introduced me to the work. A deep friendship with Bob has endured for four decades and came full circle when we co-taught a year-long TSK course for Dharma College in 2024. I also want to thank the many TSK students who have studied and practiced with me over the years, some of whom have themselves become gifted teachers and guides. Special thanks go to Gavin Anderson, Bruce Alderman, David Filippone, Elon Goldstein, Eric Lichtman, Oda Linder, and Richard Miller for their steadfast support. Special thanks to my long-time friend, Alfonso Montuori, for reading various snippets. I owe a special debt of gratitude to Dr. Peter Fenner, whose pioneering approach to non-dual wisdom I first encountered more than twenty-five years ago as a student in his inaugural "non-dual psychotherapy" cohort. His guidance, and his steady confidence in my work—especially his encouragement of this project—have been invaluable.

This book was begun within the mandala-blessing field of the Odiyan Country Center, where I was on retreat in September 2023. I was fortunate to spend mornings and afternoons writing between retreat sessions. I remain deeply grateful to the tireless volunteers at all the Nyingma centers whose devotion has enabled Rinpoche's teachings to take root in the West.

Finally, I wish to thank Kat Thurston, Merrill Peterson, Irene Imfeld, Caroline van Tuyll, Ralph McFall, and the dedicated staff of Dharma Publishing and New World Library, whose care and effort have made the publication of M*ind Space* possible.

ABOUT THE AUTHOR

Ronald E. Purser, Ph.D., is the Lam Larsen Distinguished Research Professor of Management at San Francisco State University and the internationally recognized author of *McMindfulness: How Mindfulness Became the New Capitalist Spirituality*, a book that sparked global debate and established him as a leading critic of contemporary spirituality. His essays and commentaries have appeared in more than a hundred media outlets, including *The New York Times, The Guardian, Financial Times, The Nation, Salon, The Saturday Evening Post, The Huffington Post, The New Statesman, The Irish Times, Metro, Fast Company, Vice, Truthout.org, The Telegraph, Los Angeles Review of Books, Current Affairs,* and *Tricycle*. He has been featured on the BBC, CBC, NPR, and on television with Chris Hedges, Lee Camp, and R.J. Eskrow. Purser is also a frequent guest on popular podcasts such as *The ZDoggMD Show, The Chauncey DeVega Show, The Wright Show,* and *Upstream*. Alongside his public writing, Purser is the author or editor of numerous academic volumes, including *The Handbook of the Ethical Foundations of Mindfulness, Handbook of Mindfulness: Culture, Context and Social Engagement, 24/7: Time and Temporality in the Network Society, Social Creativity (Vols. 1 & 2), The Self Managing Organization,* and *The Search Conference*.

He has studied *Time, Space, and Knowledge* since 1982, when he encountered the groundbreaking text at the Nyingma Institute in Berkeley. Since then, he has integrated TSK's experiential insights into his scholarship and teaching. Today he is a senior instructor at Dharma College in Berkeley, California, where he leads courses and seminars on TSK for contemporary audiences and the host of *The Mindful Cranks* podcast. He lives in Pacifica, California.

INDEX

The index is offered not as a catalog of concepts, but as a field of entry points, many terms a gesture toward the spaciousness and freedom the text evokes. Readers are encouraged to explore context beyond the listed pages, allowing the words to open up experience rather than fixate it. Tracking down the many references to a commonly used term, such as 'openness', may help reveal many portals into the awesome awareness this word can reveal, to the intimate, radiant presence, value, and wonder of Being.

To find out more about Dharma publishing and
the activities of Tarthang Rinpoche,
please click on the QR code
or visit www.dharmapublishing.com